ENGLISH IDIOMS
and
AMERICANISMS

ENGLISH IDIOMS
and
AMERICANISMS
for
FOREIGN STUDENTS, PROFESSIONALS
AND PHYSICIANS

By

J. E. SCHMIDT, M.D.

Vocabulary Editor, MODERN MEDICINE
Associate Editor, TRAUMA

CHARLES C THOMAS • PUBLISHER
Springfield • *Illinois* • *U.S.A.*

R
428.1
S 352 e

Published and Distributed Throughout the World by
CHARLES C THOMAS • PUBLISHER
BANNERSTONE HOUSE
301-327 East Lawrence Avenue, Springfield, Illinois, U.S.A.
NATCHEZ PLANTATION HOUSE
735 North Atlantic Boulevard, Fort Lauderdale, Florida, U.S.A.

Standard Book Number 398-02400-6
Library of Congress Catalog Card Number: 77-177903

With THOMAS BOOKS *careful attention is given to all details of
manufacturing and design. It is the Publisher's desire to present books
that are satisfactory as to their physical qualities and artistic possibilities
and appropriate for their particular use.* THOMAS BOOKS *will be true
to those laws of quality that assure a good name and good will.*

Printed in the United States of America
JJ-1

INTRODUCTION

The knowledge of standard English expressions and English grammar is only a part of what the foreign student, physician, or other professional must have in order to feel at home in an English-speaking world, especially in the United States. The other part of the language, the *sine qua non,* consists of the idioms, the colloquialisms, the so-called substandard expressions, and the unconventional speech. Without an understanding of these forms, the foreign student or physician will find himself at sea or bewildered outside the perimeter of formal communication; for most Americans—whether they are scientists, students, physicians, or salesmen—dislike formal speech as much as they dislike formal dress. Nothing in the field of communication bridges the gap between a foreign professional and his American colleague as smoothly as the American idiom.

The foreign professional soon learns that English idioms and Americanisms are the shibboleths by which he is judged and without which he cannot qualify as "one of the boys," which is the ultimate acceptance.

The following pages deal mainly with these homey terms and expressions that have the lovable but baffling characteristic of meaning, as a whole, not at all what the component words individually suggest.

Only in America, as the saying goes, can expressions such as "up a tree," "do the trick," "talk turkey," "get the works," and "wrapped up in" mean *in a difficult or unpleasant situation, accomplish that which one sets out to do, speak what is on one's mind, be the victim of harsh treatment,* and *engrossed or absorbed in,* respectively.

This book is intended to be not only a reference dictionary in which to look up expressions spoken or written by others but also a textbook for the acquisition of the necessary facility to communicate with one's American colleagues in the manner they like best, i.e. English speech in the American style.

ENGLISH IDIOMS
and
AMERICANISMS

A

Accord

of one's own accord. Voluntarily; (done) without being asked or ordered by anyone.

> "He joined the search party of his own accord."

> "It is good to know that he went back to work of his own accord."

with one accord. With everyone agreeing; with unanimity; without anyone dissenting.

> "They voted him into the club with one accord."

Account

call to account. To hold someone responsible; to request an explanation for an act or event; to reprimand.

> "The manager was called to account for the discharge of the employee."

give a good account of oneself. To conduct oneself in a proper manner; to do well, especially in difficult circumstances.

> "Although much less experienced, he gave a good account of himself in the boxing match."

3

on account of. Because of; for the sake of someone.

> "She held on to her marriage on account of the children."

on no account. Not under any conditions or circumstances; positively not.

> "On no account should you open the door, unless you know the person."

take into account *or* **take account of.** To make allowances for certain conditions or circumstances; to take circumstances or other factors into consideration.

> "You must take into account the fact that the customs of his native land are different from those of ours."

> "Taking account of the difficult terrain, they made good progress."

Act

act on *or* **upon.** To do something in accordance with; follow; obey; to affect; bring about a change.

> "The delegate acted on instruction from his government."

> "The outburst acted on the emotions of the jury."

act one's age. To behave or do something which is proper for or expected from any normal person of a particular age, especially the age of the person involved.

> "The elderly man was not acting his age when he tried to date his young secretary."

act up. 1. To behave in an unnatural manner; to become worse; to become active or painful. 2. To behave playfully; to show a fit of temper.

> 1. "Every time it rains our car acts up and stalls at every stop."

"His weak back acted up again."

2. "The children always act up when their mother is out."

"He acted up again when his offer was turned down."

Advantage

have the advantage of. To be in a better or stronger position than someone else; to have an advantage over someone.

"Being a very good speaker, he has the advantage of his political opponents in the televised debates."

take advantage of. 1. To put to profitable use when an opportunity exists. 2. To exploit unfairly; to impose upon.

1. "He took advantage of the housing shortage by renting out his basement."

2. "He took advantage of her good nature by asking her to work overtime."

Air

clear the air. To remove any doubt, misunderstanding, animosity, tension, etc., from a situation or, especially, from a discussion.

"Before we proceed any further, let us clear the air of the rumors that have been floating around."

get the air. 1. To be dismissed or discharged. 2. To be rejected.

1. "Those with the least seniority will get the air first."

2. "He finally got the air when his girl realized he was only pretending to have an education."

give oneself airs. To act in a pompous or haughty manner; to behave as if one is a very important or distinguished person.

"Many of his colleagues dislike him because he is in the habit of giving himself such airs."

in the air. 1. In a condition of being rumored or talked about; in circulation; on the tongues of people. 2. Still undecided; unsettled.

> 1. "There is a feeling in the air that an announcement will soon be made."

> 2. "The final decision about the move is still in the air."

put on airs. Same as *give oneself airs,* which see.

up in the air. 1. Same as *in the air,* definition 2, which see. 2. Emotionally upset; very excited.

> "He is very agitated and he gets so up in the air over the most insignificant remark."

walk on air. To be very happy; to see everything in the brightest light; to be filled with joy.

> "He got his promotion and he is walking on air."

Alive

alive to. Aware or conscious of; sensitive or alert to the presence or appearance of something.

> "Politicians are alive to the needs of their constituents during an election year."

alive with. Teeming or swarming with; full of living things.

> "In the evening, the park is alive with fireflies."

> "The yard was alive with the laughter of happy children."

All

above all. Chiefly; mainly; before anything else.

> "He wanted to leave for several reasons, but above all because of the severity of the climate."

after all. In spite of the situation, circumstances, etc.; notwithstanding everything; everything else being considered.

> "He managed to graduate with the top honors after all."

> "She failed to get the appointment after all."

> "After all, what do you expect from an average layman?"

all in. Completely exhausted; worn out; very tired.

> "After driving all day and most of the night, he was all in."

all in all. 1. When everything is considered and balanced; in a general way. 2. All together; counting everything.

> 1. "All in all, their financial condition is not bad."

> "All in all, it would probably be an improvement."

> 2. "There were six injuries all in all."

at all. 1. In the least; in the smallest degree. 2. For any cause; under any circumstances. 3. In any way or manner.

> 1. "That did not upset him at all."

> 2. "If that is so, why write at all?"

> 3. "That was not a threat at all."

in all. All together; counting everybody or everything.

> "There will be ten pages in all."

once and for all. Once more and now for the last time; finally.

> "Let us decide once and for all who will be our spokesman."

Alley

blind alley. An alley, street, or course closed at the far end; hence, a course of action or a project which cannot succeed.

"When he invested in that business, he went up a blind alley."

up one's alley. Suited perfectly to one's talents; in line with one's aims or interests.

"Compiling a medical dictionary was right up his alley."

"Traveling and meeting new people was right up his alley."

Allowance

make allowance *or* allowances (for). 1. To take conditions or circumstances into consideration. 2. To overlook or forgive because of extenuating circumstances. 3. To allow for; to leave enough time, money, etc., for.

1. "In judging the delay, we must make allowance for the extremely bad weather."

2. "Knowing about his marital rift, they made allowances for his bad manners and loss of temper."

3. "We should make allowance for one stopover."

Alone

leave alone. 1. To allow someone to remain by himself. 2. To refrain from interfering with; not to bother someone.

1. "It would be well to leave him alone for the time being."

   "Leave the man alone with his thoughts."

2. "He finally lost his temper when the kids refused to leave him alone."

   "Leave the dog alone or he'll bite you."

   "They won't bother you if you will leave them alone."

let alone. 1. Same as *leave alone,* definition 2, which see. 2. Not to mention or consider.

> "We weren't able to see them, let alone hear them."

> "He didn't have enough money to buy a used car, let alone a new one."

let well enough alone. To accept the existing situation without trying to improve it; not to try to improve something for fear of making it worse.

> "The situation seemed so precarious that we decided to let well enough alone."

> "If you won't let well enough alone, they may not renew your lease."

Along

all along. All the time; from the very beginning and throughout the time that followed.

> "I thought you were serious, but all along you were only kidding."

along with. Added to; together with.

> "He may come along with the other guests."

> "This, along with the other income, will see him through."

get along. 1. To live comfortably with; to have no disagreements with. 2. To manage one's affairs satisfactorily. 3. To proceed or go forward with whatever one is doing. 4. To leave; to go away.

> 1. "They are getting along with their new neighbors very well."

> "Try to get along with them."

> 2. "She has a new job and is getting along very well."

3. "How are they getting along with their research?"

4. "Get along, little boy; don't bother me."

Amuck

run amuck. 1. To lose control of oneself and run around wildly doing illogical and often violent things. 2. To rush about in a homicidal frenzy; to go on a killing spree.

1. "When the disturbance started, some of the guests ran amuck and began jumping out of windows."

2. "One of the prisoners ran amuck and started shooting into the crowd."

   "Seeing the gallows, he ran amuck, flailing at the guards and the priest."

Apart

apart from. Other than (this or that); aside from; in addition to.

"Apart from the location, we like everything about the project."

"Apart from the fact that the price is too high, I doubt that we really need it."

take apart. 1. To separate something into its parts; to disassemble. 2. To examine very carefully. 3. To criticize; to find fault with.

1. "He took the lawn mower apart but failed to locate the trouble."

2. "They took apart every detail of the alibi."

3. "Her own family took her apart for her remark."

Appearance

keep up appearances. To present to others an appearance or show of favorable circumstances, especially financial success, in spite of reverses; to act as if everything is coming along just fine.

"After going into bankruptcy, they still kept up appearances for the sake of their daughter."

"In spite of their financial reverses, they kept up appearances by remaining in their palatial home."

make an appearance. 1. Same as *put in an appearance,* which see. 2. To come in person; to appear before an audience; to visit publicly.

"He didn't make his appearance until the hall was packed and jammed."

"He refused to make an appearance unless he received top billing."

"She promised to make an appearance at the rally if an escort could be provided."

put in an appearance. To make a short visit; to be present at a meeting, social gathering, etc., for a short time, as if to satisfy a promise or commitment.

"We will have to at least put in an appearance, or they will never forgive us."

"The celebrity did put in an appearance, but that was about all."

Arm

arm in arm. Having the arm of one person interlocked or intertwined with the arm of another.

"Walking down the road arm in arm, they looked like two happy children."

keep at arm's length. To keep someone from becoming too familiar; to be on friendly terms with someone but not to allow him to get too intimate; to show a person that he is not quite acceptable as one's close friend; to discourage someone from becoming friendly.

"They treated him with consideration and courtesy, but they kept him at arm's length."

"Be polite to him but keep him at arm's length."

in the arms of Morpheus. Sound asleep (in allusion to Morpheus, the god of dreams in Greek mythology); having pleasant dreams.

"At the time that you are speaking of, I was in the arms of Morpheus."

receive *or* **welcome with open arms.** To receive with hospitality; to accept with cordiality; to take one in gladly or eagerly.

"I assure you that the university will be delighted to have you on the faculty and will accept you with open arms."

Arms

bear arms. 1. To carry weapons upon one's person; to be in possession of weapons. 2. To serve as a member of the armed forces of a country.

1. "No one is permitted to bear arms within the city limits."

2. "Although he is a religious man, he has no misgivings about bearing arms in the defense of his country."

take up arms. To prepare for, or go to, war; to rise in an armed rebellion; to take an active part in a dispute.

"This was one cause for which the small nation was ready to take up arms."

"While she had strong convictions about this matter, she was not ready to take up arms."

up in arms. Angry; excited; indignant; aroused enough to fight.

"They were up in arms about the proposal to tax insurance premiums."

"Don't get up in arms about his remark. Consider the source."

As

as for. With reference to; concerning; regarding.

"As for his failure to appear in person, we can readily explain that."

as good as. 1. Equal to; the same as; practically. 2. Reliable; true to; trustworthy.

1. "The case is as good as lost."

"The car is as good as new now."

2. "You needn't worry. He is as good as his word."

as if. As it would be if (a certain condition prevailed); as though.

"She acted as if we had never parted."

"You need not feel as if your life had come to an end."

as is. As something exists now; in the condition that it happens to be at present.

"They are willing to pay the full price for the car as is."

"If you are willing to take the property as is, you can have it for a reasonable price."

as it were. So to speak; in a manner of speaking; in a way.

"She was the lady of the house, as it were."

"He was not his usual self, as it were, that day."

as long as. Assuming or provided that; considering that; since.

"As long as you are here, you may have the room for at least a week."

"As long as he didn't mean it, we'll not hold it against him."

as regards. Concerning; with reference to; about.

> "As regards the effort involved, it is really negligible."

> "He said nothing as regards the trip he is supposed to be planning."

as such. In the role or position indicated; in itself, without other considerations; alone.

> "A person, as such, may lose his temper, but as a public servant he cannot afford such a luxury."

> "The role, as such, is not important, but it provides the actor with show business exposure."

as yet. So far; until now; up to this moment.

> "As yet, no one has offered a satisfactory explanation for the sudden reversal."

> "We have not, as yet, seen the last of it."

> "They have not agreed with us as yet, but there are indications that they will."

Attend

attend to. To make sure that something is taken care of or accomplished; to wait on or to look after (in the sense of satisfying someone's needs).

> "She will attend to the clerical work."

> "He usually attends to the checking of the doors and windows."

> "She attended to all his needs while he was sick last month."

> "But who will attend to that?"

Avail

avail oneself of. To make use of; to utilize that which is at hand; to take advantage of an opening, opportunity, etc.

> "He availed himself of the little bit of light still left."

> "He availed himself of the abundance of fresh air and sunshine."

> "She availed herself of the opportunity to ride back to town."

Average

average out. To arrive at an average or mean value over a period of time; to come to an expected value in spite of fluctuations.

> "In spite of the rainy weather that we have been having, the attendance will average out for the entire season."

on the average. Counting the highs and the lows and coming to a mean or average figure; usually; typically.

> "On the average, he receives about fifty inquiries a week."

B

Back

back and fill. To act in an indecisive manner; to vacillate between opposing views or positions.

> "You will never know his real stand, as he is prone to back and fill."

back and forth. From one side to the other; forward and backward; backward and forward.

> "Stop rocking the boat by moving back and forth from one side to the other."

> "The tide of victory moved back and forth throughout the battle."

back down. To moderate one's demands; to cease to insist on certain conditions; to reduce one's belligerence or threats.

> "In face of our determined reaction, the enemy backed down."

> "After prolonged negotiations, the other side finally backed down on its maximum demands."

back out. To change one's mind about a promise or commitment; to refuse to go along with others on a previously agreed course.

"One of the allies backed out and made a separate peace."

"You can depend on him. He will never let you down or back out."

back up. To give support to; to aid; to show to be true by supplying appropriate evidence.

"The big power backed up its clients' demands."

"Several national organizations backed up the Women's Lib movement and demands."

"The plaintiff backed up his charge with several clear photographs of the site of the incident."

back water. To retrace one's steps; to go back to a previous position or attitude; to withdraw from a threatening attitude or from a role of assumed superiority.

"Like all bullies, he began to back water when we stood up to him."

behind one's back. Without the knowledge or consent of someone; in the absence of someone; secretly.

"She was all smiles in his presence but complained bitterly behind his back."

"He will never do anything behind your back."

be flat on one's back. To be ill and lying in bed; to be completely incapacitated, especially by illness; also, sometimes, to be financially embarrassed.

"She was flat on her back for nearly two months."

"He was flat on his back himself after the market went down, and he was unable to help her in any way."

be on one's back. To be ill and lying in bed; to be in a bind or desperate condition; to be unable to help oneself.

"He was on his back for several weeks with a nasty lung infection."

"After all these unexpected reverses, he was on his back financially."

be on someone's back. To be very critical of someone's actions; to goad or harass someone continually; to annoy persistently with remarks or actions.

"He was on his back all the time, until the poor fellow quit."

break someone's back. To cause someone to be in financial difficulties; to cause someone to become bankrupt.

"The unexpected medical expenses just about broke his back."

"Such additional expenses might break the company's back."

break the back of something. To finish the hardest part of an undertaking; to overcome the most stubborn obstacle in the solution of a problem; to defeat or frustrate the principal issue of an argument; to destroy or annul the strength of an assault, movement, system, etc.

"The discovery of complement broke the back of the immunological problem."

"The agreement on the format of the negotiations broke the back of the impasse."

"The court decision finally broke the back of the movement against the dumping of the gas."

get off one's back. To stop criticizing, finding fault with, annoying, or disturbing somebody; to stop picking on somebody.

"When he apologized, they finally got off his back."

"If you don't get off his back he'll soon let you have it."

get *or* put one's back up. To become, or cause to become, angry (in allusion to a cat arching its back in anger or fright).

> "Making remarks about her weight is one way to get her back up."

go back on. To cease to support someone or something; to desert a cause or a protege; to become disloyal to.

> "Several of his supporters went back on him after he made the statement."

> "The movement lost impetus when its most active patron went back on it."

have one's back to the wall. To be in a difficult situation; to be in a disadvantageous position.

> "With so many of the creditors demanding payment, the company had its back to the wall."

pat on the back. To congratulate, praise, or encourage; especially, to feel that one has done something clever or accomplished something worthwhile.

> "He wants to be patted on the back every time he makes a sale."

> "Just as he was patting himself on the back for having put across his idea, they decided not to use his *modus operandi* after all."

turn one's back on. Refuse to assist; ignore the needs of someone; forsake someone to whom one was previously helpful; leave behind by walking away, as in anger.

> "We never thought that he would turn his back on his old and sick friend."

> "He never turned his back on any needy family."

with one's back to the wall. See under *have one's back to the wall.*

Bacon

bring home the bacon. 1. To earn a livelihood; to provide someone with living expenses or material needs. 2. To succeed in accomplishing something; to win or be victorious.

> 1. "After all, he is the one who brings home the bacon."

> 2. "You can depend on him to bring home the bacon."

> "Once again he brought home the bacon by getting a sizable appropriation for his state."

save one's bacon. To prevent someone from getting into a desperate situation; to save from embarrassment, injury, etc.; to aid a person in accomplishing his aim.

> "There is no one here now to save his bacon."

> "His was prone to shoot off his mouth, but his wife always managed to save his bacon."

Bad

bad off. 1. In poor health; seriously ill. 2. In unfavorable circumstances; impoverished; bankrupt.

> 1. "She is rather bad off and not expected to live."
> "I did not realize he is that bad off."

> 2. "Financially, they are rather bad off because of the condition of the market."

go to the bad. To degenerate morally; to become depraved or wicked; to lapse into criminality.

> "Some youngsters of the best families go to the bad nowadays."

in bad. 1. In difficulty; in distress. 2. In disfavor; in an unfriendly relationship; on bad terms.

> 1. "He is in bad with the law, but he is trying to go straight."

"At the moment, he is in bad financially, but things ought to pick up soon."

2. "He is in bad with his boss and he would not dare ask for a raise now."

not bad. Not very good, but acceptable; not really so bad as expected; having some merit.

"Her sister is prettier, but Helen isn't bad either."

"The show wasn't bad, but somehow we had expected a better performance from such a fine cast."

not half bad. Surprisingly better than expected; quite good.

"In spite of the slow start, the final result wasn't half bad."

"Considering the fact that we arrived late, the meal wasn't half bad."

to the bad. Financially, in arrears; in debt; on the wrong side of the ledger; in the red.

"In the end, he came out about fifty dollars to the bad."

"No matter what he does, he always comes out to the bad."

too bad. (It is) regrettable; disappointing.

"He started smoking again; too bad!"

"It's too bad that you didn't think of it sooner."

Bag

bag and baggage. 1. With all one's belongings. 2. Completely; wholly.

1. "He moved in bag and baggage."

2. "The house was vacated bag and baggage in a matter of hours."

be left holding the bag. To be left to bear the entire responsibility for a wrong act when there are others who should share the blame and possible punishment.

> "When his companions denied any complicity in the
> act, he was left holding the bag."

hold the bag. See under *be left holding the bag.*

in the bag. Virtually assured; definite; certain; having success almost guaranteed.

> "Stop worrying. It's in the bag."

> "After many months of uncertainty, the sale is finally
> in the bag."

Ball

ball up. To make, or become, tangled, confused, out of order, etc.

> "Now you've got the whole thing balled up."

> "The records are all balled up, and it will take
> months to straighten them out."

be on the ball. To keep one's eyes open for an opening or opportunity; to be physically and mentally able; to be alert.

> "You'll have to be on the ball to keep up with him."

> "If you had been on the ball, this would not have
> happened."

carry the ball. To perform the principal part; to carry the heaviest burden; to have the main responsibility.

> "The younger brother is always the one to carry the
> ball in an emergency."

get on the ball. To become alerted to a situation; to get ready to meet an emergency; to ready oneself.

> "You'll have to get on the ball if you want a piece of
> the action."

"He realized that unless he got on the ball he would soon be fired."

have something, *or* a lot, on the ball. To have a talent or capability for something; to be skilled or efficient.

"That young fellow has a lot on the ball."

"Aside from being charming, she has something on the ball."

keep the ball rolling. To continue with an activity in progress; to keep up with whatever one is doing.

"Although they lost interest in the project, they kept the ball rolling."

on the ball. Active; alert; able and willing.

"You will never find him off base; he is always on the ball."

play ball. 1. To begin, or to continue, playing a ball game; to begin or resume an activity. 2. To work with someone, for personal gain, in an undesirable undertaking; to abet a wrongdoing.

"The local authorities chose to play ball with the operators of the casino."

start the ball rolling. To get something under way; to begin a process; to start something moving.

"The campaign manager started the ball rolling by calling a press conference."

"The speaker started the ball rolling by writing the first check for the scholarship fund."

Bargain

bargain for. 1. To try to obtain for a lower price, by negotiation. 2. To take into consideration; to expect.

1. "While he was bargaining for the house, someone else bought it."

2. "Taking care of four children was more than she bargained for."

bargain on. To expect and count on; to depend on.

"You can't bargain on having good weather all summer long."

in *or* into the bargain. In addition to something agreed on; above that which has been stipulated.

"The new director proved to be a good fund raiser in the bargain."

"We got a lawn mower and a tiller in the bargain."

strike a bargain. To come to an agreement on terms or prices by way of concessions on both sides.

"After a prolonged session which lasted a day and most of the night, they finally struck a bargain."

Barge

barge in *or* into. 1. To enter in a rude manner; to intrude. 2. To run into; to collide with.

1. "While we were discussing the matter, he barged in without even knocking."

2. "He was in such a hurry to get out that he barged into one of the guests standing near the door."

Bark

bark at the moon. To make ineffectual appeals; to protest in vain; to expostulate without success.

"There is no point in talking to him. You may as well bark at the moon."

"Appealing to their sense of justice is like barking at the moon."

bark up the wrong tree. To apply one's efforts in the wrong direction; to criticize or accuse the wrong person.

> "Our adversaries might have beat us to the atomic bomb if they had not barked up the wrong tree."

> "You are barking up the wrong tree if you are holding him responsible."

Beam

off the beam. 1. Not following the course indicated by an electronic guiding beam; off one's course. 2. Altogether wrong; confused.

> 1. "The pilot did not realize that his craft was off the beam."

> 2. "Don't listen to him, he's usually off the beam."

on the beam. 1. On the course directed or indicated by an electronic guiding beam; on the proper course. 2. Doing well; alert; correct.

> "For a while, the team seemed to flounder, but they are on the beam now."

Bear

bear down. 1. Weigh down; push down. 2. Make a stronger effort; try harder.

> 1. "He tried to bear down on his prostrate opponent."

> 2. "Far from being discouraged, he actually bore down."

bear down on *or* upon. 1. To press down; to exert pressure. 2. To intensify one's effort toward accomplishing something. 3. To approach or gain on rapidly.

> 1. "His wife bore down on him to accept the offer."

2. "They bore down on the problem of unemployment."

3. "In spite of his rapid pace, his pursuer bore down upon him."

bear on. Have a relation to; affect; have a connection with.

"It was not clear how the new evidence would bear on the case."

bear out. Prove to be so; support; confirm that which is assumed.

"The events of the next few weeks will bear me out."

bear up. To keep going in spite of hardships; to endure without flinching.

"How is he bearing up under the added strain?"

bear with. To tolerate; be patient with; put up with.

"If you will bear with her for a while, you will realize that she is a competent typist."

"Please bear with me while I am trying to explain."

bring to bear. To exert something on a person in order to influence his action.

"No pressure was brought to bear on him to act in favor of the bill."

be a bear for. 1. To be very interested in something; to be exceptionally suited for, or capable of doing, something. 2. To be able to endure strain, punishment, adversity, etc.

1. "He is a bear for watching ball games on television."

"He is a bear for dealing with disgruntled customers."

2. "One has to be a bear for punishment to put up with her nagging."

"This tough cloth is a bear for punishment."

Bearing

lose one's bearings. To get lost; to lose one's way.

> "It is easy to lose one's bearings traveling alone at night on these country roads."

Beat

beat about. To search hurriedly or roughly; to throw things around while looking for something.

> "They found it at last, but not before they beat about for nearly a day."

beat a retreat. To withdraw hurriedly; to retreat in disgrace.

> "When they saw the police coming, the gang beat a retreat."

beat back. To drive back by force; to cause an adversary to retreat.

> "They beat back several attacks but finally had to yield."

beat down. 1. To subdue or suppress; to put down. 2. To force down, especially a price.

> 1. "They beat down every attempt to liberalize the press."
>
> 2. "He asked a great deal more than the car was worth, but they did not try to beat him down."

beat it. To leave; to run away or out; leave! get going!

> "The attackers beat it before help arrived."
>
> "Beat it! I tell you, or you'll be sorry."

beat off. To repulse; to drive off or back.

> "We had to beat off two nasty little dogs before we could get to the door."

beat out. To force out; get ahead of; be successful against.

> "They beat us out on the paving contract."

beat up. To give a thrashing; to pommel; strike with the fists.

> "They not only took his money, but they beat him up."

beat the rap. To get off without punishment, by devious means; to succeed in evading punishment for a crime.

> "This time he was unable to beat the rap although he had the best lawyer in town."

Bed

bed and board. 1. Living or sleeping quarters and meals. 2. The state or the obligations of marriage; home; charge of a home or household.

> 1. "In addition to bed and board, the players receive a small salary."
>
> 2. "A woman relinquishes most of her claims when she leaves her husband's bed and board."

bed down. To make one's sleeping place; to sleep (with).

> "He can bed down in the guest room."
>
> "While on the Coast, he bedded down with one of his former service buddies."

get up on the wrong side of the bed. To be irritable or in a bad mood from the time one gets up in the morning.

> "I have seldom seen him so cross; he must have gotten up on the wrong side of the bed."

put to bed. With reference to a newspaper, to work on a particular edition until it goes to press; to work on something up to the last minute.

> "It was late in the night before he was able to put it to bed."

make one's bed. To do something wrong knowingly or willingly and thus make oneself responsible for the consequences.

> "He was warned against it and has only himself to blame; as they say, he made his bed, now let him lie in it."

take to bed. To lie down in bed, usually because of illness.

> "She wasn't feeling well, and we finally persuaded her to take to bed."

Bee

have a bee in the bonnet. 1. To have odd or fanciful ideas; to be a little off mentally. 2. To be obsessed by an idea; to be completely preoccupied.

> 1. "She has a bee in her bonnet about some things, but she is really quite sane and practical about most matters."

> 2. "He has a bee in his bonnet about fighting Communism."

put the bee on. To put the pressure on for a donation or loan.

> "They always put the bee on the professional men in town when additional money is needed for any purpose."

Beef

beef up. To make stronger; to augment by the addition of men, weapons, etc.

> "Each side promised not to beef up its forces while the negotiations are under way."

> "The store usually beefs up its sales force before the holidays."

Beg

beg off. 1. To ask to be released from an obligation. 2. To secure a release from an obligation.

> 1. "He tried to beg off, but we insisted that he go through with it."

> 2. "We fully expected her to sing at the reception, but she begged off on the ground of being indisposed."

beg the question. 1. In a discussion, to make a statement which assumes as a fact the very point that is to be proved. 2. To evade an issue; to avoid answering directly.

> 1. "Your argument assumes that there were two men, but that is begging the question since we have not proved that."

> 2. "You are making all kinds of statements, but you are begging the question with regard to the time of the incident."

go begging. To remain without a taker; to have no offer; to be unwanted; to be in excess of the demand.

> "Many useful inventions go begging because of the relatively closed market."

Behalf

in behalf of. In the interest of (someone); in favor of.

> "Several lawyers volunteered to act in behalf of the victimized family."

on behalf of. 1. Same as *in behalf of,* which see. 2. Representing; as a proxy.

> "He spoke on behalf of all residents of the block."

Belt

below the belt. Unfairly; not in accordance with the rules of propriety.

> "Attacking a candidate's religious views is really hitting below the belt."

tighten one's belt. To accept a more austere way of life; to reconcile oneself to hardships; to reduce expenditures.

> "They tightened their belts and accepted the shortages without a grumble."

> "The continued economic depression made it clear that the company will have to tighten its belt."

Best

all for the best. For a satisfactory conclusion; good for the eventual outcome, in spite of present appearances to the contrary.

> "Certain happenings, which we resent at the time, are often all for the best."

as best one can. As well as one can do under the circumstances.

> "He tried to get along in the unfavorable environment as best he could."

> "She managed to live on her small income as best she could."

at best. Even under the most favorable conditions; at the highest possible degree.

> "He can only tie the score, at best."

> "At best, they can only break even on the deal."

be at one's best. To be in the best condition of health, in the best mood, at the peak of one's talent, etc.

> "Although he was not at his best, he won the match in straight sets."

get the best of. To get the upper hand; to defeat; to outdo.

> "He finally got the best of his opponent and won the contest."

> "His temper gets the best of him from time to time."

had best. Would be wise to do; should; ought to.

> "He had best buy it now while it is still available."

> "We had best accept what they are offering us or we will not get even that much."

make the best of. To accept, and live with, an unfavorable situation; to do as well as possible under adverse conditions.

> "She did not like her new apartment, but she made the best of it."

> "His income was much smaller then, but he made the best of it."

with the best. As well (or as ably) as the best in a particular field.

> "Although he is rather short, he can play ball with the best of them."

Better

better off. 1. Having more wealth, income, etc.; richer. 2. In happier circumstances; in a more desirable condition.

> 1. "His business is doing well. In fact, he is better off now than he ever was."

> 2. "She left him, but he is better off without her."

better oneself. To improve one's own condition, especially financially, socially, or educationally.

> "If you want to better yourself, you will have to take some special training in your field."

for the better. Toward an improved condition; leading to more desirable circumstances.

"The present situation is so bad that it can change only for the better."

"His condition will change for the better in time."

get the better of. See discussion under *get the best of.*

go someone one better. To outdo another person's achievement; to surpass.

"I'll go him one better by taking a trip around the world."

had better. Should; ought to; would be doing the better thing.

"You had better attend to this immediately."

think better of. To reconsider something and decide on a different or opposite course.

"I had just about decided to buy the property, but overnight I thought better of it. The price was not right."

Between

between ourselves. Without telling it to anyone else; confidentially.

"Between ourselves, I don't think she is quite his equal."

between you and me. Same as *between ourselves,* which see.

between you, me, and the lamppost. Same as *between ourselves,* which see.

in between. In one's way; separating one thing from another; situated in the space between two persons, structures, etc.

"I would have caught up with him, but another car got in between."

"The two houses are adjacent, but there is a lot in between."

Bid

bid fair. To appear likely to (be, become, or do something).

> "This stock bids fair to outdo all others."

bid in. At an auction, to make a bid higher than all others, as in order to retain ownership of the item or to raise the final selling price.

> "He had instructions from the owner of the property
> to bid in and retain ownership for the company."

Bilge

bilge water. 1. Silly or nonsensical talk. 2. Distasteful language; offensive words.

> 1. "I am not impressed by his argument. To me
>   it seems like so much bilge water."
>
> 2. "The play has no plot at all, and the dialogue is
>   nothing but obscene bilge water."

Bill

bill and coo. To exchange endearing words, as lovers do, especially in whispers.

> "They would sit in the car billing and cooing for
> hours, until Mother would order them in."

fill the bill. To be just right for something; to meet all requirements.

> "With regard to putting him up for the summer,
> our cottage will just fill the bill."

foot the bill. To underwrite; to pay the cost or expenses.

> "I suppose Jim will foot the bill, as always."

Bind

in a bind. In an unpleasant situation; under a strain; in a financial difficulty.

"What with her mother coming to stay with us, I
am really in a bind."

"Business wasn't very good this season, and this additional expense will surely put us in a bind."

Bird

bird in the hand. Something which one actually has, as opposed
to something one might possibly get (which is a bird in the bush).

"I would rather hold on to this. A bird in the hand
is worth two in the bush."

bird in the bush. See under *bird in the hand.*

birds of a feather. Persons having similar backgrounds, interests,
aims, etc.

"We are not surprised that they are involved in this
affair. Birds of a feather always flock together."

Bite

bite off more than one can chew. To take on a task that is beyond
one's talent or capabilities.

"In trying to argue with such a recognized authority, he bit off more than he could chew."

"She bit off much more than she could chew when
she attempted to bawl out the director."

bite someone's head off. To answer a simple question or remark
with unjustified impatience or anger.

"He is so irritable that he'll bite your head off for
asking the correct time."

bite the dust. To fail in something; to be defeated; to be bested
or humbled.

"Another magazine with a wide circulation bit the
dust."

"The class bully finally bit the dust when he picked
on the new boy."

bite the hand that feeds one. To do something against a person
from whom one benefits or accepts kindness; to harm or work
against something that is beneficial.

"When he criticizes his uncle, he is biting the hand
that feeds him."

Black

black out. 1. To forget events relating to a particular person,
period, etc. 2. To lose consciousness, usually as a result of fright,
shock, etc., rather than injury. 3. To eliminate or conceal all
artificial light in a region so as to make it invisible to an enemy,
especially in aerial warfare.

1. "He was completely blacked out with regard to
   the happenings that followed the automobile accident."

2. "The sight of the injury caused her to black out."

3. "An order was immediately issued to black out
   the capital and the surrounding towns."

Blank

draw a blank. To fail to get any kind of results in spite of trying; to be completely unsuccessful.

"He tried every possible way to locate his daughter,
but no matter what he did, he always drew a blank."

"He attempted to engage the stranger in a conversation, but he drew a blank every time."

Blast

at full blast. At top speed; at a maximum capacity; with full employment.

"He was running at full blast when he bumped into his teacher."

"The plant is no longer operating at full blast."

blast off. 1. To take off from a launching pad. 2. To explode with harsh words; to burst out with criticism.

1. "The astronauts are scheduled to blast off tomorrow morning."

2. "He was sizzling with anger and waiting to blast off as soon as she came in."

Bleed

bleed white. To take away all resources; to be deprived of all money or other assets.

"These continued medical expenses can bleed a person white."

"The racketeers are bleeding the local merchants white."

Blood

bad blood. Mutual distrust; animosity; rancor.

"In spite of the official reconciliation, there is still bad blood between them."

blood is thicker than water. Blood relationship proves to be the strongest factor in a time of crisis.

"Though they are not getting along, he won't let him down in this emergency. After all, blood is thicker than water."

in cold blood. Deliberately and without compassion; with a show of cruelty.

"Most of the inhabitants of the village, including women and children, were executed in cold blood."

make one's blood boil. To make one completely overcome with anger; to make one indignant.

> "The cruelty of the crime makes one's blood boil."

> "It makes my blood boil when I think how she deserted her child."

make one's blood run cold. To fill with terror; to frighten thoroughly.

> "To think of what they had to go through makes your blood run cold."

> "The thought of having to go through this ordeal makes my blood run cold."

sweat blood. To work very hard; to be or live under strenuous circumstances; to wait with anxiety and worry.

> "To satisfy that man a worker has to sweat blood."

> "Many a student sweats blood while awaiting the decision of his draft board."

Blow

blow hot and cold. To vacillate with regard to one's attitude toward a particular matter (or person), being in favor at one time and then opposed, only to be in favor again.

> "I can't understand him. One day he is in favor of the man and the next day he is against him. He just blows hot and cold."

blow over. To cease or subside; to vanish from the memory.

> "His anger will blow over in a few days."

> "Her notoriety will blow over in time and then she will be able to resume her career."

Blue

once in a blue moon. Once in a very long time; very seldom.

"We hear from him once in a blue moon, when he
happens to be in town."

out of the blue. Quite unexpectedly; seemingly out of nowhere.

"He just dropped in, out of the blue. We had no idea
he was coming."

Blush

at first blush. On the first impression; at first; without much
thought.

"It seemed like a good idea at first blush, but it
wouldn't really work."

Board

across the board. In horse or dog racing, betting to finish first,
second, third (i.e. win, place, or show).

"It was not his habit to do so, but this time he bet
across the board."

Body

keep body and soul together. To maintain an economically reasonable way of life; to earn enough to live on; to make barely
enough to live on.

"He doesn't work steadily, but he manages to keep
body and soul together."

"Her small pension wouldn't be enough to keep body
and soul together."

Boil

boil over. To lose control of one's emotions; to burst out with
harsh words; to lose one's temper.

"Any reference to his estranged wife causes him to
boil over."

Bolt

bolt from the blue. An unforeseen event occurring suddenly; an unexpected unpleasant occurrence.

"Her announcement that she would sue him for divorce came like a bolt from the blue, as he thought that she was quite happy."

Bone

feel in one's bones. To have an intuition or presentiment about something; to be convinced about something without good reason or demonstrable proof.

"I just feel in my bones that he won't show up."

"She felt in her bones that there was something wrong, but she couldn't quite put her finger on it."

have a bone to pick. To have something to argue about with someone; to have a complaint or grudge against someone.

"Come here, young man, I have a bone to pick with you."

make no bones about. 1. To be frank about something; to admit readily. 2. To have no objection to or dislike for.

1. "He made no bones about his being present when the incident took place."

2. "She makes no bones about holding down a job to help support the family."

"He makes no bones about babysitting when he feels it will make his wife feel better."

Book

bring to book. To demand an explanation; to exact justice; to force to account or pay for.

"Sooner or later he will be brought to book for his tyrannical treatment of his wife."

by the book. In accordance with the rules; in a formal or rigid manner; in an unvarying, routine way.

> "He showed little initiative, handling all matters strictly by the book."

close the books. To make an end to; to be through with someone.

> "After many years of unhappiness and hesitation, she finally closed the books on him."

in one's bad books. In disfavor with someone; in another person's bad regard; thought unfavorably of by another person.

> "At the moment he is in her bad books."

in one's book. In one's opinion; in one's personal opinion which, admittedly, may not be supported by the opinions of others.

> "In his book, the whole undertaking was a mistake from the very beginning."

in one's good books. The opposite of *in one's bad books,* which see.

know like a book. To know very well; especially to know the peculiarities of a person.

> "She knows him like a book and she could tell easily that he did not want to go."

> "You can't fool me. I know you like a book."

Boot

bet your boots. To be sure or certain (of something); be confident of; rely on.

> "You can bet your boots that I won't miss that performance."

die with one's boots on. To die while one is active and doing what he likes to do; to die while doing something hazardous.

> "He is a vigorous person and he often says that he would rather die with his boots on than wither away in idleness."

get the boot. To be discharged or fired; to be dismissed or kicked out.

> "He stayed there as long as he did because he is the manager's nephew, but he finally got the boot."

lick the boots of. To act in a subservient manner toward someone; to flatter excessively.

> "He'll lick the boots of anyone to get what he wants."

> "They didn't promote him anyway, although he had licked his boss's boots for years."

Bottle

hit the bottle. To drink alcoholic beverages in excess; to go on a drinking binge; to become inebriated or intoxicated.

> "The poor fellow is hitting the bottle again, since his wife left him."

> "Lately, whenever he has any kind of worry, he just hits the bottle."

Bottom

at bottom. Basically; fundamentally; in reality.

> "In spite of his recent misbehavior, he is, at bottom, a good man."

be at the bottom of. To be the inciting agent; to be the cause of.

> "Many persons hold that Communists are at the bottom of the student rebellion in this country."

bet one's bottom dollar. To be so sure that one would bet his last dollar.

> "I'll bet my bottom dollar that she doesn't show up at all."

get to the bottom of. To search for and find the real reason for something.

"You can bet your bottom dollar that he'll get to the bottom of things before too long."

Bound

out of bounds. Not to be entered; forbidden to access; outside of one's province or field of knowledge; beyond one's authority.

"The village was declared out of bounds for the soldiers at the nearby post."

"He was completely out of bounds in making that remark."

Bow

bow and scrape. To be extremely polite and respectful; to be humble.

"He refused to bow and scrape to every customer."

make one's bow. To make a formal appearance for the first time; to begin or initiate, as a career.

"The comedian was making his bow on national network television."

"She made her bow in a small club in this city."

take a bow. To stand up, bow, or otherwise acknowledge an introduction, applause, etc.

"She received a standing ovation and gracefully responded by taking a bow."

Bowel

have a bowel movement. To defecate; to expel the waste matter or feces from the rectum.

"The patient is expected to have a bowel movement at least once a day."

move one's bowels. Same as *have a bowel movement,* which see; also, to take a laxative, or any other means, to stimulate defecation.

> "He relied on the proper food and exercise to move his bowels."

Bowl

bowl over. To astonish or overwhelm; to confuse; to upset.

> "The announcement that he won first prize nearly bowled her over."

Box

box in. To confine by blocking the way; to keep in by surrounding.

> "When we came out of the store, we found that our car was boxed in, and we had to wait for nearly an hour."

box up. Same as *box in,* which see.

Brain

beat one's brains out. To try or work very hard; to try hard to remember; to try very hard to accomplish something.

> "He beat his brains out but he could not recall the man's name."

> "He beat his brains out for years to support the family and send the boys to college."

Branch

branch out. To enlarge the scope of one's activities, interests, etc.

> "His company is now branching out by entering the food processing field."

Brass Tacks

get down to brass tacks. To abandon the discussion of nonessential matters and begin to consider the really basic or important aspects of a problem.

> "We have talked about everything under the sun; now let's get down to brass tacks."

Bread

bread and butter. The essentials of one's subsistence; a livelihood; the source of one's livelihood.

> "This little business is, nevertheless, his bread and butter."

cast one's bread upon the waters. To do good deeds or to be charitable without a thought of personal gain.

> "I suspect this man. He doesn't seem to be a person who would cast his bread upon the waters."

know which side one's bread is buttered on. To realize which things are to one's own advantage.

> "He is always very respectful to his rich uncle. He knows which side his bread is buttered on!"

Break

break away. To leave or depart; to sever relations with; to give up.

> "He realized that she wasn't the right kind of girl for him, but he just couldn't break away from her."

break down. To lose control over one's emotions; to collapse physically or mentally; to stop working or functioning; to overcome resistance.

> "When she saw him, after all these years, she broke down and wept."

"The hard work finally took its toll. One afternoon he just broke down and had to be taken to the hospital."

"His car broke down and he had to stop for repairs."

break even. To come out of a business deal, gambling venture, contest, etc., without a loss or gain in money or reputation.

"They made no money on the deal, but they didn't lose either. They just about broke even."

break in *or* into. 1. Enter by force. 2. Train and adapt. 3. Interrupt. 4. Enter, or be admitted into, a business, profession, etc.

1. "They broke in and carried off his TV set."

2. "He is breaking in a new sales representative."

3. "The announcer broke in with an important news item."

4. "It is difficult to tell someone how to break into show business."

break off. To cease or stop suddenly; to discontinue a friendship or association.

"The negotiations broke off at midnight."

"Although they were going steady for quite a while, she decided to break off for their mutual benefit."

break out. 1. To develop an eruption. 2. To start and spread rapidly. 3. To escape.

1. "She always breaks out in the summer when it gets hot and humid."

2. "Cholera broke out in Russia in the summer of 1970."

3. "Three prisoners broke out during the night."

break with. To cease to be friendly with; to abandon; to repudiate.

> "He stood it as long as he could, but he finally broke with his in-laws."

> "The organization broke with a tradition of many years to admit women as members."

Breast

make a clean breast of. To confess freely, giving a complete account of the matter at hand.

> "He was convinced that he would do better and feel better if he made a clean breast of the whole thing."

Breath

catch one's breath. To rest long enough to regain comfortable breathing, after an exertion; to pause before resuming an effort or activity.

> "She ran all the way, without stopping to catch her breath."

in the same breath. Almost at the same time; simultaneously.

> "He said they would reconsider the offer, but in the same breath he said they are not likely to reverse their original stand."

out of breath. Short of breath; gasping for breath; dyspneic.

> "He was out of breath and talking so fast that we could hardly understand him."

save one's breath. To cease talking or pleading because it is of no avail.

> "We advised him to save his breath because the vacancy had already been filled."

Breathe

breathe again. To start enjoying life again; to feel relieved.

"Now that she has her divorce, she can breathe again."

"They lived under the strain so long, but now they can breathe again."

breathe freely. Same as *breathe again,* which see.

breathe one's last. To die; to cease living.

"She is a very courageous woman and she is not quite ready to breathe her last."

not breathe a word. Not to say anything; to keep a secret; remain silent.

"She promised not to breathe a word if I would confide in her."

"In spite of her tendency to gossip, she didn't breathe a word about our little secret."

Bridge

burn one's bridges. To do something which makes a reversal of one's action or opinion impossible; to make a decision irrevocable.

"After all the indecision, we decided to burn our bridges behind us by signing the agreement and mailing it at once by registered mail."

Bring

bring about. To cause something to happen; to accomplish.

"The new environment brought about a wonderful change in her disposition. She used to be so irritable."

bring around. 1. To cause someone to change his mind or have a desired opinion about something. 2. To bring back to consciousness.

> 1. "Don't worry about David, she'll bring him around to our side."

> 2. "The heat was so intense that she passed out. But we had no difficulty bringing her around."

bring to. Same as *bring around*, definition 2.

bring up. 1. To rear, as a child; to take care of during childhood.

2. To mention a subject or topic. 3. To eject from the stomach; vomit.

> 1. "She was brought up by her grandparents."

> 2. "He did bring up the subject, but they were reluctant to discuss it."

> 3. "She felt better after she brought up the contaminated food."

Broke

go broke. To lose most or all of one's assets or wealth; to become poor or bankrupt.

> "Everyone who buys that restaurant eventually goes broke."

Brood

brood over. To be preoccupied with an unhappy thought; to meditate constantly and unhappily about an occurrence or situation.

> "Although she knew it wasn't good for her, she couldn't stop brooding over the upcoming induction of her son."

Brush

brush aside. To refuse to consider; to disregard; to view as unimportant.

> "He tried to argue about the matter, but they brushed him aside."

> "Our suggestions were repeatedly brushed aside."

brush up. To study or review a particular subject or skill in order to refresh one's memory or ability.

> "He is brushing up on the basic sciences in preparation for the board exams."

> "You had better brush up on your backstroke if you are playing with him."

Bubble

bubble over. To manifest great joy, enthusiasm, good spirits, etc.

> "Although usually restrained, she was now bubbling over with excitement about her husband's impending release from the service."

> "He seemed satisfied, but he wasn't exactly bubbling over with enthusiasm."

Buck

buck up. To regain confidence or enthusiasm; to experience renewed vigor.

> "He was down at the mouth, but he bucked up after she called him."

Buckle

buckle down. To add vigor and determination to whatever one is doing; to do something with more zest and enthusiasm than before.

"He fooled around most of the semester, but he buckled down to study before the exams."

"After he married Betty, he buckled down and made something of himself."

buckle under. To submit to the will of another; to yield under pressure, intimidation, persuasion, etc.

"We knew that he would eventually buckle under and let her have her way. He always does."

Bud

in the bud. In the making; in an early but promising phase; unfinished.

"He is young and he plays very well. He may be a chess champion in the bud."

nip in the bud. To check or stop something from developing at the very beginning; to squelch at the earliest possible time.

"A bad habit in a child should be nipped in the bud."

"He is planning to go to the festival, but we'll nip that in the bud."

Buoy

buoy up. To lift one's spirits; to encourage; to cheer up.

"She tried to buoy him up, but he was so despondent that nothing seemed to help."

Burn

burn oneself out. To debilitate oneself through excessive work or intemperate life.

"At the rate he is going now he'll burn himself out before he reaches middle age."

burn up. 1. To consume by fire; to burn completely. 2. To cause someone to become very angry; to vex or annoy. 3. To become irritated or angry.

1. "Such dry grass burns up quickly."

2. "Her silly behavior in company burned him up."

3. "He burns up at the slightest provocation."

Bush

beat around the bush. To avoid getting to the point of a discussion by talking about other or related matters.

"Let's stop beating around the bush and get down to serious discussion."

Business

business is business. Friendship must be disregarded in the transaction of business; business dealings should not be influenced by personal relationships.

"I can't let you have this for less than the regular price; business is business."

have no business. To have no justification or right; have no right to do something.

"You have no business telling him what to do."

mean business. To really mean to do something; to be serious about a plan.

"This time he wasn't fooling; he meant business."

By

by and by. In a little while; before too long; after a short time.

"You will forget about him by and by."

by and large. When you consider everything; on the whole; in general.

> "There are some disadvantages in living in the country, but, by and large, we like it."

by the by. By the way; not to change the subject; incidentally.

> "By the by, have you heard from your brother?"

by the bye. Same as *by the by*, which see.

C

Cake

take the cake. Be worthy of note; to surpass; stand out above others.

"I have known selfish acts, but this takes the cake."

Call

call down. 1. To invoke; to bring something upon. 2. To criticize; reprimand; chide.

1. "The vicious act called down the condemnation of the entire civilized world."

2. "He was called down for it several times, but he paid no attention."

call for. 1. To come, or stop by, in order to get or pick up. 2. To require; be appropriate for.

1. "They will call for her at about seven."

2. "This invitation does not call for an answer."

"The situation calls for more expert and experienced craftsmen."

on call. Readily available for service when called upon.

"There is a serviceman on call at all times."

Candle

burn the candle at both ends. To exhaust one's energy by working too hard or by living a dissipating life.

"We warned him to slow down, but he continued to burn the candle at both ends until he had a breakdown."

not hold a candle to. Not to compare favorably with something or someone.

"He is a competent mechanic but he doesn't hold a candle to the man who quit."

not worth the candle. Not worth the expense, effort, or worry involved.

"With enough effort and money we could undoubtedly restore the house, but it wouldn't be worth the candle. We can get a new house for less."

Cap

set one's cap for. To try to get a man as a husband or sweetheart.

"There was something about this young man that made practically every girl in the office set her cap for him."

Capital

make capital of. To utilize something unfairly for personal gain or advantage; to make the most of an opportunity.

"The candidate made a thoughtless remark and the opposition did not fail to make capital of it in the campaign."

Card

have a card up one's sleeve. To have a secret advantage or bargaining plan in a given situation.

> "Their cool attitude suggests that they have a card
> up their sleeve. I wonder what it might be."

in the cards. Likely to happen; meant to be; destined by fate.

> "It seemed that he would succeed, but he didn't;
> I guess it wasn't in the cards."

put one's cards on the table. To be perfectly frank about one's intentions; to explain clearly and at once what one's goal, plan, etc., is.

> "He impressed everyone as a straightforward person by putting his cards on the table."

speak by the card. To speak with precision and accuracy.

> "You may expect this ex-schoolteacher to speak by
> the card."

Care

take care. To be cautious; to be alert or prudent.

> "She admonished him to take care and drive only
> during the day."

> "Take care, and we will see you next week."

take care of. 1. To provide for the comfort or safety of; to look after someone or something. 2. To see that something that needs to be done is done; to attend to.

> 1. "Although there were others, he chose to take
>   care of his elderly aunt."

> 2. "Have a good time and don't worry about the
>   business. I'll take care of it."

> "She took care of the bill last week."

Carnal

have carnal knowledge of. To have coitus with; have sexual intimacy with.

> "He was found innocent of the charge of having carnal knowledge of a minor."

> "Since he had no carnal knowledge of his wife during their brief marriage, the marriage was annulled."

Carry

carry all before one. To be very successful; to win every time.

> "He doesn't know what it is to lose as he always carried all before him until now."

carry a tune. To know how to sing; to sing on key; to emit one's singing voice properly.

> "As a boy, he couldn't carry a tune, but listen to him now!"

carry away. To influence or excite beyond reason; to enthrall; to transport.

> "We were carried away by her magnificent singing."

> "Don't be carried away by this beguiling young lady!"

carry off. 1. To be successful in winning; to handle or manage successfully; to face with courage. 2. To kill; cause the death of.

> 1. "As usual, he carried off the first prize."

> "He carried off the deal very diplomatically."

> 2. "The epidemic carried off thousands of people."

carry on. 1. To act or behave like a child; to act in an excited or unruly manner. 2. To continue or proceed with something.

> 1. "They carried on like two spoiled brats."

"They carried on and wouldn't leave until we
called the police."

2. "The negotiations were carried on in spite of
the complaints by both sides."

"After her father passed away, she carried on
with the business."

"Under these circumstances we cannot carry on
much longer."

carry out. 1. To implement; to put a plan, method, etc., into
practice or operation. 2. To perform from beginning to end; to
complete.

1. "The company is now ready to carry out its plan
for expansion and diversification."

2. "The exchange of prisoners was carried out
without any complications or incidents."

carry too far. To do something to excess; to go beyond the
limits of good taste or propriety.

"That, it seems to me, is carrying a joke too far. He
could have been hurt."

carry through. 1. To sustain a person while he is in a difficult
situation. 2. To accomplish; to put into practice; to complete.

1. "Only the hope that he might one day escape
carried him through the ordeal of the camp."

2. "He was eager to carry through his father's
plans, although he did not quite agree with all
of them."

Case

in any case. Regardless of what the situation may really be;
notwithstanding what happened; anyhow.

"In any case, we would rather not file the complaint
at this time."

"Give us a call tomorrow in any case."

in case. If it so happens that; in the event that; if.

"In case he does call, tell him that I'll be back next week."

in case of. In the event of; if it so happens that there is.

"In case of a tie, the date of the postmark will decide the winner."

in no case. Under no circumstances; not in any event.

"She should in no case be burdened with such menial work."

Cast

cast about. To search for anxiously; to look for eagerly and nervously.

"After his retirement he cast about for some kind of hobby to take up the spare time."

"He cast about for a while, but finally went into the insurance business."

cast aside. To throw away; to discard as useless.

"Many of the articles they cast aside are still usable."

"She wouldn't cast aside such a fine prospect."

Cat

let the cat out of the bag. To let a secret become known; to divulge an intimate matter.

"We planned to have the party as a surprise, but someone let the cat out of the bag."

Catch

catch it. To receive criticism, reprimand, or punishment.

"He'll catch it from his wife when he comes home."

catch on. 1. To begin to understand; to comprehend. 2. To become acceptable or popular.

> 1. "He was taking us seriously, but finally he did catch on and we all had a good laugh."
>
> 2. "The new styles had a good start and they are really catching on now."

catch up. To come from behind to assume an equal position with someone or something.

> "He was behind in his studies, because of illness, but he is catching up now."

Caviar

caviar to the general. Something having appeal only to people with a cultivated taste; something that is beyond the taste of the average person.

> "Though more popular than it used to be, the opera is still caviar to the general."

Chafe

chafe at the bit. To act angrily or to be irritable because of a delay; to be restless and eager to proceed.

> "He was so anxious to go on that even the short delay caused him to chafe at the bit."

Chalk

chalk up. 1. To score or earn, as in a game. 2. To credit or charge; to ascribe.

> 1. "He chalked up five points in the first game."

2. "We weren't satisfied with the results, and we chalked it up to plain bad luck."

Chance

by chance. Not by design; accidentally; without intent.

"I had no idea he was there. I met him by chance."

chance on *or* upon. To meet accidentally; to find or notice without intent.

"She chanced upon him in a restaurant in Paris."

chances are. It is most likely; I'll bet that.

"Chances are that you won't need it, but take it along anyway, just in case."

on the chance. Depending on the slight possibility or hope.

"We called her on the chance that he might still be there, but he had left about an hour before."

Chapter

chapter and verse. An exact reference to a published item which substantiates one's allegation; a reference to an authority justifying an action, opinion, etc.

"He couldn't give us chapter and verse, but he did provide some convincing evidence."

Character

in character. In agreement with a person's temperament, disposition, or character; in agreement with an assumed role.

"Such indifference to her plight just doesn't seem to be in character with this kindly person."

out of character. Not in agreement with a person's known temperament, disposition, or character; not in agreement with an assumed role.

> "His action is out of character with what we know about the man."

Charge

in charge. In control, authority, or command.

> "We had difficulty determining who was in charge."

in charge of. Having control, authority, or command (of something).

> "The man in charge of the department was absent."

Check

check in. To register one's presence or arrival, as at a hotel.

> "Several of the guests checked in after midnight."

check out. To perform the necessary procedures, as paying the bill, when leaving a hotel.

> "Guests must check out before noon, or they will be charged for the day."

check up. To verify; make inquiries about someone or something.

> "They usually check up on every applicant."

Cheek

tongue in cheek. In a joking manner; mockingly; not really meaning what is said.

> "He looked serious enough, but I know that he said it with tongue in cheek."

Cheer

be of good cheer. To have a cheerful disposition; be gay or cheerful.

"In spite of his personal problems, he seemed to be
of good cheer most of the time."

"Be of good cheer! We shall meet again some day."

Chest

get (something) off one's chest. To remove a burden from one's
mind or conscience by discussing the offending matter with
someone; to resort to catharsis.

"Now, tell me what happened and get it off your
chest."

Chestnut

pull (someone's) chestnuts out of the fire. To do something unpleasant or dangerous in behalf of another person in order to
rescue him from an arduous or dangerous situation.

"You won't easily find another fool to pull your
chestnuts out of the fire."

Chicken

count one's chickens before they are hatched. To regard something as achieved or as one's own before it is so; to assume that
one will be successful.

"There are several unresolved factors in this deal,
and I wouldn't count my chickens before they are
hatched."

Chip

chip in. To give, along with others, money, effort, etc. in order
to accomplish a particular purpose.

"We all chipped in and bought him a nice going-
away present."

chip off the old block. A person having the characteristics and personality of his father.

> "He is as tough as his father, a chip off the old block."

chip on one's shoulder. A belligerent attitude; an inclination to quarrel.

> "He has had a chip on his shoulder ever since they passed him up in the promotion deal."

when the chips are down. In a time of crisis; when the situation is critical and one has to make a decision.

> "You can count on him when the chips are down."

Choke

choke up. To become so emotional about something as not to be able to speak; to become speechless and be on the verge of tears as a result of an emotional trauma.

> "She was so choked up by the ovation that she was unable to respond."

Class

in a class by itself *or* oneself. Having no equal; unique; unlike anyone else.

> "With regard to hardness, the diamond is in a class by itself."

> "He is in a class by himself when it comes to helping a friend."

Clean

clean hands. A condition of innocence; without guilt.

> "The investigation proved that he came to us with clean hands."

clean out. To consume or use up; to exhaust.

"The litigations cleaned him out financially."

"The visitors cleaned out the entire stock of the local food market."

clean up. 1. To remove undesirable persons, things, features, etc. 2. To complete or finish, as with a chore. 3. To make a great deal of money; to make unusual profits. 4. To make oneself clean; to wash up.

1. "The authorities finally cleaned up the town by closing the local gambling casinos."

2. "We had to work overtime, but we did clean up the backlog."

3. "During the war, while the plant was in operation, the local merchants cleaned up."

4. "The kids cleaned up in a hurry when they heard that their favorite uncle was coming."

come clean. To confess; to admit one's guilt; to tell the truth, especially in detail.

"At first he denied everything, but eventually he came clean and showed us where he had hidden the missing articles."

Clear

clear out. To leave, especially by request; to force to leave; to depart quickly or surreptitiously.

"The gang cleared out before the police arrived."

"The judge issued an order to clear out the squatters."

in the clear. 1. Free from suspicion of guilt; absolved; exonerated. 2. Free from financial difficulties or debts.

1. "They suspected him, but the polygraph put him in the clear."

2. "They struggled with that business for many years, but they are in the clear now."

Close

close down. To discontinue the operation of something.

"The hotel closes down for the season after Labor Day."

close in. 1. To approach someone or something from several directions so as to encircle and trap. 2. To give a feeling of being trapped by moving imaginary walls or obstacles closer to a person.

1. "They closed in on the enemy cruiser and succeeded in sinking it."

2. "He was always deathly afraid of being in a small room, where he felt the walls were closing in on him."

close out. To sell goods or merchandise at reduced prices in order to dispose of them quickly.

"The store is closing out its summer stock at exceptionally attractive prices."

Coals

haul over the coals. To give a thorough scolding; to reprimand severely.

"You may expect to be hauled over the coals for leaving the back door unlatched."

drag over the coals. Same as *haul over the coals*, which see.

rake over the coals. Same as *haul over the coals*.

take over the coals. Same as *haul over the coals*.

Coast

coast is clear. No one is watching; nothing is in the way.

"The coast is clear; we can leave now."

Cold

cold comfort. Little consolation; no comfort at all.

> "It is cold comfort for me to know that the culprit was apprehended. The damage is done."

get cold feet. Lose one's courage; to become frightened of something.

> "He planned to participate in the demonstration, but then he got cold feet."

throw cold water on. To say something discouraging in relation to a matter about which another person is enthusiastic; to dampen the spirit of.

> "We were all enthused about the trip, but he threw cold water on our plans by reminding us of the outbreak of cholera."

Color

show one's colors. To reveal one's true nature or character; to reveal one's stand or opinion.

> "We always regarded him as a friend, but he showed his colors in the current emergency."

with flying colors. With a wide margin of victory; with eminent success.

> "We thought he might have difficulty with the math exams, but he came through with flying colors."

Come

come across. 1. To meet someone accidentally; to note or discover by sheer chance. 2. To give in and do or say what is demanded.

> 1. "I came across an old friend of yours the other day."

> 2. "After a while he came across and made the usual payment."

come around. 1. To regain consciousness. 2. To change one's stand or opinion so as to agree with that of another person.

> 1. "She fainted from the heat, but she came around quickly enough when we applied cold compresses."

> 2. "We had to do a great deal of talking, but she finally came around and saw it our way."

come to. Same as *come around,* definition 1, which see.

Company

keep company. To associate with in a friendly way; of members of the opposite sex, to go together, as in courtship.

> "They kept company for more than ten years before they were married."

part company. To cease keeping company (see above); to stop seeing each other.

> "They had been friends for a number of years, but they finally parted company because of some silly argument."

Conscience

have on one's conscience. To have a sense of guilt because of a wrong act or because of the omission of an act.

> "He still has it on his conscience that he did not answer the phone when she called."

in all conscience. In fairness; in accordance with reason or good sense; certainly.

> "In all conscience I must say that she was very patient and understanding."

Consideration

in consideration of. On the basis of; in return for.

"In consideration of his good record, the company decided not to prosecute."

take into consideration. To regard as a factor while making a decision; to keep in mind.

"We must take into consideration the fact that the accused is a minor."

Contrary

on the contrary. Just the opposite; as opposed to what has been stated.

"He did not say he liked it. On the contrary, he was very much against it."

to the contrary. To a different or opposite effect; in another direction.

"He claims he wasn't there, but the evidence points to the contrary."

Cook

cook up. To devise something, especially hurriedly or fancifully; to devise or invent in order to deceive, discredit, falsify, etc.

"She cooked up a novelty for the party, but she wouldn't tell me what it is."

"To discredit the witness, they cooked up a story about a previous arrest."

Corner

cut corners. To reduce expenses or effort; to use cheaper material; to utilize a shorter route.

"Manufacturers are not concerned about the consumer. They just want to cut corners and make bigger profits."

"He got to the point much quicker by cutting corners."

turn the corner. To pass a critical or difficult point safely.

"The first few years of his practice were difficult, but he has turned the corner by now."

Cost

at all costs. Without regard to the price or effort involved; by any means that may be necessary.

"Peace must be preserved at all costs."

at any cost. Same as *at all costs,* which see.

Cotton

cotton to. To agree with; to approve; to become fond of; to become friends.

"I just don't cotton to this proposal."

"After a while they began to cotton to each other."

Counsel

keep one's own counsel. To keep one's opinion or ideas a secret; to remain silent about something.

"Although she is generally talkative and gossipy, she kept her own counsel on this matter."

take counsel. To consult; to ask someone's opinion; to discuss and exchange opinions.

"She is very sure of herself and is not likely to take counsel."

Count

count on. To consider for a particular purpose; to rely on in case of an emergency.

> "You can always count on him when you need a friend."

count out. To omit from consideration; to exclude.

> "You can count me out as far as the European trip is concerned."

Counter

over the counter. (With regard to the sale of stocks) through the office of a broker rather than the stock exchange.

> "A large segment of the total sales of stock goes over the counter."

under the counter. In a surreptitious or illegal manner.

> "The material is still available, but you will have to buy it under the counter."

Course

in due course. In the normal passage of time; in the usual occurrence of events.

> "In due course, you will receive a notice that payment is due."

> "You will forget these minor worries in due course."

in the course of. During the time or interval of; as a part of a series of events.

> "In the course of checking the files, a discrepancy was uncovered."

Cover

take cover. To protect oneself by going under some kind of cover, roof, etc.

"When the storm broke, we took cover in a tool shed."

under cover. Under the protection of; under a pretense; in secret; concealed.

"They made their break under cover of darkness."

"The robbers entered the apartment under cover of repairmen."

"They remained under cover for about two months, until the uproar subsided."

Crack

crack a book. To open a book for the purpose of reading; to open a textbook for study.

"He studies hard before exams, but the rest of the time he hardly cracks a book."

crack a smile. To smile laboriously or unwillingly; make an effort to smile.

"She gave him a cold reception; she didn't even crack a smile when he greeted her."

crack down. To become stricter in enforcing the law, obedience, etc.

"So many people complained that the police eventually cracked down on the gambling interests."

Cradle

rob the cradle. To court or to marry a person (usually a girl) much younger than oneself.

"Jim robbed the cradle by marrying a girl less than half his age."

Crap

crap around. To fool around; to idle; to behave in a childish manner.

> "Stop crapping around and let's go to work."

Crazy

like crazy. With great enthusiasm; with excessive energy; at an unusual rate of speed.

> "Most of the time she just lolls about or watches television, but some days she is full of energy and works like crazy around the house."

Credit

give credit to. To acknowledge something worthwhile; to have confidence or trust in; to compliment.

> "Whatever one's opinions on this may be, I'll give credit to anyone who is at least sincere."

Creep

make one's flesh creep. To make one extremely uneasy through fright, revulsion, abhorrence, etc.

> "The details of that gruesome murder make one's flesh creep."

the creeps. A feeling of horror, revulsion, abhorrence, etc.; the uneasiness of being touched unpleasantly or of having something disgusting crawl on the skin.

> "This unsavory character gives me the creeps when he comes within twenty feet of me."

Crimp

put a crimp in. Introduce a hindrance; obstruct; interfere with.

> "Her mother's illness put a crimp in their plans to marry this fall."

Crop

crop up. To appear suddenly or unexpectedly, usually in an unfavorable way.

> "We were all ready to start when this thing about the sale of the house cropped up."

Cropper

come a cropper. To fail completely; to come to a disastrous end; to be hit by misfortune.

> "His new project, like many of the previous ones, suddenly came a cropper."

Cross

cross up. To disappoint or deceive, as by failing to keep a promise,

> "I thought he was the one man I could depend on, but he crossed me up by failing to make a hotel reservation."

Crow

eat crow. To humble oneself by admitting an error, retracting a statement, etc.

> "He is usually quite accurate, but he had to eat crow this time. His prediction was way off."

Cry

a far cry. A big difference; a long way; something that is much inferior to something else.

> "Just passing an exam is a far cry from being at the top of one's class."

> "Receiving an inquiry is a far cry from getting an actual offer."

cry one's eyes *or* **heart out.** To cry or weep constantly; to grieve painfully; to be inconsolably depressed by a separation from someone.

"She was so attached to her nephew that when he went into the service she cried her eyes out."

Cucumber

cool as a cucumber. Undisturbed; calm; in control of one's emotions.

"He is usually excitable, but throughout this ordeal he somehow remained as cool as a cucumber."

Cuff

off the cuff. 1. Without preparation; extemporaneously. 2. Not officially or formally; not *ex cathedra.*

1. "Considering that the speech was off the cuff, it was rather good."

2. "He wouldn't make an official statement, but off the cuff he said that no progress was made."

on the cuff. On credit; free; without charge.

"He was able to buy it on the cuff."

"They enjoyed the trip even more because it was on the cuff. The company paid for it."

Cup

in one's cups. In a condition of alcoholic intoxication; drunk.

"He is apt to lose his temper when he is in his cups."

Curry

curry favor. To seek by flattery or fawning; to seek to advance by belittling oneself.

"He wouldn't stop at anything to curry favor with his superiors."

Curtain

draw the curtain on. 1. To finish; to bring to an end. 2. To conceal or keep secret.

> 1. "After three years of futile attempts, they finally drew the curtains on the negotiations."

> 2. "The State Department drew the curtain on certain aspects of the proposal."

lift the curtain on. 1. To begin or start something. 2. To reveal or disclose; to make public.

> 1. "After a long delay, the company lifted the curtain on the building project."

> 2. "The commission is scheduled to lift the curtain on its findings next month."

Cut

a cut above. Slightly better than (someone or something else).

> "He is certainly a cut above the average person in this town."

cut across. To move diagonally across, to save distance; to move along a shorter route or course.

> "You will save yourself some walking by cutting across the field."

cut and dried. Following a prearranged and dull pattern; lacking challenge.

> "This cut and dried work would not suit his temperament. It would bore him."

cut back. To reduce or diminish the rate of an activity; to discontinue.

> "As the pace of the war slackened, powder production was cut back at the local plant."

cut in. 1. To thrust something in; to interrupt. 2. Of a man, to stop a couple while dancing in order to take the woman for his own dancing partner.

> 1. "The car to our right suddenly cut in front of us so that I had to step on the brakes."
>
> "She doesn't hesitate to cut in with her remarks no matter who is speaking."
>
> 2. "This fellow kept on cutting in with several of the couples until one of the boys punched him in the jaw."

cut it out. To stop doing something (that is annoying someone).

> "She asked him to cut it out, but he kept up his annoying chatter until she walked out."

cut out for. Especially suited for something.

> "He is a good talker and just cut out for the job."

cut up. 1. To cut into small parts; to cause lacerations or cuts in a tissue. 2. To cause distress; to depress or deject. 3. To play childish tricks; to play around so as to attract attention.

> 1. "His hand was cut up in the accident."
>
> 2. "When he left her, she was pretty much cut up."
>
> 3. "They continued to cut up until the teacher came in and reprimanded them."

D

Damn

damn with faint praise. To discredit or condemn something by giving it very moderate or inadequate praise.

> "The master of ceremonies damned the visiting artist with faint praise by referring to him as one of the better violin players in this part of the country."

give a damn. To be concerned (about someone or something); to consider important.

> "He doesn't seem to give a damn whether he hears from her or not."

Dance

dance attendance. To be excessive with one's attentions; to be near someone at all times so as to lavish attention and offer service.

> "She is beautiful and she always has a boy friend to dance attendance on her."

> "He is too proud to dance attendance on anyone."

dance to another tune. To change one's attitude in response to a change in circumstances.

"He used to be against the war, but now that his business is benefiting from it, he is dancing to another tune."

Dare

dare say. To regard something as likely; to consider quite probable.

"I dare say that you will hear from him presently."

Dark

in the dark. Uninformed; ignorant of; unenlightened; undisclosed.

"He preferred to keep us in the dark about his plans."

"His unsavory past remained in the dark for a long time."

keep dark. To keep undisclosed; to hold as a secret.

"The details of the proposal were kept dark."

Date

out of date. Belonging to a previous era; no longer used because superseded by modern versions.

"That dictionary was out of date five years ago."

to date. Until the present time; up to now.

"This is all we have received to date."

up to date. Containing, or in accord with, the latest information, ideas, etc.

"The yearly supplements keep the dictionary up to date."

Day

call it a day. To regard the working day as finished; to quit work for the day.

"Let's call it a day and go to the movies."

day in and day out. Every day; day after day, without respite.

"Doing the housework day in and day out got on her nerves."

from day to day. With regard only to the following day but without thought for the future.

"The future being so uncertain, he decided to live from day to day."

Deal

a good *or* **great deal.** A large amount; much; very much.

"We have already spent a great deal of money on this project."

"We cannot spend a great deal more time on this problem."

Death

to death. Very much; almost to the point of death; to the utmost.

"He was sick to death of her nagging."

"They almost worried him to death."

Deck

clear the decks. To move things out of the way and get ready for action.

"I make a motion that we clear the decks."

hit the deck. 1. To rise from sleep; get out of bed. 2. To fall, or be knocked, to the ground. 3. Prepare for action.

1. "He usually hits the deck at about seven in the morning."

2. "He landed a right to the chin and his opponent hit the deck."

3. "After a layover of several weeks, they were quite ready to hit the deck."

on deck. 1. Ready to act; prepared to proceed. 2. Standing next in line; coming up next.

1. "Only three men were on deck the next morning."

2. "Jimmy Smith is on deck."

Deep

go off the deep end. To undertake rashly; to plunge into something without due consideration; to become angry or emotional.

"He surely went off the deep end when he bought that restaurant."

"No need to go off the deep end over such a trifle."

Defiance

in defiance of. In spite of; despite; notwithstanding.

"We had a good crop in defiance of the dry weather."

Degree

by degrees. Little by little; gradually.

"The inflation got worse by degrees."

to a degree. To a certain extent; by a certain amount.

"They are both right to a degree."

Devil

between the devil and the deep. Faced by a choice between equally undesirable alternatives.

"He felt that he was between the devil and the deep, since he was sure to offend his boss if he didn't attend, and he would displease his wife if he did."

between the devil and the deep blue sea. Same as *between the devil and the deep,* which see.

give the devil his due. Acknowledge merit, talent, etc., with reference to a person one dislikes.

> "Whether you like him or not, you have to give the devil his due. He is a clever debater."

raise the devil. 1. To complain vehemently or noisily. 2. To celebrate in a boisterous manner; to make a commotion or a great deal of noise.

> 1. "He raised the devil because we didn't notify him in time."
>
> 2. "He couldn't study because the kids were raising the devil outside his window."

the devil to pay. Trouble in the future; consequences to be endured.

> "If the campus unrest gets worse, there will be the devil to pay."

Dig

dig in. To prepare oneself for a long stay or for a possible assault; to intensify one's effort.

> "The boys decided to live in the summer cottage and began to dig in for the winter."
>
> "It was his custom to dig in during the last few weeks of the semester."

dig into. To work vigorously; to undertake something with great interest.

> "He made up his mind to pass the exam and he dug into his studies."

Dilemma

on the horns of a dilemma. Same as *between the devil and the deep,* which see.

Dim

take a dim view of. To regard something as likely to fail; to view with skepticism.

"I, personally, take a dim view of his investment plans."

"Don't listen to him. He takes a dim view of practically everything involving a risk."

Distance

keep one's distance. To act in a reserved manner; to be aloof; not to get too close or familiar with others.

"He is polite enough and speaks when spoken to, but he keeps his distance."

Do

do away with. 1. Abolish; discontinue using; put an end to. 2. To kill or murder; destroy.

1. "The committee decided to do away with the preliminary registration."

2. "They did away with him in the typical gangland manner."

do without. To abstain from; to get along without something.

"We did without luxuries for a long time, and sometimes without necessities, so that we might send the boy to college."

have to do with. Have a relationship with; be associated with.

"We cannot see what this has to do with the problem at hand."

"How a person is brought up has a great deal to do with his outlook on life."

make do. To manage to get along with what one has or with what is available although it is not completely satisfactory.

"She will make do with the old typewriter until the new one arrives."

Dog

a dog's life. A very difficult kind of life or existence; an existence marked by prolonged hardships.

"We are happy that his lot has improved, for he has lived a dog's life all these years."

dog-eat-dog. Marked by ruthlessness; designating a business in which unfair methods of competition are regarded as normal.

"Advertising is a dog-eat-dog business in which nothing is sacred."

put on the dog. To behave in a manner intended to give the impression of wealth, success, etc.

"Pay no attention to them. They are just putting on the dog."

Door

lay at the door of. To put the blame on someone; to impute a wrongdoing, guilt, etc., to someone.

"The blame for car theft may often be laid at the door of careless drivers who leave the key in the lock."

out of doors. Outside of the house or dwelling; in the open air.

"She makes her children spend a great deal of time out of doors."

Dot

dot one's i's and cross one's t's. To be very careful about even the smallest details.

> "You can depend on this girl to attend to all details. She is one who always dots her i's and crosses her t's."

on the dot. Exactly on time; precise; punctual.

> "He was here at seven, on the dot, as usual."

Double

double in brass. To be able to do, or to do, work which is different from one's regular work.

> "In such a small newspaper everyone doubles in brass. The editor reads proof, the receptionist does the typing, and the delivery man does some photography."

double up. 1. To bend at the waist, as in pain or laughter. 2. Of two persons or families, to live together in a room or apartment intended for one.

> 1. "He lay in bed doubled up with pain."

> 2. "Because of the extreme housing shortage in the area, some families had to double up."

Doubt

beyond the shadow of a doubt. Very definitely; certainly.

> "It is their handiwork, beyond the shadow of a doubt."

beyond doubt. Same as *beyond the shadow of a doubt,* which see.

no doubt. Very likely; certainly.

> "They will, no doubt, make at least a formal objection."

without doubt. Certainly; without any question.

> "It is without doubt the finest example of medieval art."

Down

down and out. In a desperate condition because of illness, lack of money, loneliness, etc.

> "He was down and out when he received this lucrative offer, and from then on things turned for the better."

down in the mouth. Depressed; in a blue mood; discouraged.

> "He has been down in the mouth ever since he lost his job."

Draw

beat to the draw. To do something before another person trying to do the same; to accomplish something sooner than one's opponent.

> "Our competitor beat us to the draw by coming out first with the new toy."

draw out. 1. To prolong; to extend unnecessarily. 2. To succeed in obtaining information from an unwilling talker.

> 1. "The negotiations were drawn out over a period of several months."

> 2. "I was able to draw out an admission from her that she did hear from him on the day in question."

Dream

dream up. To devise or conceive a plan or project, especially one that is not practical; to come up with a fanciful or unrealistic story, account, etc.

"Once again he dreamed up a plan for pollution control, but no one paid any attention to him."

"I don't believe a word of it. He just dreamed it up."

Dress

dress up. To put on one's best clothes; to dress in formal clothes.

"She took special care to dress up for the occasion."

Drop

at the drop of a hat. Without delay or hesitation; in response to the slightest provocation.

"He'll start an argument with you at the drop of a hat."

drop behind. Not to be able to keep up with the pace of another; to proceed at a slower rate than another.

"Illness in the family and other worries caused him to drop behind in his studies."

drop in. To make an unannounced visit; to visit unexpectedly.

"Guess who dropped in yesterday. Jim and his wife."

drop off. 1. To decrease in amount. 2. To fall asleep.

1. "Business has dropped off at least 15 percent in the last six months."

2. "He usually drops off while watching television."

drop out. To cease being a member of; to discontinue participating.

"Much is being said in these days against dropping out of school."

get *or* have the drop on. To achieve an advantage over an adversary; to enjoy a superior position with regard to an opponent.

> "The candidate got a drop on his opponent by announcing first."

Drug

drug on the market. Something that is so abundant or plentifully supplied that it is of little interest and has small value or bargaining power.

> "In that small town, widows and other unattached women are a drug on the market. What we need is more eligible men."

Drum

drum up. To create or stimulate interest, business demand, a market, etc., by vigorous effort.

> "The mayor is on a trip trying to drum up business for the city."

Dust

throw dust in someone's eyes. To do something for the purpose of misleading.

> "Their pretended interest in the property is meant to throw dust in our eyes."

Dutch

beat the Dutch. To be very surprising; to stagger the imagination; to surpass all others.

> "How they were able to make so much money in so short a time is fantastic. It beats the Dutch!"

go Dutch. To have an arrangement whereby each person pays his own expenses.

> "In that country, boys and girls always go Dutch."

in Dutch. In a condition of disfavor with someone; in some difculty.

> "He is always in Dutch with somebody. Now it's his neighbor."

Duty

do duty. To serve the same purpose as something else; to function as a substitute.

> "The local policeman also does duty as school bus driver."

off duty. Not working in one's official capacity; not on duty; at liberty.

> "Although the officer was off duty, he apprehended the burglar."

on duty. Engaged in one's official capacity; functioning in one's role; not relieved.

> "An investigator is not allowed to drink while on duty."

Dwell

dwell on. To concentrate on a particular point; to think continuously about something; to talk at length.

> "Let's not dwell on this part of the discussion any longer."

Dye

of the deepest dye. Of the worst kind; of the most heinous sort.

> "He is a racist of the deepest dye."

E

Ear

be all ears. To listen eagerly; to be interested and attentive.

"The minute I mentioned Alice, she was all ears."

fall on deaf ears. To fail to be heeded; to get an adverse reaction.

"Her plea for her husband fell on deaf ears."

have *or* keep one's ear to the ground. To keep oneself informed about current events; to be on the lookout for an opportunity.

"He always kept his ear to the ground and was able
to acquire the property long before anyone else ap-
preciated its potential value."

have the ear of. To have access to and the attention of a person; to be in a position to talk to.

"This girl has the ear of an influential member of the
committee."

in one ear and out of the other. Listened to but not heeded; heard but quickly forgotten.

"I told him about the hazard, but it went in one ear
and out of the other."

turn a deaf ear. To pay no attention; refuse to heed; be unwilling to listen.

> "The company turned a deaf ear to the request for another extension."

up to the ears. Deeply involved; thoroughly submerged in.

> "He is up to the ears in debt already."

Earth

come back *or* down to earth. To abandon a dream or visionary plan and return to reality.

> "I advised him to stop dreaming of Utopias and come down to earth."

down-to-earth. Not visionary; practical; realistic; with both feet on the ground.

> "He is a very sensible, down-to-earth fellow."

move heaven and earth. To stop at nothing; to make every possible effort.

> "He is one person who will move heaven and earth to get what he wants."

Easy

easy come, easy go. Not particularly intent on earning money or concerned about spending it; obtained and disposed of with equal ease or unconcern.

> "He has made several fortunes and lost them. With him it's easy come, easy go."

on easy street. In good financial condition; having an easy and ample income.

> "He did have it rough for a while, but he is on easy street now."

take it easy. To abstain from hard physical or mental work; to live a life marked by rest and relaxation; to refrain from anger, emotional crises, etc.

> "When he became a 'senior citizen,' he decided to take it easy."

> "Knowing his quick temper, she advised him to take it easy in arguing his case."

Eat

eat one's heart out. To worry intensely about something; to grieve.

> "She is eating her heart out over his expected induction into the service."

eat one out of house and home. Of a visitor, to eat so much of the host's food as to impoverish him.

> "Her two guests almost ate her out of house and home."

eat one's words. To be forced to retract a previous statement.

> "When they said the boy will never make it, they did not realize that they would have to eat their words later on."

Edge

on edge. 1. Nervous; irritable; easily angered. 2. Eager; very curious.

> 1. "She is so terribly on edge that the slightest noise makes her jump."

> 2. "Everyone was on edge to hear the verdict."

take the edge off. To reduce the intensity, as of pain, pleasure, etc.

> "Hearing about the award on the radio took the edge off the surprise."

Effect

to the effect. Meaning in substance; saying in essence.

"He said something to the effect that the response to his inquiry was not clear or not definite."

Egg

lay an egg. To be utterly unsuccessful; to make a fool of oneself or fail miserably, especially in front of a group of people.

"In spite of the expensive buildup, he laid an egg as the master of ceremonies."

put all one's eggs in one basket. To invest all one's money or otherwise risk all in a single enterprise.

"A person shouldn't invest all his money in stocks. That would be putting all one's eggs in one basket."

Eight Ball

behind the eight ball. In an unfavorable or disadvantageous situation.

"With the market down and all his investments being in stocks, he is now behind the eight ball."

Eke

eke out. 1. To earn a living with difficulty; to barely make enough to live on. 2. To improvise a supplement for something.

1. "Although he has three jobs, he barely manages to eke out a living."

2. "He eked out his deficient formal education by extensive reading."

Elbow

at one's elbow. Near one's person; easily reached; nearby.

> "Having a small kitchen has one advantage: everything is at one's elbow."

rub elbows with. To be in close physical contact with; to associate or mingle with.

> "At this restaurant you will have a chance to rub elbows with some of the literary greats."

Element

be in one's element. To be in optimum surroundings; to be in a situation in which one can do his best.

> "When he is among musicians, he is in his element."

End

at loose ends. In a confused state; without definite ideas or plans.

> "They arrived in their new homeland with high hopes, but they were at loose ends as to how to acclimate themselves."

make both ends meet. To manage to live on one's income; to keep expenses within the limits of income.

> "They are able to make ends meets only because she takes in sewing."

no end. So much as to be almost without an end or limit; very much.

> "They enjoyed her visit no end."

> "He was thrilled no end by the citation."

on end. Continuously; without interruption.

> "Those youngsters can talk over the telephone for hours on end."

Enter

enter into. 1. To participate; take part in. 2. To consider or deal with. 3. To form a part of something. 4. To partake of; share in; to sympathize with.

1. "After much persuasion, he agreed to enter into the negotiations."

2. "The author enters into this phase of the discussion in the last chapter."

3. "Factors other than politics also enter into this."

4. "In her present state of mind, I did not expect her to enter into the spirit of the festivities."

Event

at all events. No matter what the situation may be; in any case.

"At all events, you can always get back the amount you invest."

in any event. Same as *at all events*, which see.

in the event of. In the case a certain event occurs; if it so happens that.

"In the event you do not hear from him, I'll take care of your problem."

Every

every now and then. Occasionally; occurring at intervals of time; not often; from time to time.

"Every now and then he calls me or writes a letter."

"He doesn't do this very often, just every now and then."

every so often. Same as *every now and then*, which see.

every which way. In all directions; in a disorderly fashion.

> "When he undresses, he throws the clothes every which way."

Exception

take exception. 1. To object to something. 2. To be offended; to feel insulted.

> 1. "They took exception to the omission of a certain provision from the final draft of the contract."
>
> 2. "He took exception to my calling him by his first name."

Excuse

excuse oneself. To leave after offering an apology for so doing.

> "He excused himself at ten o'clock, as he had a plane to catch the next morning."

Expense

at the expense of. At the loss or sacrifice of; to the impairment or injury of.

> "You can type faster only at the expense of accuracy."

Explain

explain away. To diminish the severity (as of an offense) or the significance of something by an explanation; to relieve anxiety, doubt, etc.

> "He tried to explain away his disparaging remark, but it was too late."

> "The doctor succeeded in explaining away the fear of the patient."

Extreme

go to extremes. To be drastic; to use radical methods; to be immoderate.

> "If he wants something, he'll go to extremes to get it."

Eye

an eye for an eye. Retribution or punishment which is equal to the injury or injustice; repayment for an injury by an equivalent injury.

> "They believe in the Biblical formula for justice, i.e. an eye for an eye."

catch one's eye. To succeed in attracting another person's attention; to make a favorable impression on someone.

> "I finally caught his eye across the room, and he nodded recognition."

> "For no reason that we could see, the girl caught his eye and she got the job."

feast one's eyes on. To behold with great pleasure; to look at intently and with admiration.

> "He feasted his eyes on the girls at the swimming pool."

> "They feasted their eyes on the ancient structures in the Biblical city."

give someone the eye. To look at a person with admiration; to give a person an amorous look, usually implying an invitation.

> "She was embarrassed when she noticed that the boys gave her the eye."

have an eye for. To have a special talent for discerning or noticing; be interested in.

> "She has an eye for typographical errors."

"He has an eye for shapely girls."

in the public eye. Much seen or written about; well-known.

"He is no longer in the public eye, but we remember him well."

keep an eye on. To watch over someone (and give aid if needed); to look after.

"The neighbor promised to keep an eye on the house while we are away."

keep one's eyes open. To be alert or watchful; to watch for, as an opportunity.

"We are keeping our eyes open for a good buy in the stock market."

open one's eyes. To make someone see reality or the true facts; to become aware of a situation.

"The article opened our eyes to the plight of certain minority groups in this country."

see eye to eye. Of two or more persons, to have the same opinion; to agree on something.

"They see eye to eye on at least one point: the need to combat pollution."

shut one's eyes to. To disregard advisedly; to refuse to interfere, object to, criticize, etc.

"He simply shut his eyes to his wife's unseemly behavior."

with an eye to. With special attention or interest; with a particular aim in mind.

"She looked at her customers with an eye to spotting an eligible bachelor."

F

Face

face to face. In the presence of each other or one another; looking at each other; very near something.

"The negotiators never met face to face."

"He found himself face to face with disaster."

face up to. To acknowledge; to admit; to meet something with courage; to resist with determination.

"You must face up to the realization that the investment was a bad one."

"She was ready to face up to the emergency."

in the face of. Notwithstanding (a certain condition); in the presence of something; when confronted with.

"She remains confident in the face of all the odds against her."

"He continued to plead innocent even in the face of the evidence to the contrary."

on the face of it. On the basis of outward appearances or a superficial examination; by just looking at it.

"On the face of it, he does seem guilty."

save face. To save oneself from humiliation; to prevent disgrace.

> "They gave him a choice of resigning, to save face."

> "His main object was to save face, regardless of cost."

to one's face. Directed to one in one's presence; done or said while facing the subject; directly; without fear; brazenly.

> "They talk about her, but they'll never say it to her face."

> "She is very outspoken; she'll tell it to your face."

Fact

in fact. In reality; really; in truth.

> "In fact, I believe that we paid more for the property than it is worth."

as a matter of fact. Same as *in fact,* which see.

in point of fact. Same as *in fact.*

Fade

fade out. To disappear gradually; to lose popularity in a gradual manner.

> "The extravagant musicals faded out in the forties."

> "After the trial he faded out as an attraction, though he was found innocent."

Fair

bid fair. To seem likely; to have a good chance.

> "This plan bids fair to succeed where the others failed."

fair and square. In an honest and just manner; without subterfuge.

"He got to the position he now occupies fair and square."

fair to middling. Good enough to pass but not very good; fairly good.

"Business has been only fair to middling."

Faith

bad faith. Dishonesty; lack of sincerity; deceit.

"We cannot tolerate bad faith in an employee."

"She demonstrated bad faith when she continued to date her girl friend's husband."

good faith. Sincere intentions; honesty.

"The company amply demonstrated its good faith in the project."

in good faith. With obvious good intentions; meaning well; honestly.

"He filled out the application in good faith, not knowing that he was ill."

keep faith. To remain loyal, as to a cause, promise, etc.; to adhere to one's principles.

"You can depend on him to keep faith."

to break faith. To betray one's principles, promises, etc.; to be disloyal.

"We did not expect him to break faith with his political principles, but he disappointed us."

Fall

fall away. 1. To cease being a friend; to desert. 2. To lose weight or flesh; to become sickly.

1. "Many of the candidate's supporters fell away when he declared himself against the war."

2. "We hardly recognized her as she fell away so badly."

fall back. To move backward under pressure; to withdraw; to retreat.

"The men fell back to previously prepared positions."

fall back on. To return to something upon which one formerly relied; to rely on something which is not one's first choice.

"When the plant closed, he fell back on doing odd jobs and minor repairs for his neighbors."

fall behind. To lag behind, as in progress; to fail to do something on time.

"His having to work caused him to fall behind in his studies."

"In spite of all, she never fell behind in her scheduled payments."

fall flat. To be totally unsuccessful; to fail completely.

"In spite of all the advertising, the new product fell flat."

fall for. To be strongly attracted to in an amorous way; to become infatuated with.

"Of all the girls to choose from, he had to fall for the waitress!"

fall in. To agree to abide by; to decide to follow a certain course; take proper place.

"He finally fell in with the others."

fall in with. To join as companion or member; to become a follower of.

"While he was on the road for the firm, he fell in with some bad company."

fall on. 1. To be one's obligation; to become a duty. 2. To come into a specified condition; to experience.

1. "On Tuesdays, it falls on me to stay till closing."

2. "Losses on the stock market caused him to fall on hard times."

fall out. 1. To have a disagreement or quarrel with someone; to cease having good relationship with. 2. To occur by chance; to happen.

1. "After many years of harmony, they fell out over the issue of abortion."

2. "It so fell out that I wasn't home when they called."

fall short. To fail to come up to a certain standard; fail to reach a certain level, amount, etc.

"His time fell short of the record by half a second."

"His performance fell short of the expectation."

fall through. End in failure; fail to succeed; come to nothing.

"In spite of a promising start, the negotiations fell through."

fall under. 1. To come under the influence, control, etc. 2. To be classified as; to be included in.

1. "She was a strong-willed woman, and he gradually fell under her spell."

2. "This item falls under the heading of miscellaneous expenses."

Far

as far as. To the extent that; to the degree.

"As far as one can judge on the basis of a small sample, this is satisfactory material."

by far. By a wide margin; to a great extent; very much.

> "Of the two, this is the better by far."

> "This is by far the better bargain."

far and away. By a wide margin; by far; without doubt.

> "This is far and away the better bargain."

far and wide. Covering great distances; everywhere; in all directions.

> "They searched far and wide, but were unable to locate the man."

far be it from me. I am not a person who would; I would not do (this or that).

> "Far be it from me to meddle in your business, but I don't think you should hire this girl."

> "Far be it from me to complain, but this steak is not tender at all."

far out. Far removed from the customary or conventional; odd; offbeat.

> "This form of art is too far out for me to appreciate."

go far. 1. To be successful; to accomplish much. 2. To last long; to cover much. 3. To be very helpful toward a particular aim; have a desirable effect.

> 1. "Everyone predicted that he would go far in whatever field he chose."

> 2. "This small can of paint will not go far."

> "A single coat of paint does not go far."

> 3. "A smile or a kind word goes far toward putting a patient at ease."

insofar as. To the extent that; with regard to the degree that.

"Insofar as salary is concerned, I am sure we can agree on that."

so far. 1. Up to this time; up to now. 2. As far as a certain point; to that extent or distance.

1. "So far, we are doing very well."

"We have not heard from them so far."

2. "You can go only so far on confidence alone."

"You can go so far with him, but no farther."

so far as. Same as *insofar as,* which see.

so far, so good. Up to this time everything is in good order; nothing undesirable has happened so far or until now.

"We are expecting some disturbance, but so far, so good. We are keeping our fingers crossed."

Fast

play fast and loose. To use deception in order to gain an advantage; to be irresponsible.

"He played fast and loose with the confidence of his friends, but they soon found him out."

Fat

a fat chance. A very small chance or likelihood; no chance at all.

"You have a fat chance of getting a date with that girl."

"He for class president? A fat chance!"

chew the fat. To spend time talking about insignificant matters.

"All they did was chew the fat; they didn't do a bit of work."

"Let's stop chewing the fat and get down to work."

the fat is in the fire. The thing is done and there is no turning back.

> "The fat is in the fire, as she has already filed the suit."

> "Now that we have accused him face to face, the fat is in the fire."

> "Right or wrong, we have made our stand clear and the fat is in the fire."

the fat of the land. The best of everything; ease or idleness coupled with a luxurious way of life.

> "He married a rich widow and he is living on the fat of the land."

Fault

find fault with. To criticize; to find and point out defects.

> "She seems to enjoy finding fault with whatever he does."

to a fault. To an excessive or extreme degree; too much.

> "If anything, you can say that he is meticulous to a fault."

> "She is sympathetic to a fault."

Favor

find favor. To be liked; to receive acceptance.

> "I do not believe your suggestion will find favor with your employer."

in favor of. 1. In support of; for something. 2. To the benefit or advantage of.

> 1. "The majority of people are in favor of the proposed legislation."

2. "The evidence seems to be in favor of the defendant."

in one's favor. Acting to one's advantage; exerting an effect which is to one's credit.

"Everything that we have checked out is in his favor."

out of favor. Not on good terms with someone; not liked by someone.

"At the moment, he is out of favor with his uncle."

Feather

feather in one's cap. Something that adds to one's standing; accomplishment; honor; distinction.

"His latest book is another feather in his cap."

feather one's nest. To improve one's financial condition by devious means; to grow rich by taking advantage of circumstances, especially illicitly.

"The official used his position and influence to feather his nest."

in fine feather. In good form, good humor, or good health.

"He was, as usual, in fine feather, telling jokes and cavorting with the children."

Feed

off one's feed. Marked by lack of appetite; not feeling well; depressed; sad.

off his feed lately."
"I don't know what is the matter, but he has been

Feel

feel like. To be inclined (to do something); be in favor of doing.

"I don't feel like playing today."

"He just didn't feel like arguing with her."

feel like oneself. To be in one's usual condition with regard to health, state of mind, etc.

"He hasn't felt like himself for several days, and that explains why he lost his temper."

feel one out. To use an indirect and cautious form of questioning in order to determine a person's views regarding a particular matter.

"We tried to feel him out on the subject of selling the house, but he was wary."

feel up to. To feel well enough for a particular activity; to be capable of.

"He invited me to come along on the trip, but I just didn't feel up to it."

Feet

on one's feet. 1. In a standing position. 2. In a financially secure condition; well established.

1. "He was on his feet within a second after he heard the call."

2. "The economic boom resulting from the war helped him get on his feet."

stand on one's own feet. To be able to get along without the help of others.

"You cannot always be there to manage his affairs. He will have to stand on his own feet sooner or later."

Fence

on the fence. In a position which favors neither side in a dispute; in a position from which one can join either side in a dispute.

"The previous Administration seemed to be on the fence with regard to the Middle East."

mend one's fences. To secure or improve one's position, especially by friendly overtures.

"It was obvious that she was trying to mend her fences in her relations with the in-laws."

Fend

fend for oneself. To take care of oneself without outside help; to manage one's affairs without help from others.

"Having depended on his aunt for many years, he finally decided to leave her home and fend for himself."

Few

quite a few. Very many; a large number; not a few, but many.

"I don't know how many students participated, but there were quite a few."

Fiddle

fit as a fiddle. In perfect physical condition; in the best of health.

"He isn't exactly fit as a fiddle, but he is in fairly good health."

play second fiddle. To function in a secondary or inferior role.

"Having been the manager for many years, he finds it difficult to play second fiddle to the new chief."

Field

play the field. To direct one's attention to a variety of subjects or persons; to date, or keep company with, several members of the opposite sex, rather than one person.

"When he returned to civilian life he decided to play the field for a while before deciding on marriage."

Fight

fight it out. To fight until one side or one contestant wins.

"We decided not to intervene but to let them fight it out between themselves."

Figure

figure on. 1. To count on something or someone; to rely on. 2. To take into account or consideration.

1. "He had figured on some help from his brother."

2. "We should figure on losing a certain amount of the crop by spoilage."

figure out. To calculate mathematically; to come to a conclusion; to understand.

"It would be difficult to figure out the losses at this time."

"I just can't figure out what they meant by that statement."

Fill

fill in. 1. To supply requested information. 2. To add details in order to complete. 3. To take the place of someone; to substitute for. 4. To fill an empty space with some material. 5. To bring a person up to date by supplying information.

1. "You are expected to fill in the requested information in the enclosed blank."

2. "You can fill in the shading later."

3. "She is not a regular. She is just filling in for one of the girls who is sick."

4. "Before painting, fill in the nail holes with putty or plastic wood."

5. "The young lady will fill you in on the latest developments."

fill out. 1. To become stouter, shapelier, larger, etc. 2. To complete a document by writing in the information requested.

1. "Such a diet will keep you well nourished without filling you out."

"She looks better since she filled out a little."

2. "First of all you will have to fill out this application blank."

fill up. To make full; to cause to be sated; to give a feeling of having eaten too much.

"This kind of food will fill you up real fast."

Finger

burn one's fingers. To suffer injury, insult, etc., because one is meddling in another's business or because of rashness.

"I burned my fingers once before trying to stop their quarrel. I will not try again."

have a finger in the pie. 1. To engage in meddling. 2. To have a financial interest in something.

1. "He loves to have a finger in the pie by offering gratuitous advice."

2. "He wouldn't be so interested in the project if he didn't have a finger in the pie."

put one's finger on. To point out clearly; to understand or visualize in detail.

> "I know there is something wrong here, but I can't put my finger on it."

put the finger on. 1. To point out a suspect or a criminal to the police or other authorities. 2. To designate a potential victim of a crime to the perpetrator or to point out a place of business or a home that is to be burglarized.

> 1. "One of the group put the finger on the leader of the gang."

> 2. "No one knows who put the finger on the bank president as the next victim."

twist around one's little finger. To be able to make someone do as directed; to make a person (usually of the opposite sex) behave and act in a compliant manner.

> "As self-asserted as he seems here, his wife twists him around her little finger."

Finish

finish with. To sever relations with someone, especially on a social level.

> "At last she told him that she was finished with him forever."

Fire

between two fires. Under attack from both sides, as the opponents in a controversy.

> "Neither side liked the proposal, so that the congressman found himself between two fires."

catch fire. To start burning; to become suddenly popular or successful.

> "Although he has been singing for years, he didn't catch fire until recently."

fight fire with fire. To use the same harsh methods against an opponent as he uses.

> "We had to be very firm with them. We had to fight fire with fire."

fire away. To start a vigorous speech; to start asking questions.

> "At the end of the lecture, the audience was invited to fire away with questions."

go through fire and water. To expose oneself to various hardships and dangers in order to achieve a particular goal.

> "He did not attain his goal without sacrifice. He went through fire and water."

miss fire. To fail to achieve something; to miss one's goal; to be unsuccessful.

> "His attempts to interest a sponsor missed fire several times, but he succeeded eventually."

play with fire. To handle a dangerous matter playfully; to trifle with a hazardous situation.

> "You had better be careful in dealing with these dangerous characters. Don't play with fire."

set on fire. To cause something to ignite or burn; to inflame passions; to stimulate the imagination.

> "The vision of the lovely girl set his imagination on fire."

> "The possibility of winning first prize set his energies on fire."

set fire to. Same as *set on fire*, which see.

> "The conversation set fire to her dreams."

set the world on fire. To become successful very rapidly and in various fields; to become known or famous; to make telling changes or contributions.

> "It looked very much as if he were trying to set the world on fire, although he denied it."

under fire. Under attack as by a military force; under severe criticism or accusation.

> "The college president is under fire for being too lenient."

First

first thing. Before anything else is done; as the first act; at once.

> "I'll attend to this first thing in the morning."

in the first place. As a beginning; to start with; as the first of several points.

> "In the first place, they are not interested in selling. Besides, the price would be too high for us to handle."

Fish

drink like a fish. To drink alcoholic beverages to excess.

> "You couldn't tell it by looking at him, but he drinks like a fish."

fish for. To try to obtain by sly or indirect methods; to search for cunnningly.

> "Don't pay any attention to him. He is obviously fishing for a compliment."

fish in troubled waters. To gain selfishly by taking advantage of a confused or critical situation.

> "Many speculators made money during the decline of the stock market by fishing in troubled waters."

like a fish out of water. Like a person out of his usual and familiar environment; uncomfortable; ill at ease.

"When he is not among his literary friends, he feels like a fish out of water."

other fish to fry. Other things to do; more important matters to attend to.

"He can't spend too much time arguing with you about this matter. He has other fish to fry."

Fit

by fits and starts. In a manner marked by periods of activity alternating with periods of idleness; irregularly; off and on.

"He doesn't work at it all the time, only by fits and starts."

"You can't depend on this car. It works by fits and starts."

fit to be tied. Very excited or angry; furious.

"She was fit to be tied when I told her I would not attend the party."

have a fit. To become very excited or angry and demonstrative; to go into hysterics.

"The woman had a fit when they told her the repair would not be completed till the next day."

throw a fit. Same as *have a fit*, which see.

Fix

fix up. 1. To put in proper order. 2. To arrange for a meeting with someone.

1. "Go ahead and relax. I'll fix up this mess."

2. "If you want a date, I can fix you up with a nice girl."

Flag

flag down. To use a flag or any device as a signal for a moving vehicle to stop.

> "We had to flag down a passing car in order to ask for help."

Flare

flare up. 1. To become angry again, especially suddenly. 2. To burst into activity after a cessation or a period of remission.

> 1. "The minute he mentioned her name, she flared up again."

> 2. "Fighting flares up sporadically on that front."

> "The excitement caused her illness to flare up."

Flash

flash in the pan. 1. An intense effort which attains some success and then fails, or does not succeed at all. 2. A person that is successful for a brief period; something that succeeds or is popular for a short time.

> 1. "Their successful venture with the novelty toy was just a flash in the pan."

> 2. "He was indeed popular for a short time, but he didn't last long—just a flash in the pan."

Flat

fall flat. See under *fall*.

> "All her efforts fell flat; he just wasn't interested."

Flat-Footed

catch flat-footed. To catch someone in a disadvantageous position; to catch a person in a condition of unpreparedness; to catch in the commission of an offense.

"His request caught her flat-footed, as she didn't have that much money in her account."

"This time the police caught him flat-footed, with the evidence on hand."

Flesh

flesh and blood. The tissues and structures of the body, or the body as a whole, representing something with a limited capability.

"That is obviously more than flesh and blood can stand."

in the flesh. In person, rather than through the medium of a picture, tape, etc.; present in person, not by proxy or any other way.

"Can you imagine seeing all these famous people in the flesh!"

"She looks better on television than in the flesh."

one's own flesh and blood. One's close relatives; person or persons related to one by blood.

"After all, one does not forsake one's own flesh and blood."

"Even this tyrant had a kindly feeling for his own flesh and blood."

Flotsam

flotsam and jetsam. Wreckage of a ship and its cargo floating on the water; people having no permanent residence; drifters; worthless things.

"The town has deteriorated and is occupied by the flotsam and jetsam of society."

"Every time he takes a vacation he brings back a sack of flotsam and jetsam."

Flunk

flunk out. To be dismissed from a school because of unsatisfactory work.

"This is the third time he has flunked out of college."

Fly

fly in the face of. To defy custom, authority, etc.; to oppose openly.

"He flew in the face of his family's objections and married the girl anyway."

let fly. To throw something; to strike out; to attack with words.

"The irate man let fly a book at the speaker."

"They let fly a torrent of abuse at the visiting politician."

on the fly. While moving about; while one is in a hurry.

"It is hard on the digestion to be always eating on the fly."

fly in the ointment. Something, apparently insignificant or small, which hinders or checks an important project.

"This is a good plan. The only fly in the ointment is the possibility of offending the old man."

"There is only one fly in the ointment—one of us will have to get up early in the morning."

Foam

foam at the mouth. To talk in great anger; to be in a rage.

"She literally foamed at the mouth as she related the details of the incident."

"There is no need to foam at the mouth about it. We'll make the necessary adjustments."

Focus

in focus. Clear; understandable; logical.

"Now, with the additional information, the whole situation seems to be in focus."

Fold

fold up. Of a business enterprise, to fail; of a play, exhibition, etc., to close its doors because of failure to attract sufficient attention.

"In spite of relatively good press reports, the play folded up after a run of two weeks."

Follow

follow through. To continue in an endeavor or activity until the best results are obtained.

"He made a good start, and he would have undoubtedly succeeded had he followed through."

follow up. To resume an activity temporarily abandoned, in order to attain a desired end or obtain complete information.

"The press seldom follows up the progress of a case. You hear only the beginning, but you seldom know how it ends."

Fool

be nobody's fool. To be shrewd, clever, or wise; to be able to handle any situation.

"Don't worry about him. He is nobody's fool. He won't fall for that ruse."

fool around. 1. To handle carelessly or aimlessly. 2. To spend time with a person of the opposite sex without serious intentions.

1. "Don't fool around with that gun."

"They go to school, but they don't study. They just like to fool around."

2. "She is not serious about Jim. She is just fooling around."

fool with. To associate in a trifling manner; handle without care.

"I wouldn't fool with them if I were you."

"A sharp knife is nothing to fool with, especially by a child."

Foot

put one's best foot forward. To make an effort to make the best possible impression on someone; to do the best one can.

"When you meet this man, try to put your best foot forward. If you make a good impression on him you'll get the job."

put one's foot down. To take a determined stand; to implement one's decision.

"Eventually he put his foot down and refused to let him have the car."

put one's foot in one's mouth. To say or do something embarrassing, especially habitually.

"As usual, he put his foot in his mouth when he called his boss's wife 'Dolly'."

put one's foot in it. Same as *put one's foot in one's mouth*, which see.

Follow

follow in one's footsteps. To follow the same course, take up the same profession, etc., as another person whom one respects or admires.

"He followed in his father's footsteps and became an attorney."

follow in someone's footsteps. Same as *follow in one's footsteps,* which see.

Force

in force. In effect; applicable; valid.

> "The ten o'clock curfew is still in force."

Forget

forget oneself. To do or say something not befitting one's person, as if through forgetting who one is.

> "Don't forget yourself now, and act your age when
> you are with those young girls."

Fork

fork over. To hand over, especially unwillingly; to give unceremoniously.

> "He had to fork over half of his share or risk the
> chance of being informed on."

> "They told him to fork over the amount he over-
> charged them, or he'd be taken care of, their way."

fork out. To spend, especially unwillingly or excessively; to pay an exorbitant amount.

> "He forked out fifty dollars for that front seat."

> "The company is almost forced to fork out several
> hundred dollars a year in gratuities."

Form

bad form. Conduct or behavior not acceptable in polite society.

> "I would say that addressing a lady one has just
> met by her first name is rather bad form."

good form. Conduct or behavior acceptable in polite society; proper style.

> "It is perfectly good form to interject the title 'Sir' when speaking to an older gentleman."

> "This layout is certainly good form for the purpose it is meant to serve."

Fortune

tell one's fortune. To foretell or profess to foretell what is going to happen to a person by interpreting certain omens or by any other means.

> "I do not believe it is possible to tell one's fortune by looking at crystal balls, tea leaves, or the like."

Foul

foul up. To frustrate or spoil; cause to end in failure; bungle.

> "Now look what you did! You fouled up the whole thing by mentioning it to your brother."

Free

free and easy. Free from the bonds of formality; not constrained by conventionality; casual; excessively casual.

> "He shuns formality and loves the free and easy life."

> "His behavior was just a little too free and easy to suit her."

give a free hand. To allow someone to act as he sees fit; to bestow liberty of action.

> "He wasn't quite ready to give the new man a free hand with the business."

make free with. 1. To act with reference to something as if one owns it; to be too free with someone else's property. 2. To be, or try to be, too familiar or intimate with someone.

> 1. "I advised him not to make free with his neighbor's tools."
>
> 2. "He tried to make free with her, but she put him in his place."

with a free hand. Generously; without stint; lavishly.

> "She gives to charities with a free hand."

Freeze

freeze out. To repel or exclude by successful competition; to keep away or out by an unfriendly manner or by snubbing.

> "Our company was frozen out of this deal by an unusually low bid."
>
> "They froze him out of their intimate circle by sheer aloofness."

Friend

make friends with. To become friendly with someone; to enter into a friendly relationship.

> "He is a great hand at making friends with total strangers."
>
> "I wouldn't make friends with such people!"

Frog

frog in the throat. A condition caused by the presence of phlegm on the vocal folds of the larynx, marked by difficulty in producing voiced sounds.

> "You'll have to excuse me for not talking clearly, as I have a frog in the throat."

Front

in front of. 1. Geographically ahead of. 2. Near the entrance to a house; near what is regarded as the front of a house. 3. In the presence of a person or persons.

1. "In certain countries, the man always walks in front of the lady, especially one's wife."

2. "You install this alarm in front of the house."

3. "She shouldn't chide him in front of these people."

Frying Pan

out of the frying pan and into the fire. Out of one bad situation and into another one still worse.

"What would that do! That's even worse; it's out of the frying pan and into the fire."

Full

full of. 1. Containing very much of; filled by. 2. Preoccupied with, as plans, fancies, etc.

1. "This surface is full of tiny holes."

2. "He is always full of impractical ideas and fanciful schemes."

full well. Very well; with certainty; without doubt.

"You know full well that we cannot accept your offer."

"When she took the job she knew full well that it was only for the summer."

to the full. Thoroughly; as much as possible; completely.

"It was a short vacation, but we enjoyed it to the full."

"In spite of some interruptions, she utilized her free time to the full."

G

Gab

gift of gab. A talent for glib or smooth conversation; eloquence.

"He'll persuade them yet. He has that gift of gab."

Gaff

stand the gaff. To stand up well under adverse conditions; to bear tension, difficulties, adverse circumstances, etc.

"He had to give up that job. He couldn't stand the gaff."

Gain

gain on. To come nearer to an opponent's position or score.

"We are still ahead in the scoring, but they are gaining on us."

Gallery

play to the gallery. To do something calculated to appeal to the common, rather than the refined, tastes; to appeal to the general public.

"In the past several years, television has been playing to the gallery."

"To make money in this business, you have to play to the gallery."

Game

big game. Important people; an important or influential person; anything important; a hazardous undertaking.

"You are dealing with big game when you are trying to consort with members of that family."

play the game. To act in accordance with the rules; to be just and fair.

"The negotiations broke down because one side refused to play the game."

the game is up. It is all over; the attempt is lost; the chances for success are gone.

"After losing money for three years in a row, he realized that the game was up."

Gang

gang up on. To combine as a group in order to oppose or attack someone.

"Now, fellows, don't you gang up on me!"

"When he realized that several of the boys were ganging up on the little fellow, he decided to intervene."

Gantlet

run the gantlet. To go through a period or a process of punishment or hardship; to put up with abuse or criticism from both or all sides.

"He knew that he would have to run the gantlet,

that he would be denounced by both the conservatives and the liberals, but he decided to proceed anyway."

Gas

step on the gas. To accelerate the pace of an activity (in allusion to the stepping or pressing on the gas pedal of an automobile).

"We had better step on the gas if we want this painting job finished today."

"We got there on time, but we had to step on the gas to do it."

Gauntlet

take up the gauntlet. To accept a challenge to a fight; to take up a cause which requires a defense.

"He was not one to retreat but rather one who would take up the gauntlet."

"Several lawyers were ready to take up the gauntlet for the defendant."

Gear

high gear. High speed (in allusion to a mechanical arrangement of gears yielding the highest speed).

"In spite of some delays, the construction is now proceeding in high gear."

low gear. Low speed. See under *high gear.*

"They have been operating in low gear from the very start, and I don't think they can change now."

Get

get about. 1. To move around; be active. 2. To become known to many. 3. To attend social events; to mix socially.

1. "He doesn't get about as much as he used to, although he still likes to attend games."

2. "We were naive to think we could keep it a secret. We should have known it would get about."

3. "He is getting about much more now since he met Betty."

get across. 1. To be transmitted from one to another in a clear, understandable manner. 2. To present something in an understandable manner; to convince.

1. "In spite of everything, the idea somehow didn't get across. They failed to grasp the point."

2. "He is a good speaker and he was able to get across the idea that if we don't attend to this now, we will not have another chance."

get ahead. To proceed in a successful manner; to make good progress.

"You are not going to get ahead by sitting here and waiting for an opportunity."

"To get ahead, you must work hard and be willing to make certain sacrifices."

get ahead of someone. To surpass someone; to do better than another person.

"To get ahead of him you'll have to get up early in the morning."

"Many have tried to get ahead of him, but none succeeded."

get along. 1. To proceed with whatever one is doing. 2. To have a pleasant relationship with someone. 3. To be reasonably successful in making a living.

1. "How is he getting along with his research?"

2. "He is not getting along with his in-laws."

3. "His wife went to work, as they were unable to get along without additional income."

get around. 1. Same as *get about* (all three definitions). 2. To overcome something, as by going around it. 3. To gain favor by devious means.

2. "He got around the transportation problem by renting a car."

3. "He has a glib tongue, and he got around to her by being sweet and complimentary."

get at. 1. To reach; attain. 2. To come to, as a point; to hint at. 3. To arrive, as at a conclusion.

1. "He tried, but he was unable to get at it."

2. "Here is what I am getting at. I am not convinced that he is guilty."

3. "We are trying to get at the cause of this disturbance."

get away. To leave a particular place; to detach oneself from; to escape.

"She is such a talker! I couldn't get away from her."

"No matter how he tried, he couldn't get away from his worries."

get away with. To be able to do something wrong without being discovered or, if discovered, without being punished.

"He was able to get away with it only because he is a relative of the boss."

"You got away with it this time but you won't always be so lucky."

get back. 1. To come back; return. 2. To obtain by way of return; to recover. 3. To get justice; to avenge; to retaliate.

    1. "He didn't get back till after midnight."

    2. "He didn't lose everything. He got back part of the investment."

    3. "He got back at his tormentor by asking him what his qualifications are."

get by. 1. To succeed in passing without being seen or apprehended. 2. To continue in a particular condition or existence in spite of difficulties.

    1. "He was able to get by the sentry, who was intoxicated."

    2. "The business has fallen off, but they manage to get by somehow."

get down. 1. To come down from a specified place. 2. To discourage; to frustrate; depress. 3. To direct one's energies toward a task. 4. To swallow; to make pass into the esophagus or stomach.

    1. "Get down from this table immediately!"

    2. "Nothing gets me down more than visiting someone in the hospital."

    3. "We have fooled around enough. Let's get down to business."

    4. "Water from the faucet gags me. I can't get it down."

get in. 1. To enter a place. 2. To become involved. 3. To begin an association with. 4. To arrive.

    1. "The burglars got in through a basement door."

    2. "If you don't use a budget, you will get in debt more and more."

3. "He got in with this rough bunch at the plant."

4. "They won't get in until two in the morning."

get it. 1. To be criticized or punished. 2. To understand and retain.

1. "He got it good from his wife, and he deserved it."

2. "I don't get it. Why do you have to leave now?"

"She is not one to skip over anything in her studies. She likes to get it."

get nowhere. To fail in accomplishing something attempted; to make no progress or headway.

"He talked and talked, but he got nowhere. She wouldn't listen to him."

"You'll get nowhere with that girl."

get off. 1. To help someone to escape consequences or punishment. 2. To succeed in avoiding punishment or the result of a deed. 3. To leave a conveyance, as a train. 4. To have the audacity or impudence.

1. "He knows a lawyer who promised to get him off altogether or with a light sentence."

2. "A woman is likely to get off with a light sentence."

3. "They got off the plane without incident."

4. "Where does she get off telling us what we should have done!"

get on. 1. To board; to climb on. 2. To continue with what one is doing. 3. To grow older.

1. "He got on the plane in Louisville."

"If you'll get on the chair you'll be able to reach it."

2. "We have waited long enough, let's get on with
   the work."

3. "He is not as active as he used to be; he is
   getting on in years."

get out. 1. To leave. 2. To become known. 3. To issue; publish.

1. "They got out at Baltimore or Washington."

   "He got out of the insurance business."

2. "Somehow it got out that he is quitting his job."

3. "They have a newspaper to get out each week."

get over. 1. Same as *get across,* which see. 2. To recover from.
3. To dismiss from one's mind.

2. "It will take him a while to get over this latest
   illness."

3. "He couldn't get over it that his best friend let
   him down."

get through. 1. To finish, as a task. 2. To succeed in reaching
someone or something. 3. To succeed in making oneself understood.

1. "I don't think he can get through by two o'clock."

2. "We tried to phone him, but the lines were all
   tied up and we couldn't get through."

3. "We tried our best to explain our side of it, but
   we couldn't get through to him."

get together. 1. To gather as a group; to meet. 2. To agree on
something.

1. "The remaining members still get together once
   a month."

2. "They agreed on some points, but they were unable to get together on the main issue."

get up. 1. To stand up; to rise from bed, usually after sleep. 2. To climb on something. 3. To prepare; organize.

1. "He usually gets up at seven, but he overslept today."

2. "If you will get up on the ladder, you will see it."

3. "He got up some kind of a contest or game."

Give

give and take. 1. To make concessions in order to reach agreement. 2. To exchange, as ideas, courtesies, etc.

1. "Each side must be ready to give and take if an agreement is to be reached."

2. "After the lecture, the audience had an opportunity to give and take."

give away. 1. To give something as a gift. 2. To reveal, as a secret, feeling, etc. 3. To present the bride to the bridegroom in a marriage ceremony.

1. "He gave away most of his estate during his lifetime."

2. "His loss of temper gave away his true feelings."

3. "She didn't say who will give the bride away."

give in. To acknowledge defeat; to cease fighting, claiming, etc.

"After pursuing the case through the courts for several years, he finally gave in."

give to understand. To make something understood; to explain.

"I am given to understand that there will be no classes tomorrow."

give up. 1. To cease holding on to; despair. 2. To stop doing something. 3. To surrender; to stop resisting.

1. "By this time he has given up all hope."

2. "He is trying very hard to give up smoking."

3. "When he saw that he was outnumbered, he gave up without a struggle."

Glove

hand in glove. Close association; intimacy; friendship.

"He has been hand in glove with the mayor for years."

handle with kid gloves. To handle with diplomacy; to deal with gentleness; approach tactfully.

"She is very sensitive about the subject. You will have to handle her with kid gloves."

Go

go about. To proceed; to continue; busy oneself with; move or travel.

"He goes about his business as if nothing had happened."

"He goes about the countryside in a converted camper."

go after. To try to secure or obtain; attempt to attain; pursue.

"You will not get the girl if you sit here and wait. You've got to go after her."

"I don't know what he is going after now."

go against. To oppose; to work against; to be contrary to.

"This kind of publicity will go against us."

"It goes against his principles to overlook something like that."

go along. 1. To agree; to cooperate. 2. To go in the company of. 3. To continue; proceed; move.

1. "Well, I'll go along with you on this point."

2. "No, she went along with her grandmother."

3. "We can go along at this rate for a long time."

go around. 1. To be frequently in the company of; to date a member of the opposite sex. 2. To be enough to accommodate everybody.

1. "He goes around with a rough crowd."

"Yes, he does go around with Margaret."

2. "There wouldn't be enough of the ice cream to go around."

go back on. To fail to keep a promise; to break a commitment.

"If he promised to help, he will not go back on his promise. That I can assure you."

go by. 1. To pass without being taken advantage of. 2. To depend on; to be guided by.

1. "Don't let this opportunity go by. You may not have another one."

2. "I wouldn't go by what he is saying. He is seldom right."

go for. 1. To be impressed by; to be convinced. 2. To be fond of; to be attracted by.

1. "I don't go for such sales methods."

"Somehow, she didn't go for that explanation."

2. "He goes for fancy jackets and sports clothes."

"He goes for girls with long hair."

go in for. To be fond of; to engage in; to do or take part in something.

"He doesn't go in for such wild parties."

"They don't go in for athletics or sports events."

go into. 1. To discuss; to inquire; investigate. 2. To enter a particular field, as a profession or occupation.

1. "Let's not go into that again. We discussed it at length yesterday."

2. "He considered law, but he decided to go into medicine."

go off. 1. To explode. 2. To happen in a certain way; to proceed.

1. "Luckily, the grenade did not go off."

2. "We arranged a meeting between the two, but it didn't go off too well."

go on. 1. To happen or take place. 2. To continue, as an action. 3. To talk at length. 4. To make an appearance, as on a stage; to begin showing, as a movie. 5. An expression of disbelief.

1. "We wondered what was going on."

2. "The celebration and the noise went on all night."

3. "She would have gone on for hours, if I hadn't suggested that we watch television."

4. "The feature picture goes on at seven."

5. "Go on, you can't mean it!"

go out. 1. To cease; come to an end (of a particular process). 2. Be sympathetic. 3. To go to a place of entertainment. 4. To stop being in fashion.

1. "The lights flickered, then went out."

2. "Her heart went out for him, but what could she do?"

3. "He goes out at least twice a week."

4. "That style went out in the early seventies."

go over. 1. To study again; review. 2. To occur in a successful manner.

1. "Let's go over this part of the agreement once more."

2. "The party didn't quite go over; I don't know why."

go through. 1. To search carefully. 2. To receive acceptance; to succeed. 3. To endure an unpleasant experience.

1. "We went through the house from top to bottom."

2. "In spite of all, the proposal failed to go through."

3. "They went through a great deal, but they are all right now."

have a go at. To try one's luck at something; to attempt a venture, especially one involving risk.

"The restaurant had changed ownership several times in the past few years, yet these people decided to have a go at it anyway."

let oneself go. To throw away inhibitions; to act in an unrestrained manner, usually for a short time, or on a special occasion.

"This was a time, he felt, when he could let himself go by having a few drinks with his old cronies."

Going

get going. To start; to begin, as a trip; to initiate.

"Now that you have all the information, get going!"

"Enough of this talk. Let's get going."

going on. 1. Happening; occurring; taking place. 2. Nearing (a time or age).

1. "I have no idea what is going on over there."

2. "How old is she?" "I suspect she is going on forty."

going to. Intending to; expecting to (do something); will.

"I am definitely going to make an inquiry."

"I think it is going to rain."

goings on. Activities regarded as inappropriate; mischief; boisterous conduct.

"We cannot tolerate such goings on."

Gone

far gone. Very far advanced; deeply involved; near death.

"He was too far gone to respond to treatment."

Good

as good as. The same as; practically; virtually.

"When he says he'll do something, it's as good as done."

come to no good. To end in an undesirable condition; go astray; end in failure.

"Everyone had predicted that this boy would come to no good, but he fooled them all. He is an outstanding citizen and a big success in business."

for good. Forever; permanently.

"This time, she felt, he left her for good."

good for. 1. Able to function, or valid, for a certain length of time. 2. Useful in a certain capacity; able to perform a specified function.

1. "This battery is good for about three months."

2. "He is good for a hundred dollar contribution."

make good. 1. To fulfill, as a promise or obligation. 2. To make restitution, as for damages. 3. To become successful.

> 1. "You can depend on him to make good his pledge."
>
> 2. "You needn't wory about the torn garment. The company will make good your loss."
>
> 3. "He made good in the real estate business."

no good. 1. Worthless; of no use. 2. Unworthy; bad; amoral.

> 1. "I wouldn't buy this junk. It's no good."
>
> 2. "He is a no good fellow, if I ever saw one."

to the good. Richer; better off; having an advantageous effect or influence.

> "When he liquidated the business, he was about two thousand dollars to the good."
>
> "The change in the rules will be that much to the good for us."

Goose

cook one's goose. To frustrate one's plans; to destroy a person's chances.

> "I'll tell his girl friend. That will cook his goose."
>
> "His outburst of temper cooked his goose as far as we are concerned."

Grace

fall from grace. To fall into disfavor with someone; to lose one's favor with an important person.

> "No one knows why, but he fell from grace with the political boss."

have the grace. Be kind enough (to do something); to have the decency.

> "The burglar had the grace to at least return the personal papers."

in someone's good *or* bad graces. In someone's favor or disfavor; in a good or bad relationship.

> "In spite of everything, she managed to remain in her aunt's good graces."

with bad grace. Grudgingly; not in a sporting manner.

> "He did help them with the work, but he did so with bad grace."

with good grace. Willingly; cheerfully; without reluctance.

> "He not only helped with the clerical work, but he did so with good grace."

> "She does everything with good grace and a pleasant smile."

Grade

make the grade. To be successful in attaining a goal; to do well enough.

> "He is not well prepared for this work. I doubt that he'll make the grade."

Grain

against one's grain. Contrary to one's principles; not in accord with one's inclination, temper, etc.

> "Cruel treatment, even of a criminal, goes against her grain."

Grave

have one foot in the grave. To be gravely ill; to be so old as to be in the shadow of death.

"He has one foot in the grave, but he is still anxious
to make more money."

Grindstone

keep one's nose to the grindstone. To apply oneself steadily and
conscientiously to a particular task.

"I am sure that you can succeed, but you will have
to keep your nose to the grindstone."

Grip

come to grips with. To cope with; struggle with; deal with in a
firm way.

"In your new job you will come to grips with
problems that you have not faced here."

"You cannot avoid the issue much longer. You'll
have to come to grips with it sooner or later."

Grist

grist to one's mill. Something that can be used to one's advantage;
something used profitably.

"Actually, all this controversy and the ensuing publicity is grist to his mill."

Groove

in the groove. In good working order; up-to-date; fashionable.

"After a slow start they really took off. They were
in the groove."

"To be in the groove, you'll have to get a mini bike."

Ground

break ground. To begin digging, as for a construction job; to
begin any venture; to take initial steps.

"They are breaking ground for the new school."

"By way of breaking ground for his new job, he threw a little party."

cut the ground from under one's feet. To deprive someone's argument of its validity; to nullify an effort; to frustrate.

"He cut the ground from under our feet by refusing to corroborate our statement."

"If you divulge this information, you will cut the ground from under the feet of the prosecution."

from the ground up. From the very beginning to the end; completely.

"To rejuvenate this business you will have to re-build it from the ground up."

gain ground. To advance; to make progress; to improve.

"He is recuperating slowly, but he is gaining ground."

hold one's ground. To maintain one's position; to keep from losing what one has or what one has gained.

"He is still holding his ground against a superior adversary."

on delicate ground. On a subject requiring diplomacy; in a matter requiring tact; holding an opinion or position difficult to prove or maintain.

"Now, when you speak of women's rights, you are on delicate ground."

on firm ground. In an advantageous position; on a subject about which one is safe from contradiction.

"You'll be on firm ground once you get through with the slack season."

"The additional evidence puts you on firm ground."

on the ground of. On the basis of; because.

"He justifies his action on the ground that he was dealt with unfairly in the past."

stand one's ground. Same as *hold one's ground,* which see.

Ground Floor

get in on the ground floor. To join, as a business enterprise, at the very beginning or any advantageous time.

"Well, he got in on the ground floor when the shares were selling at ten dollars."

Grow

grow on. To become more likable or lovable as time goes by.

"He doesn't make a good initial impression, but if you give him a chance, he grows on you."

grow out of. 1. To be the result of; originate from. 2. To abandon, or be freed from, as one grows older.

1. "Their dispute grew out of a careless remark."

2. "Every boy has a tendency to prevaricate. He'll grow out of it in time."

Guard

on one's guard. Alert for any possible hazard or unexpected development.

"He is always on his guard when he makes a deal with those people."

Gun

big gun. An important person; an influential politician; a high-ranking military man.

"When you deal with him, you are dealing with a
real big gun. He's the most influential man in this
town."

go great guns. To be doing very well; to be proceeding fast and
satisfactorily.

"They were going great guns in the new location,
until their competitor started cutting prices."

gun for. 1. To look for someone in order to harm or kill, as in
retribution. 2. To attempt to obtain; to seek.

1. "He is gunning for the fellow who informed on
him."

2. "She is being very sweet to her boss, as she is
gunning for a promotion."

stick to one's guns. To persist in one's opinion, stand, etc., in
spite of pressure.

"They attempted to discredit his statement, but he
stuck to his guns."

H

Hail

hail-fellow-well-met. Very amicable or sociable; easy-going and friendly, especially with strangers.

> "He is the kind of hail-fellow-well-met person who would fit this position perfectly."

hail from. To originate from; come from; be a native of.

> "He hails from your part of the country—Maryland."

Hair

get in one's hair. To get on one's nerves; to annoy; to pester.

> "He gets in my hair when he starts talking about his wild schemes."

let one's hair down. To dispense with one's inhibitions; to talk very frankly; to reveal one's innermost feelings.

> "This one time she really let her hair down and told me about what is bothering her."

make one's hair stand on end. To cause someone to be horrified; to terrify.

> "If this account will not make your hair stand on end, nothing will."

145

split hairs. Fuss about small differences; make an issue over minor things.

> "If we want to get this project going we will have to stop splitting hairs."

Half Cocked

go off half cocked. To act or speak without thinking; to speak hastily or rashly.

> "Now, let's think this over. Let's not go off half cocked."

go off at half cock. Same as *go off half cocked,* which see.

Hammer

hammer and tongs. With great vigor; with gusto; with all of one's energy.

> "As with everything else, he went hammer and tongs soliciting votes for his favorite candidate."

hammer away at. To persist in doing something; to persevere in emphasizing a point; to keep on talking about a subject.

> "He wouldn't take no for an answer and kept hammering away at it until they agreed to reconsider the matter."

hammer out. Smooth out; remove certain inconsistencies or disagreements; work out something acceptable.

> "In the end, they hammered out an acceptable contract."

Hand

at first hand. Directly from the person involved in a particular situation; not through the agency of a person not himself involved.

> "With a great deal of effort, the reporter was able to get the story at first hand, from the victim."

at hand. Nearby; close to oneself or to something.

> "I asked him because he was the only man at hand."

at the hands of. By the action of; through the medium or agency of.

> "He suffered physical hardships at the hands of his cruel captors."

bite the hand that feeds one. To be ungrateful, or do harm, to one's benefactor.

> "He wouldn't be disloyal to his uncle. He wouldn't bite the hand that feeds him."

change hands. To change ownership; to pass from the ownership of one to that of another.

> "I have lost count of the number of times this business has changed hands in the past few years."

eat out of one's hand. To be submissive to; to be so fond of one as to be dominated by him or her.

> "He turned out to be a remarkably uxorious husband; he eats out of her hand."

force one's hand. To cause someone to act before he is ready; to do something that forces another to reveal his stand or opinion.

> "We weren't actually ready to buy, but our competitor's bid forced our hand."

from hand to mouth. Without planning or saving for the future; spending all that one earns.

> "They haven't a cent in the bank, as they have lived from hand to mouth all their lives."

hand and foot. Involving the hands and the feet; using both hands and feet; so diligently as to satisfy all needs or wishes.

> "Nothing is too difficult for her where he is concerned; she waits on him hand and foot."

hand down. 1. To pass to an offspring; to bequeath. 2. To announce a decision or verdict.

> 1. "This type of disorder is handed down through the mother."

> 2. "The verdict will not be handed down till next week at the earliest."

hand it to. To compliment an undesirable person for a deserved credit; give credit unwillingly.

> "You have to hand it to that scoundrel. He does have a beautiful garden."

hand out. To give something to many people; to distribute.

> "The attendant will hand out the questionnaires."

hand over. To surrender something; to give up; to deliver unwillingly.

> "The teller was instructed to hand over all paper money."

hand over fist. In abundance; in large quantities; easily and copiously.

> "That little store is making money hand over fist."

hands down. Without any, or much, effort; very easily.

> "It was hardly a contest. He won hands down."

hands up! A directive, usually by a gunman to his victim, to raise the hands above one's head to forestall resistance.

> "If you hear the man say 'hands up!', you had better reach."

have one's hands full. To be as busy as one can be; to be engaged in something requiring all one's energy or time.

> "With the four children to take care of, you'll have your hands full this summer."

lay one's hands on. 1. To acquire possession of; obtain. 2. To get a hold of and punish.

> 1. "I would like to lay my hands on a few thousand dollars so that I could buy that house."

> 2. "Wait till I lay my hands on that rascal!"

not lift a hand. To exert no effort (in behalf of someone); to do nothing.

> "He wouldn't lift a hand in her behalf."

not lift a finger. Same as *not lift a hand,* which see.

on hand. Present at this time; available now; ready.

> "We have none on hand now, but we expect another shipment."

on one's hands. In one's care or sphere of responsibility.

> "He has on his hands no less than three emergency cases."

on the one hand. Considering the matter from this point of view.

> "On the one hand, this is a relatively safe investment."

on the other hand. But considering the matter from another point of view.

> "On the other hand, the dividends are rather low."

out of hand. 1. Immediately; without delay. 2. Out of control; unmanageable.

> 1. "It is still available, but you will have to act out of hand."

> 2. "The situation was threatening to get out of hand."

show one's hand. To reveal one's true intentions; to divulge one's motives.

> "When the issue comes up for discussion, he will
> have to show his hand."

throw up one's hands. To recognize one's failure and give up;
to cease trying because of despair.

> "He will fight to the very end. He is not one to
> throw up his hands."

try one's hand at. To try one's capabilities at something; to engage in.

> "When he lost his job, he decided to try his hand at
> writing."

upper hand. The more advantageous position; the benefit.

> "He had the upper hand over the others because of
> his education and experience."

wash one's hands of. To disengage oneself from something; to
stop being interested in or supporting; to renounce further responsibility.

> "When the client still refused to cooperate, he
> washed his hands of the entire case."

with a heavy hand. 1. Sternly; without tact; indelicately. 2. Clumsily; awkwardly.

> 1. "He ruled his household with a heavy hand."

> 2. "He broke the bad news with a heavy hand."

with a high hand. In a dictatorial fashion; arrogantly; arbitrarily.

> "The chairman of the board managed the firm's busi-
> ness with a high hand."

with clean hands. Without the taint of guilt; in a state of innocence.

> "We investigated him before he was hired, and he
> came to us with clean hands."

Handgrip

come to handgrips. To engage in physical combat; come to hand-to-hand fighting; to enter into a conflict of any kind.

> "In the local office, he will no doubt come to handgrips with the old manager."

Handle

fly off the handle. To lose one's temper; to become very angry, especially suddenly and without sufficient reason.

> "He has been irritable of late, and he is liable to fly off the handle at the slightest provocation."

Handwriting

see the handwriting on the wall. To realize that misfortune is impending; to foresee a disaster.

> "When the nearby plant began to lay off many of its workers, the local merchants thought they saw the handwriting on the wall."

Hang

hang around. To frequent, as a place; to be in the company of, as a celebrity.

> "He usually hangs around the local candy store."

> "He loves to hang around the members of visiting teams during tournament games."

hang on. 1. To keep holding; to be unwilling to give up. 2. To proceed with something one is doing. 3. To depend on for comfort. 4. To remain for a long time.

> 1. "He decided to hang on to the smaller of the two farms."

> 2. "I'll try to hang on for another few months. Business may improve after the first of the year."

3. "She hangs on to her few friends with desperation."

4. "This pain in the back is hanging on too long."

hang out. To spend a great deal of one's time (with or in); frequent.

"He likes to hang out at the drug store."

"We are discouraging him from hanging out with that bunch of kids."

hang over. To persist in a threatening manner; to remain undecided.

"The uncertainty over his induction into the service still hangs over him."

"The court decided to let the suit hang over till its next session."

hang up. 1. To put a garment on a hanger or a hook; to suspend. 2. To terminate a telephone conversation by replacing the receiver on the hook or cradle.

1. "She taught her children to hang up their clothes properly."

2. "The best thing to do in such a case is to hang up."

Hard

be hard on. To be stern or harsh with; to be difficult or painful for.

"He is known to be hard on second offenders."

"It will be hard on her when the children leave."

go hard with. To be severe with; to cause discomfort or pain.

"The jury is bound to go hard with the defendant."

"This climate will go hard with his arthritis."

hard and fast. Not varying; always the same; always effective or applicable.

> "There is no hard and fast rule on how to deal with this type of emergency."

> "We have one hard and fast rule: not to extend credit."

hard of hearing. Not hearing very well; partly deaf; having impaired hearing.

> "He often pretends to be hard of hearing when he doesn't want to hear."

hard put to it. In considerable difficulty; in a quandary; at a loss.

> "For a while he was hard put to it as to how to handle the situation."

> "They will be hard put to it to make the proper choice."

hard up. In desperate need, usually of money; to be lacking in.

> "He'll be hard up no matter how much he earns."

> "This region, especially, is hard up for doctors."

Hark

hark back. To return in discussion or thought; to go back to a previous subject or point.

> "Let's not hark back to those days. We should try to forget them."

> "No matter what you talk about, he always harks back to his life in California."

Harness

in harness. Occupied with one's usual work; working energetically.

"He dislikes vacations and he is not really happy unless he is in harness."

"Wait till he gets in harness again. He'll forget all about her."

Haste

make haste. To hurry; to do things fast; to move rapidly.

"As the Romans used to say, *festina lente,* make haste slowly, or take it easy."

Hat

pass the hat around. To take up a collection of money; to stage a benefit.

"He is doing well. Nobody will have to pass the hat around for him."

take one's hat off. To show respect or admiration; to congratulate.

"I take my hat off to him. He gave a splendid performance."

talk through one's hat. To say nonsensical things; to talk foolishly; to be silly in one's statements.

"As usual he was talking through his hat, making all sorts of silly prognostications."

throw one's hat into the ring. To commit oneself to something; to enter a contest or become a candidate.

"At long last he threw his hat into the ring by announcing his candidacy for mayor."

Hatchet

bury the hatchet. To cease fighting; to dismiss the cause of discord.

"I am all for burying the hatchet, and the sooner the better."

Have

have it in for. To feel animosity for; to have a grudge against someone; to be eager to get even with someone.

> "He has it in for a neighbor who complained about him to the police."

have it out. To settle an issue by open discussion; to have a fight about something.

> "This has been on our minds for a long time. Let's have it out right here and now."

have on. 1. To be clothed in; to wear. 2. To have secret information about.

> 1. "What do you have on right now?"
>
> 2. "They must have something on him, or he wouldn't do as they tell him."

have to do with. To have a relation to something; to associate with; keep company.

> "What does this case have to do with our discussion!"
>
> "I wouldn't have anything to do with him."

Hay

hit the hay. To go to sleep; retire for the night.

> "If you'll excuse me, I'll hit the hay now."

make hay while the sun shines. To take advantage of a situation while the opportunity exists.

> "During the war years, he held down three jobs, trying to make hay while the sun shone."
>
> "You had better work a little overtime and make some extra money. One should make hay while the sun shines."

Head

come to a head. Come to the highest point; reach a point where something has to be resolved one way or the other.

> "This condition of uncertainty will have to come to a head very soon."

> "The meeting came to a head in utter confusion."

go to one's head. To intoxicate; to cause one to become unduly vain or haughty.

> "Don't let this initial success go to your head. There are plenty of hard knocks ahead."

> "His success with Norma went to his head. Now he fancies himself a Don Juan."

hang one's head. To lower one's head, literally or figuratively, in shame or embarrassment.

> "Selma is not a girl to hang her head, even when she makes a faux pas."

head and shoulders above. Very much superior; much better.

> "In stamina and determination, he is head and shoulders above the other contestants."

head off. To put oneself in a position to check something or turn someone back; intercept; prevent something from happening.

> "If we act immediately, we might be able to head off the impending confrontation."

head over heels. 1. Completely; utterly. 2. Hastily; carelessly.

> 1. "He is head over heels engrossed in the new project."

> 2. "Is he in love? I would say head over heels."

keep one's head. To retain self-control; keep one's cool; act with good sense.

"You can depend on him to keep his head no matter
what happens."

keep one's head above water. To keep oneself from going into
debt; to manage to survive financially; to make a living.

"In spite of all the reverses, he still manages to keep
his head above water."

lose one's head. Lose one's self-control; become excited and confused.

"I have never seen him lose his head, no matter what
came up."

make head or tail of. To comprehend or understand; to make
sense of; to distinguish.

"I can't make head or tail out of this double talk.
Can you?"

on *or* upon one's head. On one's conscience; as one's responsibility.

"If you don't help this man, you may have his death
on your head."

"Taking care of her sick mother fell, as always, on
her head."

over one's head. 1. Omitting contact with the person usually in
charge of a particular function and going directly to one in a
superior position. 2. Beyond one's ability to understand; beyond
one's capability to handle.

1. "Going over the head of his editor, the author ap-
   pealed to the publisher."

2. "The study of nuclear physics was over his head."

   "The reference to the mythological figure went
   over his head."

   "Buying that business put him in debt over his
   head."

put heads together. To conspire; plan or scheme together.

> "When they put their heads together, you may be sure that they will come up with something."

take it into one's head. To decide upon something; to form a notion, usually an unreasonable one.

> "She took it into her head to become a practical nurse."

> "He took it into his head that someone is spreading false rumors about his wife."

turn one's head. 1. To cause one to behave it a silly manner; to cause one to depart from his usual, sensible ways. 2. To cause one to become overly confident or conceited.

> 1. "You leave it to a redhead to turn a man's head."

> 2. "A few lucky investments in the stock market seem to have turned his head. He believes he is quite an authority."

Hear

not hear of. To be so opposed to something as not to wish to consider it or hear it discussed.

> "I tried to tell him to see a doctor, but he would not hear of it."

Heart

after one's own heart. Pleasing one perfectly; just as one likes it.

> "Now, there is a politician after my own heart!"

at heart. Basically; divested of outside or extraneous influences; in one's innermost feelings.

> "He may act tough, but at heart he is a kindly person."

> "At heart, he is still a little boy who likes a good detective story."

break one's heart. To cause one keen sorrow; to inflict profound grief; to become ill because of grief; die; kill.

> "The induction into the service of her only son almost broke her heart."

by heart. From memory; without visual or auditory aid; through the aid of memorizing.

> "He has made the speech so many times that he knows every word of it by heart."

change of heart. A change of mind, opinion, outlook, etc.

> "Judging by the latest speech, the Senator must have had a change of heart on the subject."

do one's heart good. To please immensely; to delight; to make happy.

> "It would do his heart good to see you now."

eat one's heart out. To grieve without respite; to brood; to have some anxiety or misfortune torment one's soul.

> "I wish you would stop eating your heart out over that unworthy girl."

from the bottom of one's heart. With the deepest feelings; most sincerely; with the utmost appreciation.

> "For this noble effort, I thank you from the bottom of my heart."

have a heart. To be merciful; to act with compassion; to be kind and sympathetic.

> "Have a heart! Let the boy have the car."

have one's heart in one's mouth. To be extremely fearful or anxious; to be nervous with apprehension or anticipation.

> "He acted as if he didn't have a fear, but all the time, as he admitted later, his heart was in his mouth."

have one's heart in the right place. To be basically kind and generous.

> "Never mind his blustering. I know that his heart
> is in the right place. He'll come through."

heart and soul. With great enthusiasm; fervently; with all of one's energies.

> "He works in behalf of retarded children heart and
> soul."

> "She entered heart and soul into the political cam-
> paign."

near one's heart. Close to one's aims and aspirations; of great concern; in one's affection.

> "Such a good cause is likely to be near his heart."

set one's heart at rest. To be rid of one's fears and anxieties; to be reassured; to reassure.

> "The telephone call from her son set her heart at
> rest."

set one's heart on. To make up one's mind to do or achieve something; to make a decision to attain something.

> "He set his heart on winning top honors in college."

> "He set his heart on that beautiful car."

take heart. To renew one's optimism or courage; to regain lost confidence.

> "He was despondent for a long time, but then he
> took heart when he read about the new drug."

take to heart. To be worried; to regard as very important; to grieve.

> "I didn't think he would take to heart such a minor
> loss, but he did."

> "Don't take every little thing to heart."

to one's heart's content. As much (of something) as it takes to satisfy; as long as one wishes.

> "You can listen to the good music to your heart's content."

wear one's heart on one's sleeve. To be so frank as to reveal one's innermost feelings; to be prone to fall in love and to admit it.

> "You can't tell how she feels. She doesn't wear her heart on her sleeve."

with all one's heart. With profound sincerity; devotedly; with cordiality.

> "I wish you the best of luck with all my heart."

> "She welcomed me with all her heart and made my vacation a memorable one."

Heavy

hang heavy. To drag on boringly; to oppress with tedium.

> "Time hangs heavy when you have no one to talk to and nothing to do."

Heel

cool one's heels. To be forced to sit and wait, especially as a gesture of disregard or as a means of enforcing discipline.

> "He was furious because the manager let him cool his heels for nearly two hours before seeing him."

down at the heel. In bad financial circumstances; shabbily dressed; run-down.

> "Your visitor seemed to be rather down at the heel."

kick up one's heels. To be unusually gay and lighthearted; to have fun; to be boisterous and merry.

> "He is usually morose, but once in a while he likes to kick up his heels."

on the heels of. Following closely; close behind; occurring in quick succession.

> "First we had the inflation, and on the heels of that came the business recession and unemployment."

Hell

be hell on. To be difficult on or harmful to; to be unpleasant or painful.

> "Those noisy kids will be hell on her nerves."

> "This terrible climate will be hell on his arthritis."

catch *or* get hell. To receive a severe scolding; to be the target of a harsh reprimand; to be bawled out.

> "He'll catch hell from his boss for being absent the other day."

play hell with. To cause disorder or difficulty; to injure or damage.

> "Some of these drugs play hell with the sympathetic nervous system."

> "Washing the hands so frequently plays hell with my skin."

Help

cannot help but. Cannot do anything except (the following); must; be obliged to.

> "A few kind words cannot help but improve the situation."

> "The application of cold compresses cannot help but reduce the swelling."

help oneself to. To take something by one's own initiative; to partake of something without permission; to serve oneself food or drink.

"I don't think he should help himself to his neighbor's lawnmower while he is away."

"Don't you think you had enough? You have already helped yourself to three servings of chicken and mashed potatoes."

Hem

hem and haw. To speak equivocally, without committing oneself; to avoid making a definite statement; beat around the bush.

"He did nothing but hem and haw; I have no idea where he stands on the issue."

Here

here and there. In some or various places; at various or irregular intervals.

"Here and there you can still find an old-fashioned tailor who mends clothing, but they are rare."

"The surface is cracked here and there, but it is not in too bad a condition."

neither here nor there. Not applicable to a particular situation; beside the point or issue; not relevant to the subject at hand.

"The fact that it was done before is neither here nor there. Every case must be judged on its own merit."

High

fly high. To be filled with cheer and high hope; to be looking to the future with confidence and expectation.

"Her financial situation and married life have improved greatly; she is flying high these days."

"He was flying high when this reversal occurred, and now he's down at the mouth again."

high and dry. In an uncomfortable situation and without any prospects for getting help; helpless and deserted.

> "One day he just walked out, leaving her high and dry with three children and no means for subsistence."

high and low. In every place one can think of; everywhere.

> "We looked high and low, but we never found the missing letter."

high and mighty. In an arrogant manner; conceited; arrogant.

> "He acts so high and mighty; I despise him!"

> "You mean this high and mighty rascal actually apologized to you?"

History

make history. To do something sufficiently important to be a part of history or recorded events.

> "His contribution to this effort will not exactly make history, but it is important."

Hit

hit it off. To be very successful in getting along with someone; to suceed in making friends with.

> "They hit it off and are the best of friends now."

> "He hit it off with his new partner right from the start."

hit or miss. In an unorganized way; without regard to method or detail.

> "The search has to be done methodically, not hit or miss."

Hog

go the whole hog. To risk all; to go as far as possible; do or embrace completely.

> "If you feel so certain of your method, why not go the whole hog; bet all you've got."

> "He decided to go the whole hog and buy the most expensive model."

hog wild. Extremely excited; totally unrestrained; maniacal.

> "At the mere mention of the subject he went hog wild and pulled out a gun."

> "Now, don't go hog wild and spend all your money on souvenirs."

Hold

catch hold of. 1. To obtain; get; grasp. 2. To make contact with; to meet.

> 1. "I caught hold of him as he brushed by me."

> 2. "I'll certainly explain it to him, if I can catch hold of him. He is always out."

get hold of. 1. To get in one's possession; to acquire. 2. To put a grasp on.

> 1. "If you can get hold of an empty oil drum, you might use it as an incinerator."

> 2. "Get a hold of his arm and keep him there until I arrive."

hold back. 1. To retain; fail to surrender. 2. Keep from; restrain.

> 1. "I held nothing back. He got all I had."

> 2. "She couldn't hold herself back from telling her mother about her plans."

hold down. 1. To continue keeping or having; retain. 2. Keep at a low level; restrain; keep under control.

> 1. "For some reason he is finding it difficult to hold down a job."

> 2. "Hold down your temper, fellow!"

> "I'll hold him down while you call the police."

hold forth. To talk at length and enthusiastically; to talk repeatedly.

> "He has been holding forth on the evils of smoking for the past two hours."

> "Once again he is holding forth on his favorite subject, how to combat inflation."

hold off. 1. To resist; to repel, as an attack. 2. To delay; to postpone an action; to schedule for a later time.

> 1. "Try to hold him off in the front office."

> "They were able to hold off the intruder long enough to call for help."

> 2. "We shall hold off publicizing the sale until you are ready."

hold on. To keep one's possession of something; to retain one's grasp or hold.

> "I would suggest that you hold on to the property."

> "He held on to his opinion for a long time, but eventually he came around and acknowledged his mistake."

hold one's own. To be able to do as well as another; to continue without falling behind another person.

> "In mathematics, at least, he can hold his own with the other boys."

> "I assure you that she will do more than hold her own if given half a chance."

hold out. 1. To continue without stopping or surrendering; to remain firm; to keep going. 2. To retain something that one is expected to surrender; to keep secretly.

> 1. "If they can hold out for another six weeks, they'll make it."
>
> 2. "The boys beat him up because they thought he was holding out some details of the deal."

hold over. 1. To keep something for future action; to postpone. 2. To remain for an additional length of time; to stay in office beyond the regular term. 3. To keep something as a threat to another person.

> 1. "The decision is to be held over till the next session."
>
> 2. "The play was held over for two more weeks."
>
> 3. "He knew well that they were holding the incident over him, and so he had no choice but to go along."

hold up. 1. To present for consideration or comparison. 2. To last or endure. 3. To delay. 4. To expose. 5. To keep from collapsing. 6. To stop by force or threat in order to rob.

> 1. "She held up his work as a good example to follow."
>
> 2. "This floor covering will hold up as long as the house."
>
> 3. "What in the world held you up so long!"
>
> 4. "I wouldn't hold up a young boy to public ridicule."
>
> 5. "He received so much punishment, I don't know what's holding him up."
>
> 6. "It's no fun to be held up, especially twice in one week."

Hole

burn a hole in one's pocket. To make a person desirous of spending (money).

> "He is not used to having money. As soon as he gets a dollar, it begins to burn a hole in his pocket. He must spend it immediately."

hole up. To retire to a secluded place; to hide out from the police.

> "He holed up for the winter with his aunt, in the country."

> "The police think the robber is holed up with some buddies in Philadelphia."

in the hole. Financially deficient; in debt; in the red.

> "With this additional expense, I'll be a hundred dollars in the hole for the next six months."

make a hole in. Reduce by a large amount; consume a good portion of.

> "Buying a color TV set will surely make a hole in his budget."

pick holes in. To find faults or flaws in; to disparage by pointing out deficiencies.

> "You can pick holes in practically any proposal, but this one seems to be especially vulnerable."

Hollow

beat all hollow. To excel by far; to outdo or outstrip; to surpass.

> "In typing, she can beat anyone here all hollow."

Home

bring home to. To emphasize, as by a convincing example; to impress; convince.

"The gravity of the situation was brought home to
the public by the recent violence in the streets."

see one home. Escort a person, especially a girl, home; to see to
it that a person gets home safely.

"It will be my pleasure to see Nancy home tonight."

Honor

do the honors. To perform the functions of a host, as in presiding, introducing, serving at table, etc.

"Last year, you did the honors at the Christmas
dinner; now it is his turn."

on *or* upon one's honor. At the risk of losing one's good name
(if something promised is not fulfilled or something stated is not
true).

"They were on their honor not to drink at the party
and to be home not later than one o'clock."

Hook

by hook or by crook. In any way possible, whether honest or dishonest, ethical or unethical, etc.

"We have to get those people out of there by hook
or by crook."

hook, line, and sinker. All the way; completely.

"The con man offered him a very attractive deal,
and the poor fellow fell for it hook, line, and sinker."

on one's own hook. On one's own responsibility; at one's own
risk; without the help of others.

"He could have continued in business with his uncle,
but he decided to branch out on his own hook."

Hope

hope against hope. To continue to be optimistic although there is no reason for hoping; to persist in hoping in spite of reverses.

> "We still hope against hope that a way will be found to rescue the trapped men."

Horn

blow one's own horn. To boast about one's own talents, achievements, etc.

> "He is a very modest person and is not likely to blow his own horn, even in the case of an outstanding achievement."

horn in. To intrude; to push oneself into a situation where one doesn't belong; to try to become a beneficiary of a lucrative business; to interrupt.

> "When the business started to make money, several persons who had refused to join in the beginning tried to horn in."

> "Don't think that you can finish the story without her horning in."

pull in one's horns. To become less belligerent; to curb one's hostile attitude; to restrain one's animosity.

> "She pulled in her horns after her husband chided her for her intemperate behavior and unfriendly attitude toward his mother."

Horse

back the wrong horse. To support a losing candidate, contestant, etc.; to favor, or bet on, a losing side.

> "I surely backed the wrong horse when I supported the challenger."

be on one's high horse. To be arrogant; to treat others with disrespect or disdain.

"Having won a few cases in a row, he is on his high horse again."

hold one's horses. To exercise restraint; to curb one's impulses; to calm down.

"He was told to hold his horses or leave."

"Hold your horses now! We are working as fast as we can."

horse around. To engage in rough or boisterous play; to perpetrate boisterous pranks.

"Stop horsing around and get to work!"

"They usually horse around while waiting for a call."

horse of another *or* a different color. Not the same at all; entirely different; an entirely different situation.

"Now, when you speak of jogging as an exercise, that is a horse of a different color."

Host

reckon without one's host. To make a plan, or decide on something, while omitting an important factor.

"When you decided to take a vacation in Europe before asking your parents, you were reckoning without your host. They'll have something to say about it."

Hot

get hot. To perform at the top of one's ability; to do something very well or efficiently; to get into the spirit of one's act; to become inspired or enthused.

"The band didn't get hot until the last few days of their engagement."

make it hot for. To make things difficult or unbearable for someone.

"He shouldn't have told the boss who broke the window. The boys will now make it hot for him."

Hour

after hours. After the time when a business, school, office, etc., is open for its usual functions; after business hours; after office hours.

> "His schedule is very tight at the office, but he may be able to see you after hours."

> "The cleaning and the restocking of the store are done after hours; that is, after closing."

hour after hour. One hour after another; all the time; without respite.

> "She sat home, waiting for the call, hour after hour."

of the hour. Of the present time; of this day or period; of the current season.

> "He is certainly the hero of the hour."

> "The war was certainly the uppermost topic of the hour."

the small hours. The early hours of the morning; the hours of the morning immediately following midnight.

> "Somehow, he found the small hours of the morning especially serene and relaxing, and he was fond of reading at that time."

House

bring down the house. Make so much noise as to almost cause the house to collapse; to receive tumultuous applause.

> "The neighbors are complaining that you are bringing the house down."

> "His first appearance on the stage brought the house down.

"He didn't exactly bring down the house, but he was received well."

clean house. To rid of undesirable conditions; to put things in order.

"Before we criticize them, we had better clean house ourselves."

keep house. To attend to the affairs of a home or household; to be a housekeeper or housewife; do housework.

"She prefers to be a career woman. Keeping house is not her chosen profession."

on the house. At the expense of the business or establishment; free; as a gift of the management.

"To celebrate the occasion, drinks are on the house."

"Flowers for the ladies were on the house."

set one's house in order. To improve one's own conditions by removing undesirable elements; to make oneself right or proper.

"We should set our house in order before launching the campaign."

How

and how! Yes, very much; more than you can imagine; terrific!

"Yes, I liked that girl. And how!"

"Do I want to go? And how!"

how come? How does it happen that? Why? How do you explain?

"If you like the girl, how come that you don't ever call her?"

how so? How do you explain it? How do you account for it? Why is it so?

"You say that they will not be able to attend. How so?"

Hoyle

according to Hoyle. In accordance with rules or regulations; fair; proper.

> "Making an exception in his case is not according to Hoyle, but we'll do it."

> "Well, that wouldn't be exactly according to Hoyle."

Huddle

go into a huddle. To enter into a private discussion; to confer.

> "Before giving me an answer, he went into a huddle with members of the staff."

Hue

hue and cry. An intense or heated public protest; a popular outcry; a general alarm.

> "I don't know what this hue and cry is about! Teachers have struck before."

Hunt

hunt someone *or* something down. To chase or pursue someone until he is caught; to search for something until it is found.

> "They hunted him down in the home of his estranged wife, somewhere in Illinois."

> "They are still trying to hunt the error down in last month's entries."

I

Ice

break the ice. To say or do something to relieve the awkwardness in dealing with a person just met; to get something started by overcoming initial obstacles.

> "It was his custom to break the ice by telling a humorous story or anecdote."

> "They broke the ice by tearing down the old building and clearing the lot."

cut no ice. To have no effect; to make no difference; to fail to influence.

> "The addition of a few dollars will cut no ice with them."

> "That cuts no ice. I am still opposed to the plan."

on thin ice. In a precarious condition; in a risky situation; not well supported; not convincing.

> "If you have nothing more than the one case to support your hypothesis, you are rather on thin ice."

Ill

go ill with. To be bad for; to be to the disadvantage of; to work against.

"Such a display of bad taste will go ill with his plans
for a promotion."

ill at ease. Unable to relax; tense or nervous; uncomfortable; feeling not at home.

"Being in a strange country and unable to communicate would make anyone ill at ease."

Impatient

impatient of. Easily annoyed by; unwilling to put up with; intolerant of.

"When she plays, she is impatient of any noises inside or outside the house."

In

in for. Sure to have an unpleasant experience; certain to face something undesirable.

"He is in for a good scolding from his wife when he gets home."

ins and outs. The various details or complexities of a business or enterprise.

"We showed him as much as we could, but he'll have to learn the ins and outs of this business from experience."

in with. In a friendly relation with; on close terms with; in favor with.

"It is good to be in with this family. They own half of the town."

"In spite of his humble origin, he is in with the finest people in this part of the country."

Inch

by inches. 1. Very narrowly; by a small margin. 2. Gradually.

1. "He didn't win, but he missed only by inches."

   "You escaped bumping into him by inches."

2. "Somehow, he has a way of winning one's confidence by inches."

every inch. In every respect; thoroughly or completely.

"That boy is every inch his father's son."

"Our new member is every inch a champion."

inch by inch. Gradually; by a series of small advances; slowly.

"He worked his way to the top inch by inch."

within an inch of. Very near to; close to; within a very short distance.

"He came within an inch of losing his entire investment."

within an inch of one's life. Very near to one's death; almost to the point of losing one's life.

"The robbers beat him mercilessly, within an inch of his life."

Increase

on the increase. Becoming more prevalent; increasing; multiplying.

"Crime in the streets is on the increase."

"The incidence of venereal disease is on the increase."

Incumbent

incumbent on *or* upon. Falling as a duty or obligation upon; expected of as a matter of justice.

"It is incumbent upon every member of this community to contribute to the drive for cleanliness."

Inquire

inquire after. To make an inquiry regarding the condition or health of someone.

> "Whenever we talk, he never fails to inquire after you."

Inside

inside of. Within a specified space; within, or in less than, a specified time.

> "He was completely exhausted inside of a mile."

> "We were there inside of five minutes from the time he called."

inside out. 1. So turned that the former inner side is now outside. 2. In every detail; completely.

> 1. "If you'll turn the socks inside out, you will have a smoother surface against the skin."

> 2. "He was born in this business. He knows it inside out."

Interest

in the interest *or* interests of. For the benefit of; for the promotion of.

> "We should make some concessions in the interests of world peace."

> "In the interest of his own welfare he should be on better terms with the people of the community."

Iron

iron out. To come to an agreement about a dispute; to settle inconsistencies; to remove obstacles.

> "They are meeting now in order to iron out their differences."

"We have agreed on the main issues, but some minor
details still need to be ironed out."

irons in the fire. Business undertakings, projects, etc., in which
one has an interest.

"This business isn't his only source of income. He
has many irons in the fire."

strike while the iron is hot. To proceed quickly while an opportunity presents itself.

"You let the opportunity slip by you. You should
strike while the iron is hot, my friend!"

Issue

at issue. 1. Undecided; under discussion; in dispute. 2. Having
opposing viewpoints; not in agreement.

1. "The matter of legalizing the drug is still at issue."

2. "Authorities are at issue about the effects of the
    drug."

take issue. To dispute; to disagree with; to assert an opposing
view.

"I would take issue with you on your statement that
we know all the facts about this matter."

J

Jack

jack up. 1. To raise or elevate by means of a mechanical device, as a jack. 2. To raise prices; to increase demands.

1. "Anyone can jack up a car with this simple jack."

2. "They took advantage of the shortages and jacked up the prices on all items."

Jib

cut of one's jib. One's manner of dressing or general appearance.

"One could easily tell by the cut of his jib that he came from the Midwest."

Jig

the jig is up. All possibilities for a successful end, an escape, etc., are gone; it's all over.

"When the prosecution was able to produce three reliable witnesses, the defendant and his attorney knew that the jig was up."

180

Job

odd jobs. Various kinds of work; miscellaneous jobs involving different skills.

> "Since he lost his old job at the plant, he has been doing odd jobs, as painting, house repairs, etc."

on the job. 1. Doing one's regular work. 2. Alert; attentive to one's duties or the demands of one's job.

> 1. "The accident occurred while he was on the job."

> 2. "The guards were on the job and foiled the escape."

Jump

get the jump on. To gain an advantage over someone by getting started earlier; to get a head start.

> "This company got the jump on the competitors and has been ahead in sales from the start."

jump at. 1. Arrive at hastily. 2. To be eager to accept.

> 1. "I wouldn't jump at such a conclusion without more evidence."

> "You have a tendency to jump at conclusions."

> 2. "I know that he would jump at such an offer."

jump all over someone. To scold or criticize, especially without giving the subject a chance to answer.

> "As soon as I entered his office, he jumped all over me."

jump in with both feet. To join an enterprise eagerly and without giving the matter any thought; to enter into hastily.

> "When the offer was made to him, he jumped in with both feet—and he has been sorry ever since."

jump on. To rebuke or scold, especially in a loud voice.

> "Even his own mother jumped on him for getting involved in the brawl."

jump on the bandwagon. To join a popular cause; to join a group or side which is certain or likely to win.

> "There were a few holdouts, but they also jumped on the bandwagon toward the end of the campaign."

jump the gun. To begin something before the set time; to get a head start before the proper time.

> "The company jumped the gun by submitting its bid several days before the set date."

on the jump. Very busy; moving about all the time; always in a hurry.

> "Between the store and the home, she is on the jump all the time."

> "The roomers and the children keep her on the jump."

Just

just now. 1. At this time; only at this time. 2. A little while ago; no more than a moment ago.

> 1. "This is available just now, on this sale. The offer expires tonight."

> 2. "Indeed, he was here, but he just now left, a moment ago."

just the same. In spite of it; nevertheless; however it may be.

> "You have a point there, but I have to go by the book just the same."

> "Just the same, if he had called me in time, I might have been able to do something about it."

Justice

bring to justice. To apprehend an offender and make him stand trial for his wrongdoing.

> "Because of international legal complications, the suspected murderer was never brought to justice."

do oneself, someone, *or* itself justice. 1. To treat in a just or fair manner. 2. To comprehend and appreciate fully. 3. To do something or to behave in a manner worthy of the person involved; to be fair to oneself.

> 1. "We are not doing him justice by letting him do this menial work."

> 2. "To do this portrait justice, you must view it from a certain angle and in the proper lighting."

> 3. "This is the work which will demonstrate his talent and in which he will do himself justice."

K

Keel

keel over. To collapse suddenly as a result of fainting or shock.

"It was all so sudden. We stood there and talked, and suddenly he keeled over, apparently because of the excessive heat."

"When I told him about you and me, he almost keeled over from surprise."

on an even keel. In a stable manner; smoothly; steadily.

"Like any publication of mass circulation, this magazine has had its ups and downs, but it is definitely on an even keel now."

Keep

for keeps. To be retained permanently; forever; for good.

"This time I am giving it to you for keeps."

"Let's decide who gets what for keeps."

keep in with. To be or to remain on friendly terms with.

"In his business, he's got to keep in with the influential people of the community."

184

keep to oneself. 1. To shun the company of others. 2. To refrain from revealing; to keep as a secret.

1. "You might call him a loner. He certainly likes to keep to himself."

2. "If you tell her, you may as well tell it to everybody, as she is not one to keep things to herself."

keep up. 1. To continue at a steady or unslackening rate. 2. To manage to keep clean and orderly. 3. To persevere in doing something. 4. To see to it that one is informed on the latest developments or current events. 5. Not lag behind.

1. "It would be difficult to keep up this pace for very long."

2. "It takes two experienced men to keep up these grounds."

3. "If you keep up this horsing around, you won't get any cooperation from me."

4. "He keeps up with the latest development in pharmacology."

   "He keeps up on the standing of the various teams."

5. "I don't know if he'll be able to keep up with you. He is just a boy."

Key

key up. To cause to become excited or nervous; to energize.

"This prolonged tension and uncertainty has him so keyed up that he cannot keep his mind on his work."

"He was rather disappointed by the cancellation, as he was all keyed up to go."

Kick

kick around. 1. To treat someone unjustly or disrespectfully; to take advantage of. 2. To discuss or consider something, usually not too seriously.

> 1. "You won't have him to kick around any longer."

> 2. "We did kick the idea around for a while, but it's not practical."

kick back. 1. To move suddenly backward; to recoil. 2. To give part of a fee or payment to someone, usually as a reward for arranging a deal, recommending a client, etc.

> 1. "The gun usually kicks back. Watch out for it."

> 2. "Everyone suspects that the contractor kicks back a certain amount to his friends on the board of directors, but there is no concrete evidence."

kick in. To contribute one's expected share; to pay off.

> "Everyone kicks in for the annual Christmas party."

> "He knows what will happen if he doesn't kick in."

kick off. To begin something; to proceed with the first stages of an undertaking, especially a campaign, benefit, etc.

> "The director decided to kick off the telethon with a humorous political sketch."

kick out. To dismiss, as from membership in a group; to force to leave.

> "He laughed and said he was kicked out from better places than that."

> "When the manager of the restaurant found out what the waitress had been up to, he kicked her out."

kick up. To cause some specified unpleasantness; to stir up, as a ruckus.

> "The kids kicked up a terrible pandemonium outside his study."

> "You'll have to handle him diplomatically, or else he'll kick up a lot of trouble."

Kill

kill off. 1. To kill or destroy on a large scale. 2. To squelch; to neutralize; to drain of (something).

> 1. "That late frost in May killed off all of our tomato plants."

> 2. "She is a pretty girl, to be sure, but her sloppy appearance killed off my interest in her."

kill with kindness. To be so excessively kind as to annoy or harm someone; to arouse resentment by acts of injudicious kindness.

> "You had better stay clear of her, as she can kill you with kindness."

> "His aunt is a kindly soul, but she is so solicitous and persistent that she virtually kills you with kindness."

at the kill. At the end of an action, especially of something spectacular.

> "The fight was all but over, with one of the boxers badly battered, but no one was leaving. The spectators obviously wanted to be present at the kill, a knockout."

in at the kill. Present *at the kill*, which see.

Kin

near of kin. Related by blood; closely related.

> "They are related, but I don't think they are near of kin."

next of kin. A person's nearest relatives or relative.

"The name of the victim was not released, pending notification of next of kin."

of kin. Belonging to the same family; related.

"Although their family names are not identical, I have reason to believe that they are of kin."

Kind

in kind. 1. Involving something of the same kind; in a manner similar to a specified something. 2. Using produce or merchandise as a payment medium, instead of money.

1. "We will make some kind of an exchange, perhaps of properties in kind."

   "They will be repaid in kind for their lack of co-operation."

2. "In the country, doctors are still occasionally paid in kind."

kind of. In some small way; to a certain extent; somewhat.

"Their styles are kind of alike, as I remember them."

of a kind. 1. Of the same sort or kind; of like character. 2. Of a sort that is not desirable; of poor quality; so called, but not really.

1. "I wouldn't trust either of them. They are two of a kind and totally unreliable."

2. "It is help of a kind but certainly not sufficient to remedy the situation."

Kingdom

kingdom come. The next world; the existence that follows death.

"There is enough powder in that shed to send us all to kingdom come."

Kiss

kiss off. To disregard; ignore; reject.

"They are influential people, and it wouldn't be advisable for us to kiss off their complaint."

kiss of death. An injurious or destructive influence; a fatal relationship; an undesirable offer of help; a lethal sign.

"The support of the candidate by that political party is tantamount to a kiss of death."

Kit

kit and caboodle. All of a certain group of persons or things; the whole lot of.

"We took everything with us—the whole kit and caboodle."

Kith

kith and kin. Relatives; relatives and friends; relatives, friends, and acquaintances.

"She has so many kith and kin that even I sometimes become confused."

"She maintains a brisk correspondence with her numerous kith and kin."

Knee

bring one to his knees. To force someone to yield; to bring into a state of submission.

"The company held out against its competitors as long as it could, but the dip in the stock market brought it to its knees."

Knock

knock around *or* **about.** 1. To live or exist in a condition of aimless wandering; to move from place to place or from one country to another without a particular aim. 2. To treat someone unkindly; to kick around.

>   1. "After his discharge he decided to knock around for a while before joining his brother in the insurance business."
>
>   2. "The refugees had been knocked around by the several countries which gave them temporary asylum."

knock down. 1. To disassemble for convenience in transporting. 2. To earn; to make a specified amount of money. 3. To reduce the price of merchandise.

>   1. "The furniture will be knocked down and crated."
>
>   2. "I imagine that he knocks down about two hundred per week."
>
>   3. "All items bearing a red label were knocked down for this sale."

knock it off. To stop doing whatever one is doing; to cease.

> "Knock it off, fellows, or the neighbors will call the police!"

> "I told him to knock it off, but he wouldn't listen. So I clobbered him."

knock off. 1. To stop working. 2. To take off a specified amount from. 3. To bring about; to accomplish. 4. To murder.

>   1. "We knocked off a little earlier today because of the bad weather."
>
>   2. "He'll knock off a couple of dollars if you tell him I sent you."
>
>   3. "He knocked off a pretty good deal, I must say."
>
>   4. "They are liable to knock him off if he talks."

knock oneself out. To exhaust oneself trying to do something; to try one's best.

> "He knocked himself out all summer cramming for the examinations only to learn later that his application was turned down."

knock out. 1. In boxing, to render an opponent unfit or unable to continue fighting at a specified time, as at the count of nine or at the beginning of a round. 2. To put out of action; to damage.

> 1. "The challenger knocked out the champion in the fifth round."
>
> 2. "The broken main knocked out the water supply to the town for several hours."

knock over. 1. To upset; to cause to fall from a vertical to a horizontal position. 2. To overwhelm; to overcome emotionally.

> 1. "In his hurry to get out he knocked over the night table and smashed the radio."
>
> 2. "They were completely knocked over by the news of the kidnapping."

knock together. To construct something in a hurry, without much attention to the appearance of the product.

> "If they come, we can always knock together a few crude bunks."

knock up. 1. To bruise or scratch; to damage or mar. 2. In the United States, to have coitus with a female; in Britain, to impregnate a female.

> 1. "The furniture was pretty much knocked up by the time it arrived."
>
> "Her arm was knocked up a bit, but not seriously."
>
> 2. "He likes to have us believe that he knocked her up on the first date."
>
> "No one would have known about their affair if he hadn't knocked her up."

Know

in the know. In a position to know; privy to secret information.

"I wonder how much we can depend on his opinion. Is he in the know?"

Knowledge

to the best of one's knowledge. To the extent that one knows about a particular matter (and admitting that the information may not be complete).

"To the best of my knowledge no such letter was received here or at the main office."

Knuckle

knuckle down. To intensify one's effort; to start working harder.

"If you'll knuckle down, you can finish the job by the end of the week."

knuckle under. To submit; to give in; to yield.

"I don't think they are about to knuckle under, no matter what you do."

L

Labor

labor under. To harbor or maintain; to be under.

> "He is laboring under the false impression that all he has to do is ask for it."

Lace

lace into. To enter forcefully, as into an argument; to upbraid; castigate; scold vehemently.

> "As soon as the opportunity presented itself, Jim laced into him for neglecting their mother while he was out of town."

Lacing

give a lacing. To beat up; to give a thrashing.

> "He gave the boy a lacing he'll not soon forget."

Laid

laid up. Sick in bed; out of work or circulation because of illness.

> "He was laid up for several weeks with a sprained ankle, I believe."

Lam

on the lam. Avoiding or escaping from the police or other authorities; in hiding.

> "You can't get in touch with him now; he is on the lam."

take it on the lam. To escape or get away from the police or other authorities; to keep moving or go into hiding.

> "He probably took it on the lam as soon as he heard that the police got his name."

Lamb

like a lamb. 1. As a lamb would, i.e., gently. 2. Naive; easily duped.

> 1. "She broached the subject very timidly, like a lamb."

> 2. "When it comes to matters like these, he is like a lamb. He'll believe anything."

Lap

in the lap of luxury. Living in, or enjoying, luxury; surrounded by things conducive to sumptuous living.

> "He had his rough days, financially, but he struck it rich. You might say that he is in the lap of luxury now."

in the lap of the gods. In the hands of fate; beyond human power to control or influence.

> "We have done everything humanly possible for him. Now it is in the lap of the gods."

lap up. To receive eagerly; to accept avidly without analysis or evaluation.

> "She was hungry for compliments, and she lapped up everything his glib tongue dished out."

Large

at large. 1. At liberty; not confined; not in custody. 2. In detail; in full. 3. In general; on the whole. 4. Representing an entire state or district.

> 1. "The authorities know who the culprit is, but they have not located him. He is still at large."
>
> 2. "There is no time to discuss the subject at large at this meeting."
>
> 3. "The young generation, at large, is a bright group."
>
> 4. "Which district does he represent?" "He is a congressman at large."

Lash

lash out. To burst forth with angry words; to rebuke; to attack verbally.

> "He took it for a while without saying a word, but finally he lashed out at his critic."

Last

at last. After a long time; eventually; finally.

> "They ignored the annoyance for a long time, but at last they decided to take action."

at long last. 1. Same as *at last*, which see. 2. After a prolonged period marked by difficulties and vagaries; after a period of uncertainty or anxiety.

> 1. "At long last they decided to do something about it."
>
> 2. "At long last she heard from him, but she spent many a sleepless night before she did."

breathe one's last. To die.

> "He wants to do something spectacular before he breathes his last."

see the last of. To see the end of something; to see for the last time.

> "We haven't seen the last of the winter yet."

> "I am afraid you haven't seen the last of this fellow."

> "Will she ever see the last of his kind!"

Latch

latch on to. 1. To obtain; to get into; to get possession of. 2. To attach oneself socially to someone; to follow persistently as a companion.

> 1. "When he bought that business, he latched on to something good. It's a gold mine."

> 2. "In desperation and loneliness, she latched herself on to a friend of the family who is at least ten years younger than she."

> "We warned her not to latch on to just any man who smiled at her."

latch onto. Same as *latch on to,* which see.

Latest

at the latest. Not later than a specified time; at the most, as late as.

> "He should be there by seven, at the latest."

> "At the latest, we leave by six o'clock."

the latest. The nearest to the present time; the most recent; the most modern.

> "This is not the latest figure but it is recent enough."

"Women are forever seeking the latest styles rather than the most flattering."

"The latest news dispatch arrived here about ten minutes ago."

Laugh

have the last laugh. To be successful in the end, especially after initial failures; to win ultimately.

> "As usual, he had something up his sleeve and he had the last laugh on his competition. He got the property."

laugh at. 1. To ridicule; to make fun of; to regard as amusing. 2. To regard as unworthy or impractical; to be indifferent to or unimpressed by.

> 1. "They laughed at him when he sat down at the piano."
>
> "They laughed at the idea that man will someday fly to the moon."
>
> 2. "Most men still laugh at the idea of having women employed as jockeys, bartenders, barbers, etc."

laugh away. To attempt to dismiss, or show disregard for, something embarrassing or uncomfortable by laughter.

> "There is no point in trying to laugh away this problem. It is real, and it has to be dealt with realistically."

laugh down. To rebuff with laughter; to reject or silence by responding with laughter.

> "His suggestion was laughed down just a few months ago, but now they are thinking about it seriously."

laugh in *or* up one's sleeve. To laugh at something privately; to regard secretly with contempt and amusement.

> "He laughed up his sleeve at their attempts to purchase the building, since he had no intention of selling it."

laugh off. To regard as unworthy of consideration; to express contempt for something by laughter.

> "Telephoned bomb threats usually turn out to be the work of cranks. Nevertheless, no one laughs them off and a search is invariably made."

laugh on the other side of the mouth. To change one's attitude from levity to seriousness, from pleasure to resentment, etc.

> "He'll laugh on the other side of the mouth when he finds out that it was his car that was bumped."

laugh out of the other side of the mouth. Same as *laugh on the other side of the mouth,* which see.

laugh out of court. To dismiss, laughingly, as completely unfounded, impractical, etc.; to reject with scorn or derision.

> "He'd be laughed out of court with that kind of complaint."

no laughing matter. Something too serious to be regarded as amusing.

> "An allergic condition, though often made light of, is no laughing matter to the victim."

Laurel

look to one's laurels. To be worried about the possibility of being outdone or surpassed.

> "The younger scientists are very talented and alert. Some of the older ones had better look to their laurels."

rest on one's laurels. To be gratified or content with what one has already achieved and, hence, not to try for more.

> "He has written several successful plays, and now he is retired and resting on his laurels."

Law

be a law unto oneself. To disregard established customs and follow one's own rules or inclinations.

> "In his seclusion and in his vast financial empire, he follows no established pattern of behavior; he is a law unto himself."

lay down the law. 1. To give uncompromising orders; to order with authority. 2. To upbraid; to direct severe criticism to.

> 1. "The only way to get him to do anything is to lay down the law. He doesn't respond to gentle appeals."

> 2. "Wait till he gets home. His wife is going to lay down the law to him for making a fool of himself."

take the law into one's own hands. To punish or mete out justice in accordance with one's own feelings or views and without regard to the conventional legal processes.

> "In the old West, a man often had to take the law into his own hands to obtain justice. The established legal procedures were mighty slow."

Lay

lay about. To strike, hit, or deliver blows in every direction.

> "The burglar broke away from the policeman and cut through the crowd, laying about as he ran."

lay a course. To follow a certain course; to formulate a course of action.

"He laid a course which, he felt, would take him to
the top echelons of the organization."

lay aside. 1. To put out of the way; to decide to forget; to abandon. 2. To put away for use at a later time.

1. "Let's lay aside this prickly issue and proceed with
the other matters."

2. "We decided to lay aside a certain amount each
week for any emergency that may arise."

lay away. 1. Same as *lay aside,* definition 2. 2. To put a piece of
merchandise aside until such time as the prospective customer
is ready to buy it.

1. "He laid away a few hundred dollars in his emergency account."

2. "The store would be glad to lay away this dress
for you till Christmas."

lay before. To present something to someone for consideration.

"This proposal was laid before the committee several
times, but they refused to consider it."

lay by. To put away for use at a later time; lay aside.

"With the living costs being so high, she was unable
to lay by a single dollar during the entire summer."

lay close. To remain close or near to someone or something; to
follow closely; to remain relevant to.

"If you lay close to the guide, you'll get more out of
this tour."

"Let's lay as close as possible to our original plan."

lay down. 1. To give up by putting down one's arms or weapons.
2. To store; to accumulate a supply of something. 3. To formulate, as rules; to declare. 4. To sacrifice. 5. To bet or wager.

1. "The besieged garrison agreed to lay down its
arms."

2. "During the winter, we like to lay down a supply of staples, in case of bad weather."

3. "We should follow the rules that we, ourselves, laid down."

4. "The men who laid down their lives for this cause, and for us, deserve this special honor."

5. "How much are you ready to lay down on the home team?"

lay for. To be in hiding and waiting for someone to attack, arrest, etc.

"They were apparently laying for him in his own apartment and attacked him when he came home."

"The police are laying for him at the airport."

lay in. To put away a supply of something; to accumulate and store.

"In anticipation of the strike, most companies have laid in a good supply of coal."

lay into. To assail physically; to abuse with words.

"She laid into him with her usual invective as soon as he opened the door."

lay it on. To exaggerate or be effusive in describing something; to overwhelm with praise or compliments; to flatter.

"You have to take everything he tells you with a grain of salt, as he is prone to lay it on."

"Do give the girl a compliment, but don't lay it on, or she'll see that you are a phony."

lay it on thick. Same as *lay it on,* but more so.

lay off. 1. To dismiss a worker from his job, especially for a while, usually because of a temporary slowdown in business. 2. To cease badgering, teasing, importuning, etc. 3. To outline by means of markers, lines, stakes, etc.; to designate the limits or boundaries of.

1. "At least a thousand men are to be laid off at the plant during the next three months."

2. "She asked him to lay off, but he didn't, so she slapped him."

   "If you don't lay off him, he'll let you have it!"

3. "We were able to judge the size of the proposed structure, as the builder had laid off the area with markers."

lay on. To cover by spreading a material on; apply.

"You can lay on this adhesive with a brush."

lay oneself open. To render oneself vulnerable to attack, criticism, etc.

"By doing this, you'll lay yourself open to charges of racism."

lay oneself out. To put forth considerable effort; to try hard; to do one's best in order to accomplish something.

"He may want the job, but I haven't seen him lay himself out trying to get it."

lay out. 1. To spend money on something that another person needs, with the understanding that it will be repaid. 2. To prepare a plan; to make an outline or sketch. 3. To put down or arrange something in such a way that it is amenable to inspection or ready for use. 4. To knock down by a blow; to knock out. 5. To prepare a body for burial.

1. "You needn't be afraid to lay out the money for him on this material. He'll pay you, I'm sure. He is as good as his word."

2. "He laid out his project to us in some detail."

3. "She always lays out his clothes for him in the morning."

4. "I am afraid he'll lay you out if you continue to badger him. He can do it, you know."

5. "The deceased was laid out in a local funeral
home."

lay over. 1. To make a brief stop somewhere while traveling.
2. To postpone.

1. "We decided to lay over for a couple of days in
New York on our way to Europe."

2. "The discussion and vote will have to be laid
over until the chairman recovers from his illness."

lay to. 1. To ascribe credit or blame; to attribute. 2. To make
a determined effort; to proceed vigorously.

1. "You may lay this to lack of cooperation on the
part of our allies."

2. "You can still be ready for the exams if you will
lay to during the remaining three weeks."

lay up. To cause to be disabled, as by illness; to confine to bed.

"He was laid up for nearly a month with a sprained
ankle."

Lead

lead off. To begin or initiate an action; to be the first to do.

"How about you leading off the proceedings with
a few words of welcome for the visitors?"

lead on. To encourage someone to initiate, or proceed with, an
action which is destined to be futile or disappointing.

"She denied that she had ever led him on, but he
insists that she did."

lead someone a chase. To make a fool of someone in his quest for
something by supplying false clues or leads, thus wasting his
effort and time.

"The various crank calls led him a chase through
half a dozen cities without a shred of success."

lead up to. To prepare the way for something; to come to a point in a gradual and roundabout way.

> "He led up to the announcement by telling us a few jokes and quoting a passage from Shakespeare."

Leaf

take a leaf from one's book. To follow the example of someone; to imitate.

> "We admit that we took a leaf from our competitor's book, and it was very successful, but he copied many of our models. That makes us even."

turn over a new leaf. To make a new start, usually toward a more desirable goal; to discard an old way or method in favor of something regarded as an improvement.

> "My friend decided to turn over a new leaf by leaving his father's business and striking out on his own."

League

in league. In association with someone for the purpose of achieving a goal that is of interest to both or all.

> "We are in league to keep pornography out of the mail."

> "He would be in league with the devil if that would help him get rich."

Lean

lean over backward. To counter an undesirable tendency (as that resulting from prejudice or personal dislike) by an excessive effort in the opposite direction (as actually favoring the person involved).

> "In his effort not to be impolite to his mother-in-law, whom he disliked, he leaned over backward and did more for her than he did for his own mother."

Leap

leap in the dark. A risky act, the consequences of which cannot be predicted because the surrounding circumstances are unknown.

> "The investment was, admittedly, a leap in the dark, but it paid off well."

leaps and bounds, by. In a very fast manner; rapidly.

> "After the first year, his practice grew by leaps and bounds."

Lease

new lease on life. An opportunity for a better and happier life created by an improvement in one's financial circumstances, health, surroundings, etc.

> "His new job and change in location gave him a new lease on life."

> "The settlement of her claim against the company gave her a new lease on life."

Leash

hold in leash. Curb an impulse or action; hold in restraint; control.

> "He is very anxious to get started and I doubt that she'll be able to hold him in leash much longer."

strain at the leash. To be ready and eager to start; to be resentful of restraint or lack of freedom.

> "As spring is approaching, he is straining at the leash to begin the construction job."

> "Having been a bachelor so many years, he is straining at the leash now that he is married."

Least

at least. 1. At the lowest level or figure. 2. Bad as it is, still; in any event.

> 1. "You should get at least one week off."
>
> "This is worth at least fifty dollars."
>
> 2. "Hard as the work is, at least you can knock off and take a rest when you want to. I can't."

not in the least. Not even in a small way or in the smallest degree; not at all.

> "His response does not affect my opinion of him in the least."
>
> "She was not in the least interested in his explanation."

Leave

leave off. 1. To dispense with; stop using or wearing. 2. To omit; to desist from.

> 1. "It's getting rather warm. You may want to leave off your topcoat."
>
> 2. "If you would leave off smoking, your bronchitis would surely improve."

leave one alone. To cease annoying or disturbing; not bother.

> "Leave him alone! He is not feeling too well."
>
> "I told him to leave me alone, but he wouldn't listen."

leave out. To exclude; omit; refuse or fail to consider (for something).

> "You can leave out the details; just give us the main facts."
>
> "This year he was left out of the list of the top ten."

on leave. Away from one's job or post, but absent with permission.

> "The superintendent is on leave, but may I help you?"

take leave of. To say farewell to; to leave behind; to depart from.

> "I have already taken leave of the fellows at the office."

> "He must have taken leave of his senses, to act like this!"

take one's leave. To separate oneself from; to say good-by to and depart from.

> "She found it painful to take her leave from her old friends and neighbors."

Leg

not have a leg to stand on. To have no justification for doing or saying something; to have no basis for a given opinion or action.

> "I told him that he'll be laughed out of court. Without witnesses he doesn't have a leg to stand on."

on one's *or* its last legs. Near the end; in the last days of one's or its existence; almost totally exhausted.

> "After such a long and hot day, the poor fellow was on his last legs."

> "Our black-and-white TV set is on its last legs anyway, so let's trade it in and get a color TV."

pull one's leg. To deceive someone in an innocuous way, for laughs; to kid; to tease someone for fun.

> "It is hard to tell whether he is serious or is just pulling your leg. He is such a good actor."

shake a leg. To hurry; to speed up one's activity.

> "Come on! Shake a leg! We haven't got all day."

stretch one's legs. To get some exercise, especially to take a walk, after being sedentary for some time.

> "Well, it's time to stretch my legs; I have been sitting all day."

Leisure

at leisure. 1. Without haste or hurry. 2. Not employed; out of work.

> 1. "You don't have to do it now. You can read it at leisure when you feel like it."

> 2. "A number of scientists formerly employed in various space projects are now at leisure."

at one's leisure. When one is not busy; when one finds it convenient.

> "He does such small jobs at his leisure, after hours."

Lend

lend itself to. To be suitable or useful for; to be open or amenable to.

> "Such a statement lends itself to various interpretations."

> "This type of plot doesn't lend itself to adaptation for television use."

Length

at length. 1. In great detail; completely; fully. 2. In the end; after a considerable time; finally.

> 1. "He didn't have the time today to go into it at length, but he gave us an idea about the plan."

> 2. "At length we know who is responsible for this."

> "He tried to make a comeback at length, but the reception he received was not encouraging."

go to any length. To make every effort; to stop at nothing; to disregard any obstacles.

"He will go to any length to get what he wants."

Less

less than. 1. Not as much as. 2. Falling far below a specified standard or level; by far short of being as described, anticipated, etc.; not at all.

1. "The total is less than the amount we need."

2. "Whatever you may think of him, he is less than a hero to me. In fact, he is a cad."

"I would say this is less than a satisfactory job."

no less a person than. 1. A person of a rank or importance not lower or less than another, specified person. 2. The very person named or specified.

1. "No less a person than a governor can commute a sentence."

2. "No less a person than the President himself made the statement."

Let

let be. To allow to remain undisturbed, alone, etc.; to refrain from dealing with.

"Let him be tonight; he is not in a good mood."

"When he doesn't feel like talking, we just let him be."

"He is not the kind of boy you should associate with. Let him be."

let down. 1. To fail to do what one ought to do; to disappoint. 2. To desert in a time of need. 3. To relax; abate; cease to be alert.

1. "He will not let you down, I assure you."

2. "I don't know the man. He may let us down when we need him most."

3. "You must not let down for a minute, or he will take advantage of you."

let in. 1. To permit to enter, flow in, etc. 2. To involve in, usually something undesirable.

1. "Let the man in. He is one of our guests."

   "Open the window and let in some fresh air."

2. "By buying the restaurant, he let himself in for both a headache and financial loss."

let off. 1. To release from duty or responsibility; to allow someone to leave his work for a while. 2. To permit someone to escape with little or no punishment; to be lenient with. 3. To emit; release.

1. "He refused to let me off for the day, but I left anyway."

2. "They will probably let her off with a reprimand or a suspended sentence."

3. "He wanted to let off a little steam, but he's harmless."

let on. 1. To reveal; to make something known. 2. To pretend; to make an appearance of.

1. "He didn't let on that he recognized her."

   "If he knew that we were kidding him, he didn't let on."

2. "They tried to let on that they meant to buy the property, but we knew better."

let out. 1. To reveal; to make known; to publicize. 2. To free, as from confinement. 3. To enlarge a piece of clothing by releasing material at the seams. 4. To end, as a session, course, etc. 5. To let come forth; emit. 6. To rent out.

1. "He promised not to let any of the details."

2. "Who let the dog out?" "The cattle are let out to graze at dawn."

3. "The way you have been eating lately, you will soon have to let out your trousers again."

4. "Have you asked the girl when the last show lets out?"

5. "She let out such a scream that the neighbors came running."

6. "To augment her small income, she lets out two rooms."

let up. To slacken; diminish; stop; cease.

"This cold wave is bound to let up soon. It's almost spring."

"It snowed all day, and it seemed that it would never let up."

let up on. 1. To reduce pressure; to ease up. 2. To start treating or dealing with more leniently.

1. "If you'll let up on the accelerator, I'll appreciate it."

2. "This boy will react better to a sympathetic attitude. If you will let up on him, you'll find out that I am right."

to let someone have it. To punish physically; to beat up; to bawl out; to upbraid; to censure.

"When he refused to surrender his wallet, they let him have it."

"She has a big mouth, you know, and she let him have it."

Letter

to the letter. 1. Exactly as written; precisely as directed. 2. In every particular; to the last detail.

> 1. "He followed the assembly instructions to the letter, but still he couldn't put it together."
>
> "You are translating this to the letter, without re-regard to the idiomatic significance."
>
> 2. "In spite of its idiosyncrasies, the will was executed to the letter."

Level

find one's level. To attain the position in life that one's background, industry, and talents deserve.

> "When he moved to the West Coast and joined the faculty of the university, he at last found his level."

level off. To stop rising or falling; to resume an even course.

> "They say that inflation has been licked and that prices will soon level off. Humbug!"

one's level best. The utmost a person can do; a person's best or greatest effort.

> "He is doing his level best to find another job, but it won't be easy at his age."

on the level. Without subterfuge; reliable; sincere.

> "Can we depend on this man? Is he on the level?"

Liberty

at liberty. 1. Free to do as one desires. 2. Not in captivity; not confined. 3. Out of a job; unemployed.

> 1. "We are recommending this procedure, but you are at liberty to use any method that you prefer."
>
> 2. "Two of the escaped prisoners are still at liberty."

3. "Unemployed actors are fond of referring to themselves as being 'at liberty'."

take liberties. To be unrestrained; to let oneself act, with regard to another person, in a manner that is too intimate for the existing relationship.

"He likes to take liberties with the interpretation of the law."

"When he attempted to utilize his position to take liberties with her, she decided to quit her otherwise good job."

Lick

lick into shape. To bring to perfection or proper condition by meticulous attention, repeated revision, etc.

"One more revision will lick this manuscript into shape."

lick and a promise. An incomplete or hastily done job; a perfunctory manner of doing something; a poor substitute.

"The road needs a complete resurfacing, but the department lacks the needed money, so all we get is a lick and a promise."

lick up. To accept avidly; to listen to eagerly; to consume completely.

"She ought to know better, but she surely licks up his compliments."

Lie

lie down on the job. To do less, with regard to a particular piece of work, than one can or should do; to loaf or kill time on a job.

"Now, fellows, let's not lie down on the job. The painting must be finished by Saturday."

"If you don't keep after them, they lie down on the job every time!"

lie in. To be in bed in anticipation of childbirth; to be in the process of giving birth.

> "This is a hospital for women to lie in, or a lying-in hospital."

lie over. To remain waiting for another time; to be held over for future action.

> "The final decision will have to lie over until we hear from the auditor."

lie with. 1. To be in the jurisdiction of; to be up to; to be the function of. 2. To have coitus with.

> 1. "The choice of format and typeface lies with the publisher."
>
> "It lies with the State Department to give asylum to political defectors."
>
> 2. "That scoundrel, forsooth, would lie with any wench!"

take lying down. To yield without serious resistance; to accept, as an insult, without reprisal.

> "You may rest assured that he will not take the threat lying down."

to give the lie to. 1. To accuse someone of lying; to charge with a false statement. 2. To prove to be a lie; to demonstrate the falsity of.

> 1. "He didn't explicitly give the lie to the report, but he implied that he would do so in a few days."
>
> 2. "The absence of any cuts or bruises gives the lie to his story that he had a scuffle with an intruder."

to lie out of. To extricate oneself from an embarrassing or difficult situation by concocting false excuses or circumstances.

> "He'll lie himself out of this predicament, as he has done before. He is an expert in this field."

Life

a matter of life and death. A matter on the outcome of which the life of a person depends.

> "The delivery of the vaccine in time is a matter of life and death."

> "Whether this works or not is a matter of life and death."

as big *or* large as life. In person; actually present; in fact or reality.

> "The doorbell rang. I opened the door. And there he was, unexpectedly, as large as life!"

bring to life. 1. To restore to life; to rehabilitate. 2. To bring zest or vitality to. 3. To bring to mind or memory.

> 1. "He brought her back to life by artificial respiration."
>
> "It will take a long time and a great deal of money to bring him to life, but it can be done, I am sure."

> 2. "The party was dying of the doldrums until he came. He brought it to life."

> 3. "This play brings to life an experience I had many years ago."

come to life. 1. To recover consciousness; to begin to show signs of life. 2. To show zest, vigor, or vitality. 3. To appear lifelike.

> 1. "After we watered them, most of the plants came to life."
>
> "The application of cold compresses helped him come to life."

> 2. "He was down at the mouth all evening, but as soon as his girl friend came in he came to life."

> 3. "The characters of *The Merchant of Venice* came to life on the stage."

for dear life. With desperate energy; with the utmost speed; so as to save one's life.

>"You'd be surprised at the strength that a person dipslays when he fights or runs for dear life."

for the life of one. Even if it would save one's life; even if one's life depended on a specified action; even if one tries as hard as he can.

>"For the life of him he couldn't recall the man's name."

>"For the life of me, I can't understand why you can't stay overnight."

from life. From a natural scene or phenomenon; from a live model.

>"This courtroom scene was sketched by the artist from life, during the morning session."

not on your life. By no means; never; absolutely not; under no circumstances.

>"Will he accept this paltry offer? Not on your life!"

see life. To observe how different people live; to travel and see the world; to have experience in living and in dealing with people.

>"To help him with his proposed novel, he plans to see life by traveling and talking to as many people as possible."

take a life. To kill; to murder; to cause the death of someone.

>"He is opposed to taking a life whether the life is outside the uterus or inside."

take one's own life. To commit suicide; to kill oneself.

>"Some people regard the taking of one's own life as being as much of a crime as killing another."

true to life. In accord with what happens in real life; corresponding to real events or to reality.

"You have to admit that these sketches are true to life."

to take one's life in one's hands. To risk losing one's life; to face death knowingly in order to accomplish something.

"He was warned that he'll be taking his life in his hands if he doesn't pay off."

Light

bring to light. To reveal; to make public.

"The trial brought to light many unknown details of the crime."

come to light. To become known; to be revealed; to be discovered.

"His amnesia came to light during the interrogation."

in the light of. In consideration of something specified; considering.

"In the light of more recent discoveries, the older theory of the earth's creation may have to be revised."

light up. 1. To make light or bright; to turn on a light. 2. To ignite a cigaret, cigar, etc. 3. To become cheerful or joyous.

1. "The sky was lighted up by the furiously burning warehouse."

2. "Whenever he becomes nervous he lights up a cigaret."

3. "His face lights up when he talks about his favorite project."

see the light. 1. To appear; to come into existence. 2. To become known; to come to public knowledge or view. 3. To begin to comprehend and accept a proposal, opinion, etc., formerly not understood and opposed.

> 1. "These famous letters first saw the light about fifty years ago, when they were discovered and published."
>
> 2. "Many of the findings are classified, and will not see the light till the end of this century."
>
> 3. "Many people who were always opposed to the abolition of censorship are now beginning to see the light."

shed light on. To clarify by additional information; to add to the understanding of.

> "Your statement does not shed much light on the subject."

throw light on. Same as *shed light on,* which see.

throw *or* shed new light. Offer additional facts or information; to justify a new interpretation.

> "The confession throws new light on the case."
>
> "We might have been wrong. The coroner's report certainly throws new light."

stand in one's own light. To decrease one's chances or to mar one's reputation through improper or silly behavior.

> "A politician stands in his own light when he opposes a popular cause, however right he may be morally."

to light into. To attack physically or verbally; to tear into.

> "As soon as the speaker finished, a member of the audience lighted into him with threats and invective."

to make light of. To describe as unimportant; to belittle; to regard or refer to as trifling.

> "To soothe her fear, he attempted to make light of the subject, but it seemed to me that he was greatly concerned."

Like

and the like. And other things of the same kind or similar to.

> "They repair various kinds of appliances, as fans, mixers, radios, and the like."

like anything. Very much; as much as anything that one can mention.

> "He wanted like anything to ask him how much, but he realized it wouldn't be polite."

like blazes. 1. With great intensity; very eagerly; extremely fast. 2. Like hell; never; no.

> 1. "He ran like blazes but he was late anyway."
>
> "It shook like blazes but it did not collapse."
>
> 2. "Like blazes, I will! I am not going."

like crazy. With great energy or speed; furiously.

> "They danced and shouted, and carried on like crazy."
>
> "He talked like crazy; I couldn't make out what he said."

nothing like. Not at all similar to; altogether different.

> "This dress is nothing like the one they advertised."

something like. A little bit similar to; resembling somewhat.

> "Now, this hat is something like the one we saw in the window."

the like *or* likes of. Something or someone similar to; an equal of.

> "I have never seen the like of this effrontery in all my life!"

> "We don't want the likes of him in this organization."

Limb

out on a limb. In a position in which it is difficult to defend oneself; in a vulnerable or compromising situation.

> "You'll be putting yourself out on a limb if you undertake to defend such an unpopular act."

> "By investing too heavily in the stock market, he found himself out on a limb with regard to his other operations."

Limit

the limit. Something that is extreme in either a pleasant or an unpleasant way; a person who is delightful; a person who is extremely exasperating.

> "We have seen examples of impudence before, but this demand is the limit."

> "He is always a funny man, but when he is in the mood he is the limit."

Line

all along the line. At every point or turn; everywhere in the course; at every occasion.

> "He proved to be troublesome all along the line, from the moment we left until we arrived in Los Angeles."

> "The directions turned out to be inaccurate all along the line."

bring, get, *or* **come into line.** 1. To bring or come into a straight line or row. 2. To bring into conformity; to agree; to behave properly.

1. "If you will get these two trees into line, you will have a straight row."

2. "We will have to bring these two troublemakers into line before we can expect the team to work as a unit."

draw the line. To set a boundary or limit; to restrict.

"They would probably not draw the line at anything in order to attain their goal."

"We have to draw the line somewhere. We can spend so much and no more."

draw a line. Same as *draw the line,* which see.

get a line on. To investigate and get information about someone or something.

"You will, of course, have to get a line on this man, but I think he is just the person you need."

hard line. An uncompromising course; a strict interpretation; a rigorous pursuit.

"He was willing to make concessions on some issues, but he took a hard line on the matter of overtime."

hold the line. To retain an existing situation in the face of an attempt or tendency to change it; to resist an attempt at a breakthrough.

"In spite of all efforts to hold the line against inflation, prices continue to rise."

in line. 1. In accordance with; in agreement. 2. Under control.

1. "The statement doesn't seem to be in line with the professed aims of the organization."

2. "We will hold you responsible for keeping your
men in line."

"We advised her to keep her temper in line."

in line of duty. In the course of performing the duties required
by one's occupation or trade; while doing one's assigned work.

"The detective sustained the injury in line of duty,
while making an arrest."

lay it on the line. 1. To pay in money. 2. To be frank; to state
something clearly.

1. "He laid it on the line, to the tune of a hundred
dollars."

2. "In that case, let me lay it on the line. We have
done our share and we expect you to do yours."

line up. 1. To arrange in a row or line. 2. To get the promise of
support for something; to make ready. 3. To assume a stand or
position, usually against something.

1. "By noon, more than a hundred people lined up
at the entrance."

2. "We lined up quite a number of people who are
willing to campaign for the passage of the proposed ordinance."

3. "Most of the Democrats were lined up against the
nominee."

out of line. 1. Not in a straight line; projecting from a straight
line. 2. Not in accordance with; not in agreement. 3. Rebellious;
impertinent.

1. "Only one post is out of line and will have to be
moved."

2. "Their action is sometimes out of line with their
announced policy."

3. "The gangland boss may regard such an act as out
of line."

read between the lines. To infer an unexpressed but implied meaning; to deduce a hidden purpose or meaning from something written, said, or done.

> "Although he did not say so, I read between the lines that he was sorry they had broken up."

toe the line. To comply unwillingly with an order; to conform strictly to a command; to tolerate certain things because of devotion, affection, etc.

> "He needed the job desperately, so he had no choice but to toe the line."

> "He is a proud man, but, like most men who are in love, he toes the line."

Lion

beard the lion in his den. To challenge an opponent or to defy a formidable adversary in his own familiar territory.

> "Attacking this candidate in Boston is like bearding the lion in his den."

twist the lion's tail. To provoke, or tax the patience of, a formidable opponent.

> "Some small countries enjoy, or at least get away with, provoking the United States in a game of twisting the lion's tail."

Lip

bite one's lips. To hold back the impulse to express one's annoyance or anger; to repress an emotion.

> "He wanted very much to answer the charge, but he bit his lips in order to avoid a public argument."

button one's lip. To make sure not to reveal a secret; to become very secretive.

> "He had better button his lip, or the boys will take care of him."

hang on the lips of. To listen attentively and respectfully; to listen to every word of.

> "You ought to see her hang on the lips of her boss.
> She is a devoted employee if I ever saw one!"

keep a stiff upper lip. To remain courageous in adverse circumstances; to face misfortune with fortitude.

> "Throughout their ordeal, the passengers kept a stiff
> upper lip."

smack one's lips. To express one's enjoyment of something; to express enjoyment at the mere recollection or anticipation of something.

> "Stop smacking your lips. You don't even know if
> you'll like my cooking."

Little

little by little. Gradually; by a series of small steps or amounts.

> "His resources dwindled little by little."

make little of. 1. To regard or describe as small or unimportant.
2. To fail to get much out of; to comprehend in a limited way.

> 1. "I do not mean to make little of your complaint,
>   but we must attend to the more serious problems
>   first."

> 2. "We make little of this cryptic statement."

not a little. Very much; by a considerable amount; enormously.

> "It pleased him not a little to know that she still
> remembers him."

think little of. To regard as a matter of little importance; not to be deterred by.

> "He thinks little of such remarks, certainly not
> enough to lose sleep about."

Live

live and let live. To be tolerant of the views, conduct, etc., of others; to be broadminded or forbearing.

> "He does not approve of their policy, but he does not actively oppose it. He believes that one should live and let live."

live down. To succeed in causing other people to forget or forgive one's misbehavior, offense, etc., especially by living an exemplary life.

> "It was unlikely that he would be able to live down his past in this narrow-minded community."

live high. To live as wealthy people do, i.e., in luxury.

> "Although they can barely afford it, they try to live high."

live in. To reside, or spend the nights, at one's place of employment.

> "Our maid does not live in because we do not have a suitable room for her."

live it up. To make an effort to have lots of fun; to live in a noisy and extravagant manner.

> "Since he got his divorce he is really living it up."

live out. 1. To reside or sleep away from one's place of employment. 2. To live to the end of a particular period.

> 1. "Our maid prefers to live out although we have plenty of room for her."

> 2. "They would like to live out the winter in their present location."

live through. To pass through or endure an experience or a certain period; to survive.

"They lived through many hardships in the old country."

"It may not be easy, but we'll live through it."

live up to. 1. To satisfy or fulfill something promised or expected. 2. To behave or live in accordance with certain principles or ideals; to turn out to be what one is reputed to be.

1. "As he grew older he failed to live up to the promise he showed in his childhood."

2. "The new manager did not live up to the reputation that preceded him."

live well. To live a life abounding in material comforts; to live in luxury.

"I don't know how they do it, but they live well."

live with. 1. To share a home with; to reside with. 2. To accept as inevitable; to reconcile oneself to something; to endure and make the best of. 3. To live together as husband and wife without being married.

1. "She expects to live with her sister while her home is being redecorated."

2. "He learned to live with his disability, saying that what cannot be cured must be endured."

3. "Everyone knows that she lives with this man."

Load

get a load of. 1. To look at; take a look at something. 2. To listen to; be attentive to.

1. "Charlie, get a load of this bunny!"

2. "I wasn't listening. Did you get a load of what he was driving at?"

Lock

lock out. 1. To keep someone from entering by locking the door. 2. The closing of a business or any place of employment by the owner in order to keep the workers out because of a disagreement about the terms of employment.

> 1. "We didn't mean to lock him out; we simply forgot to unlock the door."

> 2. "The company threatened to lock out the employees if they did not report for work by next morning."

lock, stock, and barrel. Including everything; completely.

> "He was so tired of the business that when he got rid of it he sold everything, lock, stock, and barrel."

lock up. To secure something, as a door, lid, etc., by means of a lock; to put behind the locked doors of a prison or jail.

> "Will you lock up tonight, please? I have to leave early."

> "Since he didn't reveal his identity, they locked him up overnight with the rest of the suspects."

under lock and key. Put away in a safe place, usually behind a locked door or in a box secured with a lock.

> "You should keep these securities under lock and key, as it is troublesome and expensive to replace them."

Loggerhead

at loggerheads. Engaged in a quarrel; disputing.

> "They are still at loggerheads over the proper disposition of the farm."

Loin

gird up one's loins. To get ready for something difficult, as a test of one's strength, endurance, stamina, etc.

> "He girded up his loins for the ordeal of a lengthy court battle."

Long

as *or* so long as. 1. During the time that (something is taking place). 2. Since; inasmuch as.

> 1. "So long as they are paying the rent, we have no cause to complain."
>
> 2. "So long as they are here, we may as well invite them."

before long. Soon; before much time passes.

> "You should have the manuscript finished before long."
>
> "Before long, it will be spring again."

the long and the short of. The whole of; the sum and substance of; the gist of.

> "The long and the short of it is that we don't have enough evidence to justify taking the case to court."

Look

it looks like. It appears that it is; it is likely that it will.

> "It looks like a good idea, but who can tell."
>
> "It looks like rain to me."

look after. To give the necessary care; to watch over.

> "Our neighbor will look after the flowers while we are on vacation."

look back. To turn one's thoughts to the past; to consider things of the past; to recall.

> "When we look back at those years now, they seem like happy years."

look daggers. To look with an expression of anger; to glare menacingly.

> "She looked daggers at me when I mentioned his name, so I quickly dropped the subject."

look down on *or* upon. To look upon someone as inferior; to regard as unworthy; have contempt for.

> "They look down on people who earn their living in the trades or non-professional occupations."

look for. 1. To try to find; to search. 2. To expect; anticipate.

> 1. "You might try to look for it in this drawer."

> 2. "May I look for you at the party tomorrow?"

> "I look for the unemployment rate to go up even higher."

look forward to. To wait for with pleasure or eagerness.

> "On the contrary, I don't mind it at all. In fact, I am looking forward to this meeting."

look in *or* into. To have a glimpse inside of.

> "We looked in the closet but it wasn't there."

> "I saw him when I looked into the window."

look in on. To visit someone briefly, especially to inquire about one's health.

> "Her neighbors will look in on her at least twice a day, so you needn't worry."

look into. To make an investigation of; to inquire into.

> "He promised to look into the incident, to see who was at fault."

look on. To watch or observe without intention to participate; to be a spectator.

> "Several bystanders looked on, but no one offered to help."

look oneself. To have one's usual or normal appearance; to appear to be in good health.

> "For the first time in several weeks she looked herself."

> "You don't look yourself today. What is the matter?"

look out. 1. To gaze from the inside to the outside. 2. To be on the alert; to be careful. 3. To take care of; to be mindful of.

> 1. "Don't look out the window, as this has a tendency to aggravate motion sickness."

> 2. "At the station, you should look out for panhandlers and pickpockets."

> 3. "Everyone should look out for his financial security."

look over. 1. To inspect; to examine and evaluate. 2. To gaze upon lustfully; to leer amorously.

> 1. "Look over these items. You may find something here that you like."

> 2. "I caught his eye as he was looking her over, from top to bottom."

look to. 1. To turn one's eyes in a specified direction. 2. To attend to; to take care of. 3. To turn one's hopes to; to focus one's expectations. 4. To depend or rely on; to utilize or resort to.

> 1. "Before crossing the street you should look to the right and to the left."

> 2. "His task is to look to the physical condition of the properties."

3. "We are all looking to the day when he'll be sufficiently rehabilitated to stand on his own feet."

4. "I look to the weight of public indignation to
stop these atrocities."

look up. 1. To turn one's eyes upward; to direct one's glance at
someone entering or speaking out. 2. To find and read an item
of information, as in a reference book. 3. To show signs of improvement; to become more prosperous. 4. To find a person
and to visit him.

1. "Everyone present looked up when he blurted
out the unexpected challenge."

2. "If you don't believe me, look it up in the dictionary."

3. "Economists say that things are looking up, but
you can't prove it by those lined up at the unemployment counters."

4. "I wish you would look up my nephew while
you are in L.A."

look up and down. 1. To search for diligently; to look everywhere. 2. To inspect a person with a searching eye; to scrutinize
amorously.

1. "We looked up and down the beach but we
couldn't spot him, for a good reason—he wasn't
there!"

2. "The personnel manager looked him up and
down before hiring him."

"She hates to walk by that corner, as the boys are
always leering and looking her up and down."

look up to. To regard someone as superior or deserving respect;
admire.

"Most women, except the 'libies,' like men they can
look up to."

look upon. To regard; to have an opinion of; to consider.

> "It is hardly realistic to look upon college students as 'kids'."

to look sharp. 1. To be on the alert; to be ready; to be quick in seizing an opportunity. 2. To look all dressed up; to be primped.

> 1. "There will be opportunities, and you will find them if you look sharp."

> 2. "My, but you are trying to look sharp tonight. What is the occasion?"

Loose

break loose. To disengage oneself from; to free oneself from someone's hold by force; escape.

> "In the turmoil resulting from the collision, the arrested man broke loose and ran off."

cast loose. 1. To untie and let go. 2. To let go and do as one pleases.

> 1. "That brat cast the rowboat loose again! Let's get it."

> 2. "We decided that the best thing to do with this boy is to cast him loose and let him try his own way."

cut loose. 1. To release someone from the control or authority of another. 2. To become, or render oneself, free from the domination of another. 3. To escape. 4. To enjoy oneself in an unrestrained manner. 5. Cut the ties or leash; unfasten.

> 1. "The commissioners decided to cut the community loose from the metropolitan authority."

> 2. "The girl decided to cut loose from her domineering mother."

3. "It is believed that the prisoner managed to cut loose during the night."

4. "The boys were in the habit of cutting loose at the local tavern on Friday nights."

5. "We found the guard tied to a chair and we cut him loose."

"The dog is gone! Someone cut him loose during the night."

let loose. To allow to go; to release; set free; become free; give way; yield.

"They won't hold him very long. In fact, they'll probably let him loose within a week."

"The roof let loose under the weight of the snow."

let loose with. To give forth; to emit; to call out; to shout.

"On the top of that, he let loose with a barrage of invective."

on the loose. Free to move or roam; enjoying oneself in an unrestrained manner.

"Your pony is on the loose again. You'd better get him."

"Watch out for this fellow. He's on the loose and anxious to go."

turn loose. To release from confinement or restraint; let do as one pleases.

"We kept the fowl in the barn all winter, but we'll turn them loose as soon as it gets warmer."

"The children shouldn't be turned loose like this, without supervision."

set loose. Same as *turn loose,* which see.

Lose

lose oneself. Lose one's way or bearings; to become confused or bewildered; to become absorbed in some work or in meditation.

> "It is easy to lose one's way driving in a strange city."

> "He lost himself trying to explain the theory of relativity."

> "I don't often lose myself in reveries, but I did this time."

lose face. To be embarrassed or humiliated; to suffer disgrace.

> "It will be difficult to get out of this situation without losing face."

lose out. To fail to achieve something desired; to fall short of gaining something sought.

> "We lost out in our last try, but we must win this time."

> "In face of such formidable competition it is no disgrace to lose out."

Loss

at a loss. 1. At a price which involves losing money. 2. In a condition of perplexity; bewildered.

> 1. "The season is over and we will have to sell the remaining summer stock at a loss."

> 2. "He, too, was in the dark and at a loss for an explanation."

at a loss to. Unable to; not certain how to (do something).

> "Even the accountant was at a loss to provide a solution."

Lost

lost in. Thoughtfully absorbed in; engrossed; engulfed in.

"He was lost in his reading and did not hear the knock on the door."

lost on. Wasted on; without an influence or effect on.

"Such refinements in production would be lost on them."

"The literary allusion was lost on him."

lost to. 1. No longer open or available to. 2. Unfeeling or insensible to.

1. "That option was lost to us when we did not exercise our rights."

2. "Their savage behavior demonstrates that they are lost to all sense of decency."

Lot

cast in one's lot with. To associate oneself with someone; to join and share the fortunes of.

"He decided to cast in his lot with the younger group of dissidents."

throw in one's lot with. Same as *cast in one's lot with,* which see.

cast lots. Same as *draw lots,* which see.

draw lots. To decide who or what by means of lots.

"They drew lots to decide who would be their spokesman."

the lot. All of a group or a class; everyone; everything.

"I won't have anything to do with the lot of them."

"If the price is right, I'll take the lot."

Love

fall in love. To begin to feel love for someone; to develop a strong interest in or desire for something.

> "He did not plan to fall in love with this girl; it just happened."

> "I just couldn't help falling in love with that magnificent painting."

for love. Without payment; (done) as a favor; because it is pleasant.

> "I couldn't get him to do it for love or for money."

for the love of. Out of consideration for; for the sake of.

> "If not for the love of justice, then do it for her sake."

> "For the love of heavens, where did you get this monstrosity of a necktie!"

in love. 1. Having the feeling of love for someone; feeling a strong affection. 2. Having a keen interest in something; feeling a strong desire.

> 1. "He says he is in love with her, but is he mature enough to know what love is?"

> 2. "He never married because he is so in love with his work."

make love. To embrace, kiss, or touch a person of the opposite sex; to have coitus.

> "The girl said that she is fed up with him because all he wants to do is make love."

> "The police arrested the couple for making love in a public park."

no love lost. No affection or friendship; animosity; bad relations.

> "There was no love lost between the two in their quest for advancement."

Low

lay low. 1. To knock down; to kill. 2. To overcome; to make ill; to confine to bed. 3. Same as *lie low*, which see.

> 1. "He laid the attacker low with a punch to the jaw."

> 2. "It doesn't take long for the virus to lay you low."

lie low. To be in hiding; to remain inactive; to keep quiet; to bide one's time.

> "It was his custom to lie low for a while after each job."

> "This is probably not the right time to make the announcement. Let's lie low for a month or so."

Luck

crowd one's luck. To be too eager to exploit an opportunity; to try too hard to get every possible benefit from a lucky situation.

> "You've made good money in this store, now don't crowd your luck by planning to branch out in other locations."

down on one's luck. In a difficult situation; in a poor financial condition.

> "Jim is down on his luck these days; I don't think he can help you."

in luck. In fortunate circumstances; lucky.

> "You are in luck. I know just the man who can help you with your problem."

out of luck. In unfortunate circumstances; unlucky.

> "You are out of luck. He just left and he won't be back for two weeks."

push one's luck. Same as *crowd one's luck,* which see.

try one's luck. To attempt to do something for the first time, with some hope for, but no assurance of, success.

> "Having failed in several other endeavors, he now decided to try his luck in insurance."

worse luck. Unfortunately; untowardly; unpropitiously.

> "We tried every physician in town, but, worse luck, not one was available."

Lung

at the top of one's lungs. In as loud a voice as one can muster; as loudly as one can speak or shout.

> "He shouted at the top of his lungs but the roar of the engines drowned him out."

Lurch

leave in the lurch. To abandon a person in need of help; to leave a person stranded; to forsake or desert.

> "We were left in the lurch when two of our best men quit shortly before Christmas."

M

Mad

like mad. As a madman would; with a madman's fury; with great enthusiasm, impulsiveness, energy, etc.

> "She talked like mad all afternoon, then she went to bed exhausted."

mad as a hatter. Completely demented; extremely foolish; silly.

> "He must be mad as a hatter to propose such a thing. Who ever heard of a wedding ceremony under water!"

Make

make a fool of. To cause someone to seem like a fool; to take advantage of, as by guile; to manipulate someone for selfish reasons.

> "She never did like him. She merely wanted to make a fool of him."

make after. To follow; to run or go after someone; to chase.

> "If you won't watch him, he'll make after every pretty girl."

"He threw the ball into the pond and the dog made after it."

make a meal of. To eat and regard as a meal something that is generally less than a complete meal.

"He can make a meal of a loaf of rye bread if the bread is the kind that he likes."

make as if. To pretend; to act as if (a certain condition exists).

"He tried to make as if he had not noticed her absence, but we knew better."

make away with. 1. To get rid of. 2. To murder or kill. 3. To steal. 4. To consume or devour completely.

1. "We got this dog to make away with the birds that pick our strawberries."

2. "He was accused of being a police informer, and some say that he was made away with."

3. "In the ensuing confusion, someone made away with the cash box."

4. "While watching television, we made away with the box of chocolates that you left here."

make believe. To pretend; to allow oneself a dreamlike thought of a desired situation.

"She used to set the table for two and make believe that he was with her again."

make book. To take bets, usually illegally, on certain events, contests, etc.; to bet.

"Ostensibly it is a confectionary, but their business is to make book."

"It does seem logical, but I wouldn't make book on it."

make fast. To tie, as a boat; to fasten; secure.

"I think I forgot to make fast the back door."

make for. 1. To move toward; to be headed for. 2. To lunge or charge at in a menacing way. 3. To favor or promote; to help accomplish.

> 1. "He tried to make for the door but was stopped by a plainclothes man."
>
> 2. "As the two thugs made for the cashier, he managed to pull a gun on them."
>
> 3. "Lack of candor on either side will not make for better progress in the negotiations."

make heavy weather. Of a ship, to roll and pitch in rough seas; to make progress slowly and laboriously; to struggle along.

> "My own impression is that I am making heavy weather with these reports. They are quite complex."

make it. To succeed in achieving a goal; to be successful in a general way.

> "This carton is rather heavy. Do you think you can make it to the car?"
>
> "He is a very resourceful man. I am sure he'll make it if nothing untoward happens."

make like. To do as someone does; to imitate; to play the role of.

> "Sometimes she likes to make like a movie star or a Mata Hari."

make off. To depart stealthily; to run away; to sneak away.

> "You stay here, and don't even think of making off before we get back."

make off with. To carry something off without permission; to steal.

> "We forgot to lock the door of the tool shed and somebody made off with our new lawn mower."

make or break. To bring noted success or complete failure.

"This is too small an investment to make or break anyone."

make out. 1. To succeed. 2. To get along. 3. To barely see; to discern. 4. To hear. 5. To understand. 6. To write out; to fill out. 7. To establish; to present. 8. To show, or attempt to show, that one is. 9. To kiss and neck.

1. "I have no doubt that he'll make out. He is clever."

2. "I was just wondering how he is making out at his new job."

3. "I can make out most of the letters but not clearly."

"He made out the shadow of a cowering man behind the counter."

4. "I can make out the voices of a man and a woman."

5. "Can you make out the meaning of this sentence?"

6. "Shall I make out this check in your name or the company's?"

7. "We must admit that he made out a good case against the suspect."

8. "They made him out to be some kind of a dolt, which he isn't."

9. "After ten years of marriage, they were still making out like young lovers."

make out with. 1. Of a man, to be successful with girls. 2. To persuade a girl to surrender.

1. "I don't know what his secret is, but he makes out with the ladies."

2. "Surprisingly, he failed to make out with this one."

make over. 1. To alter, as a garment; to change; to remodel. 2. To convey; to transfer ownership of. 3. To demonstrate one's affection for; to show concern; to fuss over.

1. "If you wish, you can make this over into two apartments."

   "You can't really make a man over with regard to basic convictions."

2. "She wants to make over this house to her son."

3. "He is embarrassed when she makes over him in public."

   "She makes over her children a little too much."

make up. 1. To compose; to constitute. 2. To compile; to put together. 3. To invent; fabricate. 4. To compensate for. 5. To complement or complete. 6. To put in proper order; to arrange in a desired pattern or manner. 7. To reach, as a conclusion; to decide. 8. To resume friendly relations, as after a quarrel; to settle a dispute in a friendly manner. 9. To prepare for a role by the use of cosmetics and an appropriate costume; to beautify one's face with cosmetics. 10. To arrange printed matter, set type, illustrations, etc., in preparing a page for a book, magazine, etc. 11. To take a course which one has missed; to take an examination again which one has missed or failed.

1. "Six chapters make up the first part of the book."

   "This plywood is made up of six thin layers."

2. "Each department is supposed to make up a list of needed supplies."

3. "He made up this story to justify his absence."

4. "One way to make up for a mediocre memory is to study more diligently."

5. "This replacement will make up the original order."

6. "Whose turn is it to make up the beds?"

7. "You don't have to make up your mind now. Think it over for a few days."

8. "Lovers always make up sooner or later. Just give them time."

   "This rift will be difficult to make up."

9. "She spends over an hour in making up for the role."

   "A girl has to make up for her dates, and that takes time."

10. "He edits the copy and makes up the pages for this special edition."

11. "He still has to make up the two exams that he missed because of illness."

make up to. To try to become friendly with someone, as by flattery, little favors, etc.; to make amorous advances.

"Don't take him seriously. He is merely trying to make up to you because you can help him with his work."

"He has been trying to make up to the new girl at the office, but so far she is giving him a cold shoulder."

make water. To empty the bladder; to urinate.

"In this part of the country, they use the expression 'to make water,' meaning to urinate."

make with. 1. To use; to move; to apply. 2. To flaunt; to show off; to demonstrate with pride.

1. "Watch that cheerleader make with the baton!"

2. "There he goes again, making with those big
   words. I'll bet he doesn't know what they mean."

on the make. 1. Trying to promote or better oneself in an aggressive way. 2. Trying to find a sweetheart or lover.

1. "Have you noticed that Garry is on the make with
   the executive group?"

2. "Watch out! She is a divorcee and on the make."

Man

as one man. Unanimously; in complete agreement; all together.

"There was complete unanimity. They voted it down
as one man."

be one's own man. 1. To be independent or autonomous. 2. To
be in complete control of one's faculties.

1. "In this company, each branch manager is his own
   man."

2. "Well, you awakened him in the middle of the
   night and I am sure he wasn't his own man."

man and boy. As a boy and as a man; from childhood on; ever
since boyhood.

"He was practically born on stage and has been in
show business, man and boy, for some forty years."

to a man. Including everyone; with not a single man excepted.

"They were opposed to the company's suggestion to
a man."

Manner

by all manner of means. Certainly; of course; without hesitation.

"If we find that we can get away, we will do so by
all manner of means."

by no manner of means. Certainly not; definitely not; by no means.

> "We have by no manner of means made a final decision about this offer."

in a manner of speaking. More or less; in a certain way; in a sense.

> "They are, in a manner of speaking, newcomers in this part of the Midwest."

to the manner born. Accustomed by virtue of birth to a particular way of life; naturally suited for a particular role or position.

> "He is a patron of the arts to the manner born."

> "When it comes to mathematical niceties, he is an expert to the manner born."

Many

a good many. A considerable number, as of persons or things; relatively many.

> "A good many of the local residents have never heard of the incident."

a great many. A very large number, as of persons or things; many.

> "A great many items in this exhibit are on loan from other museums."

one too many. Too much; too formidable; too difficult to surmount; too strong.

> "The local team found the visitors one too many for them."

> "These questions proved one too many for him. He flunked the test."

Map

put on the map. To make a place well known; bring to the attention of the public.

"The construction of the ammunition plant here put
the small town on the map."

March

on the march. Advancing vigorously; moving ahead rapidly.

"In spite of all the measures taken, inflation is still
on the march."

steal a march on. To gain an advantage over someone without
being detected.

"One of the contestants stole a march on the others
by working out at night."

Mark

beside the mark. Not relevant; not to the point.

"This statement may be quite true, but it is beside
the mark. The point is, has there been a violation?"

hit the mark. 1. To be right; to be accurate. 2. To achieve one's
goal; to succeed in an attempt.

1. "You hit the mark with that prophecy about the
change in the front office."

2. "I would like to see him hit the mark in his latest
venture."

make one's mark. To become successful; to achieve fame; to
reach one's goal.

"He always wanted to make his mark as a director.
I am glad that he made it."

mark down. 1. To make a note in writing; to record. 2. To reduce
the price of merchandise, as for a special sale.

1. "We should mark these things down or we'll forget them by next week."

2. "Not all items in the store were marked down for this sale."

mark off. To indicate the limits of something, as by drawing lines.

"Before we do anything, we should mark off the location of the vegetable garden."

mark time. 1. To cease doing something for a time, usually in order to await developments. 2. To pretend to be working while actually doing little or nothing.

1. "Production was stopped and management is marking time in the hope of receiving a new order."

2. "They actually stop working at three, then mark time till five, when they go home."

mark up. 1. To inscribe notations; to mark with symbols. 2. To increase the price of an article. 3. To set the selling price of an article by adding a certain amount to the cost.

1. "The child used his new crayons to mark up the kitchen walls."

2. "While some articles in this store are being sold at relatively low prices, other items are actually marked up."

3. "The non-pharmaceutical merchandise is usually marked up 40 percent in most stores."

miss the mark. 1. To be inaccurate. 2. To be unsuccessful in achieving a goal; to fail in an attempt.

1. "He is usually accurate, but this time he missed the mark by a mile."

2. "He tried hard enough, but he missed the mark. I suppose he never had what it takes to be a professional singer."

wide of the mark. Wrong by far; not at all to the point.

"I realized later that my explanation was wide of the mark."

Market

in the market for. Wishing to buy; looking around in order to find and buy.

"He is in the market for a good used car."

on the market. Available to those who wish to buy; offered for sale.

"This vaccine won't be on the market for another six months."

put on the market. To make it possible for the public to buy; offer for sale openly.

"We expect to put this car on the market within a year."

seller's market. A condition in buying and selling marked by a heavy demand so that the seller can demand and get relatively high prices.

"The housing shortage puts real estate in a seller's market."

buyer's market. A condition in buying and selling marked by a heavy supply so that the buyer benefits from the resulting competition and lower prices.

"At this time of the year, there is a buyer's market for eggs."

Matter

for that matter. With regard to a particular point or issue; as far as that (i.e. a particular issue or subject) is concerned.

> "For that matter, even if they paid us for the lost articles, we would not be able to replace them."

Mean

mean well by. To have a favorable aim or intention; to have friendly feelings.

> "We are convinced that he meant well by it, even though he used strong language."

Means

by all means. 1. Certainly; without doubt; of course. 2. At any price; without fail.

> 1. "We should accept it, by all means."

> 2. "You should, by all means, get a copy of the letter."

by any means. In any way at all; without regard to cost or effort.

> "They'll stop at nothing. They will try to get it by any means."

by means of. By the use of; with the aid of; relying on.

> "He didn't get to where he is now by means of flattery. He is talented and well qualified for the job."

by no means. Same as *not by any means,* which see.

means to an end. A way of attaining a certain goal; a method by which one accomplishes something.

> "This gesture on his part is not a whim. It is a means to an end in his attempt to get the nomination."

not by any means. Not in any way imaginable; in no way.

> "He is not by any means comparable to the masters, but he is an outstanding painter."

Measure

beyond measure. Too much to be counted or measured; extremely.

> "The insults to which they were subjected are beyond measure."

for good measure. To make sure it's enough; as something additional to the normal or expected.

> "She hugged him, and gave him a kiss for good measure."

> "They not only robbed him but beat him up for good measure."

in a measure. To a certain, i.e. small, degree; to some extent; somewhat, but not entirely.

> "In a measure, he does look like your fiance."

> "They are both right in a measure."

made to measure. Of a garment, made in accord with the measurements of one's figure; custom-made.

> "You can have a suit made to measure for just a few dollars more than the ready-made garments."

measure out. To deliver or eject a measured quantity; to hand out stingily.

> "After the coin is inserted, the machine measures out the correct amounts of chocolate syrup and hot water."

> "In spite of his good salary, he measures out every dollar needed for household expenses."

measure swords. 1. To test one's strength or preparedness for a contest. 2. To engage in a fight; to compete.

> 1. "I believe that he does not mean to start a war. He is merely measuring swords."

> 2. "With the confidence characteristic of youth, he was eager to measure swords with his competitors."

measure up. To be qualified for something; to be sufficiently capable.

> "He is a good worker, but as a manager he didn't quite measure up."

measure up to. To meet certain specifications; to fulfill expectations; to come up to the excellence or qualifications of another.

> "He was investigated by our personnel department and found not to measure up to the scholastic standards set by the board."

take measures. To do what is necessary in order to accomplish a particular purpose; to take steps or action.

> "If we don't take measures now to combat pollution, it may be too late."

take one's measure. To make a judgment or to form an opinion regarding a person's qualifications, character, etc.

> "All through the discussion he had the feeling that they were taking his measure as a possible replacement for their retiring dean."

Medicine

give someone a dose of his *or* her own medicine. To punish or get even with someone for an injury or insult by retaliating in kind, i.e. by using the same method.

"She didn't answer his letter for several days to give him a dose of his own medicine."

take one's medicine. To accept without resentment punishment deserved because of one's own misbehavior.

"Having admitted that he failed to do his part, he was willing to take his medicine and pay for the resulting damage."

Meet

meet halfway. To make a partial concession; to yield in part in return for an opponent's partial concession.

"We are certainly willing to meet them halfway, if they will give a little ground on their side."

meet with. 1. To encounter; to meet by chance or accidentally. 2. To experience; to face; to confront.

1. "They met with all sorts of obstacles and hostility."

"We met with unexpected good luck on the last trip."

2. "The ball team met with exceptionally cold and rainy weather which caused the cancellation of several games."

Mend

on the mend. 1. Recovering; improving in health. 2. Getting better, in a general way.

1. "Yes, he was quite ill, but he is on the mend now."

2. "The relation between the two countries isn't exactly amicable, but I would say it's on the mend."

Mercy

at one's mercy. Completely subjugated to, or in the power of, someone.

> "Looking at the burly and armed kidnaper, she realized that she was at his mercy."

at the mercy of. Same as *at one's mercy,* which see.

> "The passengers realized they were at the mercy of their captors."

Merry

make merry. To behave in a gay or joyous manner; to be in a festive mood.

> "While the guests were making merry in the living room, a thief entered through a back door and made off with some jewelry and fur coats."

Mess

mess around. 1. To be doing something without purpose or interest; to waste time with useless activity. 2. To make love to a girl; to neck or touch a girl in a libidinous way.

> 1. "Stop messing around with these pictures and do your homework."
>
> "He isn't really doing anything worthwhile. He is just messing around."
>
> 2. "She is not the kind of girl that will let you mess around."

mess with. To meddle; to associate oneself with an undesirable activity.

> "I wouldn't mess with that project if I were you."

> "He is always messing with things that are none of his business."

Midst

in our, your, *or* **their midst.** Among us, you, or them.

> "There must be an informer in your midst."

> "There is no room for jealousy in our midst."

in the midst of. Surrounded by; beset by; in the course of; while engaged in.

> "Against our will, we found ourselves in the midst of the howling mob."

> "The subsidy was cut off while they were in the midst of the research."

Milk

cry over spilt milk. To grieve over some mishap or act that cannot be rectified.

> "The thing is done. It cannot be corrected, so why cry over spilt milk?"

Mill

through the mill. Through trials, tribulations, or severe difficulties; through painful but beneficial experience.

> "She has been through the mill before when she had to get a job to support the family."

Mince

not mince words. To speak frankly, in explicit terms; to express oneself without equivocation.

> "This time he didn't mince words about his displeasure with our behavior."

> "She is not one to mince words. When she has something on her mind, she lets you know."

not mince matters. Same as *not mince words,* which see.

Mind

bear in mind. To regard as a factor; to consider something in relation to something else; to remember.

> "You should bear in mind that he is no longer a young man. He should slow down."

keep in mind. Same as *bear in mind,* which see.

> "Keep in mind that the papers have not been signed yet and that the deal may fall through."

be in one's right mind. To be sane; to be normal mentally.

> "I don't think he was in his right mind when he said this."

be of one mind. To have a unanimous opinion; to be in agreement.

> "On this particular issue they are of one mind."

be out of one's mind. 1. To be insane; to be temporarily deranged. 2. To be extremely upset or mentally agitated.

> 1. "He must have been out of his mind to say anything like this."
>
> 2. "He was out of his mind with worry about his son, and we must keep this in mind in passing judgment."

cross one's mind. To come to one's mind; to enter the mind as a possibility.

> "It did cross my mind that he may be ill, but I did not deem it likely."

change one's mind. To change one's plans, opinion, intention, etc.

> "I do not think that changing one's mind indicates lack of mental stability."

give someone a piece of one's mind. To inform a person about one's disapproval of his action, opinion, etc.; to rebuke.

> "She gave him a piece of her mind for talking too much."

have a good mind to. To have a strong impulse to do (something); to be tempted to.

> "I have a good mind to call him this minute and tell him what I think of his behavior."

have half a mind to. To be disposed, to some extent, to do something.

> "I have half a mind to ask him to leave at once."

have in mind. To plan or intend; to think about.

> "He didn't make an effort to explain what he has in mind."

keep one's mind on. To be attentive to something; to be thinking about something.

> "He was so worried that he found it difficult to keep his mind on his work."

know one's mind. To understand oneself and one's own desires, intentions, etc.

> "There is no point in asking him to explain. I doubt that he knows his mind."

make up one's mind. To decide what one wants to do; to formulate an opinion.

> "He can't make up his mind whether to go or stay."

meeting of minds. An understanding between two or more persons with regard to some plan or action; a complete agreement.

> "A meeting of minds was not reached during the first session, but another session is scheduled for tomorrow."

never mind. Don't do anything; just forget it; it doesn't matter.

> "He doesn't seem to want to do it." "Well, never mind, I'll take care of it myself."

on one's mind. In one's thoughts; causing one to be worried or anxious.

> "There is something on your mind. I can tell."

set one's mind on. To decide to achieve or do something; to focus one's attention on.

> "He set his mind on becoming a candidate for the office."

speak one's mind. To be frank in saying what one thinks, or in expressing one's feelings.

> "It is not always advantageous to speak one's mind."

take one's mind off. To divert one's thoughts from something.

> "Pleasant company does help take one's mind off a worrisome subject."

Minute

the minute that. As soon as; without delay.

> "The minute that we hear from him we will call you."

up to the minute. Up-to-date; conforming to the latest methods, style, etc.

> "The plant is up to the minute with regard to the equipment used."

Missouri

be from Missouri. To be a type of person who is not easily convinced; to be inclined to require proof.

> "Well, I am from Missouri, and I don't believe it. You'll have to prove it to me."

Mitten

give *or* get the mitten. To jilt or to be jilted; to reject or be rejected as a suitor.

"Watch out, boy, you'll get the mitten from this girl."

Mix

mix up. 1. To confuse. 2. To mistake one for another. 3. To involve.

1. "Stop this chatter, you are only mixing me up!"

2. "I am often mixed up with my cousin, who really doesn't look like me."

3. "How in the world did he ever get mixed up in this scandalous affair?"

Money

for one's money. If one had to buy, it would be his choice; in one's opinion.

"For my money, this apartment house is the better investment."

in the money. 1. Earning much money; rich. 2. In a contest, especially a horse or dog race, in the first, second, or third place, i.e. among the winners.

1. "He made several good deals and he is in the money now."

2. "You are out. You aren't even in the money."

make money. To derive a good profit; to have a good income; to get rich.

"It may not be the most elegant job, but you'll make money at it."

Month

month after month. Continually; without cessation; every month.

"It wasn't something that he did for just a while. He continued with it month after month."

month in, month out. Occurring or repeated every month.

"Month in, month out he used to give me an excuse for not paying the rent."

Mop

mop the floor with. To defeat thoroughly; to overwhelm; to subjugate completely.

"There is no question about it, our man can mop the floor with him."

mop up. 1. To complete an undertaking, endeavor, etc. 2. In warfare, to clear territory of scattered pockets of resistance.

1. "He decided to remain on the West Coast for another week to mop up some unfinished business."

2. "The government troops are still mopping up, but aside from that the fighting is over."

More

more and more. To an increasing extent; an increasing amount or number.

"The public is becoming more and more conscious of the dangers of pollution."

"More and more people reject cigaret smoking."

more or less. 1. Perhaps more, perhaps less, but certainly to some extent. 2. About; approximately.

1. "This is more or less what I had in mind."

"The description is more or less accurate."

2. "Both analyses gave more or less the same results."

Most

at the most. At the highest degree, point, etc.; at the highest limit.

"This would not cost more than a dollar or two, at
the most."

for the most part. Mostly or mainly; in the majority of cases.

"There are some rough spots, but for the most part
the surface is smooth."

make the most of. To utilize to the best advantage; to accept
what one has, get the most out of it, and be contented.

"Try to make the most of this opportunity, as you
will not have a better one."

"Now, someone else, with less adaptability, might
have been crushed. But he accepted the situation,
made the most of it, and is getting along."

Mouth

down at the mouth. Without spirit; discouraged; blue.

"He has been down at the mouth, but he wouldn't
tell me what the trouble is."

down in the mouth. Same as *down at the mouth,* which see.

give mouth to. To express a thought in spoken words; to utter
or say.

"He didn't give mouth to his anger, but I know that
he was tempted to do so."

have a big mouth. To be in the habit of expressing one's feelings
rudely and freely; to talk excessively and brazenly.

"He has a big mouth, but he means well. Just don't
pay any attention."

Move

get a move on. 1. To start going some place; to start doing. 2. To expedite; to hurry; to increase the pace.

> 1. "If you want to get there before he leaves, you'd better get a move on."

> 2. "Get a move on! You are already two hours behind schedule."

on the move. 1. Constantly moving from one place to another. 2. Making progress; moving on. 3. Actively engaged in something.

> 1. "He isn't happy unless he is on the move."

> 2. "Those were the years when the space industry was on the move."

> 3. "He is always doing something, always on the move. Otherwise, he feels he is wasting time."

Much

make much of. 1. To speak about or treat as of great importance. 2. To treat with tenderness, fondness, etc., especially to excess.

> 1. "They made much of the fact that some terms of the agreement were violated."

> 2. "The child was spoiled by his grandmother and so was used to being made much of."

Muddle

muddle through. To manage to finish or accomplish something but with some difficulty and without marked success; to get through somehow, without a purposeful effort or much interest.

> "Somehow he muddled through the first year in office."

Mum

mum's the word. Nothing is to be said or divulged; say not a word!

"Remember our agreement. Mum's the word!"

Murder

get away with murder. To be able to do as one pleases, especially in a reprehensible way, without restraint, criticism, or punishment.

"The new teacher, being uncertain of himself, let the children get away with murder."

murder will out. Any secret or wrongdoing perpetrated in secret will eventually become known.

"Their secret engagement was finally revealed. I always say murder will out."

Music

face the music. To stand up and accept the consequences of one's action.

"Sooner or later he will have to face the music, that is, the consequences of his shiftless life."

N

Nail

hit the nail on the head. To say the right thing at the right time; to do something that satisfies the taste or fulfills a need perfectly.

> "Your response hit the nail on the head."

> "That dish of ice cream hit the nail on the head."

> "That shower last night hit the nail on the head. The plants were nearly parched."

on the nail. Immediately; at once; at the proper time or place.

> "He accepted the offer on the nail, without hesitation."

> "It was good luck that the officer was on the nail when it happened."

Name

by name. 1. Personally; well; familiarly. 2. Not in person, but as a name or through one's reputation.

> 1. "He knew every employee not only by sight but also by name."

> 2. "I didn't know the man personally, only by name. They told me about him."

call names. To address someone with derogatory or abusive names; to curse or swear at.

> "It is not polite to call someone names, but it does release tension."

in the name of. 1. For the sake of; in deference to. 2. As the agent of; by the order or authority of.

> 1. "In the name of God, have you no respect for decency!"
>
> 2. "The goods were confiscated in the name of the law."

to one's name. That one may call his own; in one's possession or ownership.

> "He has only debts and not a penny to his name."

Nature

by nature. By one's inherent characteristics, not by the influence of the environment.

> "She may act tough, because her job requires it, but by nature she is a kindly person."

in a state of nature. 1. Without clothes; nude. 2. Wild; untamed.

> 1. "The kids were still in a state of nature when the police arrived."
>
> 2. "In that part of the world, and nowhere else, these animals are still in a state of nature."

in the nature of. Having the significance of; bearing the message or intent of.

> "The perfunctory invitation was in the nature of a rebuff."

of the nature of. Same as *in the nature of,* which see.

Near

near at hand. 1. Not far away; nearby; in the vicinity. 2. Not far removed from the present; soon.

1. "They told us that there is a restaurant near at hand."

2. "The day when he will have to face the music is near at hand."

Necessity

of necessity. As a logical and unavoidable result; inevitably.

"Now that he is gone, our plans must of necessity be revised."

Neck

break one's neck. 1. To make an extreme effort to accomplish something. 2. To get hurt; to give a beating.

1. "He broke his neck to finish the work on time, and look at the thanks he gets."

2. "You'll break your neck one of these days standing on this rickety chair."

   "He is likely to break your neck if you say that again."

get it in the neck. 1. To sustain a loss. 2. To be chastised or severely reprimanded. 3. To be rebuffed or rejected.

1. "It is always the middle-income group that gets it in the neck."

   "The small businessman usually gets it in the neck. He is the one sure loser."

2. "You think this is something? Wait till he gets home. He'll really get it in the neck from his wife."

3. "Many an ambitious lover got it in the neck from that gal!"

   "He made a serious effort to present his plan to management, but he got it in the neck."

neck and neck. In a contest, of the contestants, to be close to each other with regard to winning; to be side by side.

"The two ran neck and neck until the very end."

stick one's neck out. To declare one's stand or opinion with regard to a controversial matter, with the realization that the consequences may be dire; to take a chance.

"If you are foolish enough to stick your neck out on this issue, you should see a psychiatrist."

win by a neck. To win over an opponent by a small margin; to gain a close victory.

"I am going to win this race, and I don't aim to win by a neck!"

Need

if need be. If the situation demands; if it becomes necessary.

"If need be, you can always get a loan from the local bank."

Negative

in the negative. Expressing a negative (i.e., opposite of affirmative) response; saying, in effect, no; denying; rebuffing.

"I can assure you, on the basis of what he told me privately, that his answer will be in the negative."

Neighborhood

in the neighborhood of. 1. In the vicinity of a particular place; near. 2. About; approximately.

1. "I think I saw him in the neighborhood of the shopping center."

2. "She said that the price would be somewhere in the neighborhood of fifty dollars."

Nerve

get on one's nerves. To cause someone to become irritable or jittery, as by some action, words, etc.

> "That guy gets on my nerves even if he doesn't open his mouth."

> "Your incessant jabbering gets on his nerves. Cut it out."

strain every nerve. To alert oneself to the utmost; to make the strongest effort.

> "He strained every nerve but he couldn't make out what the man was trying to say. It was so noisy."

> "She strained every nerve to keep up with him, but he was a little too fast for her."

Next

get next to. To become friendly with someone; to get into one's good graces; to become intimate with someone, often with ulterior motives.

> "He was rather aloof, and difficult to get next to."

next door to. Adjacent to a specified house or any similar structure; near to.

> "The place we are talking about is next door to the duplex home on Main Street."

> "Such an act is next door to insanity. It will never work."

Nick

in the nick of time. Not a moment too soon; at the very last moment to do good.

> "The police arrived in the nick of time to prevent a showdown between the two gangs."

Nip

nip and tuck. With reference to a contest, having one competitor or another gain temporary advantages; very close; neck and neck.

> "For the first half of the course it was nip and tuck, but after that the challenger pulled definitely ahead and was never threatened."

Nose

by a nose. Just barely; by a very small or narrow margin.

> "Somehow he managed to win, but only by a nose."

count noses. To count the number of persons present in a particular place.

> "They didn't exactly count noses, but the audience numbered at least five thousand."

cut off one's nose to spite one's face. To do something rash for the relief of anger, or in retaliation, that would in the end be to one's own disadvantage; to do something harmful to oneself in the long run in order to retaliate and have a momentary feeling of triumph.

> "As much as I would have liked to dismiss the impudent repairman, I had to let him proceed with the work, for to do otherwise would have meant to be without water for days. I wasn't about to cut off my nose to spite my face."

follow one's nose. 1. To move straight forward. 2. To act in accordance with one's intuition; to abide by one's instinct rather than reasoning or logic.

> 1. "Just follow your nose; you can't miss it."

> 2. "I don't know how we came through it all. We had so little to go by. We just followed our noses."

lead by the nose. To exercise complete control over; to dominate.

> "What a shame! I never thought anyone could lead him by the nose. But apparently his wife can."

look down one's nose at. To regard something with disapproval or disdain.

> "He looks down his nose at people who have no formal education."

on the nose. Exactly; accurately; precisely on time.

> "He got it on the nose. It does weigh sixty-five pounds!"

> "We got there almost on the nose, about five minutes late."

pay through the nose. To pay a high price; to pay unwillingly; to pay incessantly.

> "They didn't stock up when the price of the merchandise was reasonable; now they are paying through the nose."

> "They are paying through the nose to keep that old truck running."

put one's nose into. To meddle; to interfere with the activities of another.

> "I don't like him to put his nose into my affairs."

poke one's nose into. Same as *put one's nose into*, which see.

put one's nose out of joint. 1. To replace a favored person by assuming his role; to become the favorite of someone by displacing an existing favorite. 2. To frustrate the hopes or plans of another.

> 1. "He is crazy about the girl and no one is going to put her nose out of joint."

> 2. "Whether he meant it or not, he surely put John's nose out of joint with that remark."

turn up one's nose at. To look upon with contempt; to regard as unworthy.

> "She turned up her nose at him because he didn't have an elegant car."

under one's very nose. So close to one as to be plainly visible.

> "Why, they snitched it from under his very nose, but he didn't see or hear a thing."

Note

compare notes. To exchange and compare views, impressions, opinions, etc.

> "After the opening show, we usually have a little celebration during which we also compare notes."

strike the right note. To set the right mood or background; to say or do the thing that is right for the occasion.

> "His short speech somehow struck the right note; everybody seemed to relax."

take notes. To make a written record of what is being said or done; to write down impressions.

> "He spoke so rapidly that it was difficult to take notes without missing something or other of what he said."

Nothing

for nothing. 1. Free of any charge. 2. Without a satisfactory result; fruitlessly; to no avail. 3. For no reason; without an apparent cause.

> 1. "Do you mean to say that they gave you this book for nothing?"

> 2. "We tried our best to keep the business running, pouring good money after bad, but it was all for nothing."

3. "The police were unable to discover any motive
for the assault. They decided it was for nothing."

make nothing of. 1. To treat or regard something as if it were
of little importance. 2. To be unable to understand or comprehend.

1. "In spite of our apprehension, the doctor made
nothing of the symptoms."

2. "We made nothing of all the shouting and ges-
ticulations."

nothing but. Only the following and nothing else; only this and
none other.

"He gave us plenty of trouble, and nothing but
trouble."

nothing doing. 1. Definitely no; you are not changing my mind!
2. No response; no success; no action or activity.

1. "If I told you once I told you a dozen times, I am
not going. Nothing doing!"

2. "We tried that other number too, but nothing
doing."

"It's slow everywhere. There is nothing doing in
this town either."

nothing less than. 1. Nothing inferior to; no fewer than. 2. The
same as.

1. "Our cat will eat nothing less than the highest
quality wieners."

2. "Their answer is nothing less than a rejection."

nothing short of. Same as *nothing less than,* which see.

think nothing of. To consider unimportant; to be inclined to overlook.

"He thinks nothing of driving twenty or more miles
just to see a movie that he read about."

"He thought nothing of that remark, I am sure."

Notice

serve notice. To make a declaration of one's intentions; to notify; to warn.

> "The company served notice that such practices will no longer be tolerated."

take notice. To become aware of; to pay attention to; to heed.

> "He ignored the first incident, but he began to take notice when it was repeated."

Now

now and then. Occasionally; from time to time; sporadically.

> "He doesn't write often, but we do hear from him now and then."

Nth

to the nth degree. To the utmost; to the highest degree or extent.

> "He is a perfectionist to the nth degree."

Number

a number of. Some, several, or many; an unspecified quantity or amount.

> "When the announcement was made about the new school, a number of residents banded together to protest."

beyond number. So many as to defy an attempt at counting; too numerous to be reckoned.

> "The advantages of being located here are beyond number."

get one's number. To come to recognize a person's motives, usually ulterior.

"He had me fooled for a while, but I finally got his number. He wants me to recommend him for promotion."

have one's number on it. Of a lethal instrument (as believed by some), to have the name of a victim impressed upon it by fate so that the intended victim must sooner or later perish by it.

"This soldier was killed in a most unusual way. The bullet surely had his number on it."

one's number is up. One's time of death has arrived; one's time of good fortune or luck is ended.

"His doctor's optimism didn't fool him a bit. He knew that his number was up."

"You got away with this long enough, fellow, but now your number is up. You'll have to face the consequences."

the numbers. A kind of illegal lottery in which money is wagered on the appearance of certain numbers in a certain way in daily newspaper reports and tabulations.

"The authorities are aware of the flourishing activities in the numbers, but they do nothing about it."

without number. Same as *beyond number,* which see.

"Men without number have tried to find a medicine that would make hair grow on bald heads."

Nut

hard nut to crack. 1. A problem that is not easy to solve; a job difficult to accomplish. 2. A person difficult to convince; a person difficult to understand or fathom.

1. "Reconciling these two men will be a hard nut to crack."

2. "I don't quite understand him. He is a hard nut to crack."

tough nut to crack. Same as *hard nut to crack,* which see.

off one's nut. Mentally deranged; crazy; wrong; unreasonable.

> "He must have been off his nut to let such an opportunity slip by."

> "I am not off my nut; I can see what's going on!"

Nuts

be nuts about. To be preoccupied with; to be very fond of; to be passionately in love with.

> "He is nuts about electronics and electrical circuitry."

> "He is nuts about chess; he'd rather play than eat."

> "He is nuts about his new girl, the redhead."

nuts! Same as *nuts to,* which see.

> "To the German commander's demand that his company surrender, his answer was a crisp 'Nuts!'."

nuts to! An exclamation or response indicating rejection, disapproval, or anger.

> "Nuts to you, my friend! I am not falling for that bit."

> "Nuts to that! We tried it before, but it never worked."

O

Oak

sport one's oak. In student circles, to close the door of one's room or apartment in order to indicate that visitors are not welcome.

> "Hey, fellow, you have been sporting your oak rather frequently of late. You haven't got a girl in your room, have you?"

Oar

put in one's oar. To offer gratuitous advice; to meddle; to stick one's nose in the affairs of another.

> "Watch out for that guy. He is likely to put in his oar while you are discussing this matter. Just tell him to shut up."

rest on one's oars. 1. To stop working in order to rest or relax. 2. To remain idle while enjoying the fruits of one's past efforts.

> 1. "He is not working just now. You might say that he is resting on his oars."

> 2. "He is taking it easy and having a good time. The income from his earlier works is more than sufficient. And he really enjoys resting on his oars."

Oats

feel one's oats. 1. To be gay; to act in a lively manner. 2. To be aware of one's importance and to act accordingly.

> 1. "After a couple of drinks, he was feeling his oats."

> 2. "Having been promoted, he is now feeling his oats. He won't even talk to you!"

sow one's wild oats. Of a young man, to be promiscuous (before marriage); to philander or be dissolute in one's youth, especially with the realization that marriage will soon check such activities.

> "Well, he is overdoing it a little, but then every young man likes to sow his wild oats. Let's be tolerant."

Occasion

on occasion. At certain times; occasionally; now and then.

> "We usually eat at home, but on occasion we do eat out."

rise to the occasion. To do or perform better than one usually does, because of the demand of the situation; to meet an emergency successfully.

> "You can depend on him to rise to the occasion, if need be."

take occasion. To utilize a suitable opportunity for a particular act, statement, etc.

> "When he comes here next, I'll take the occasion to acquaint him with the problem we are facing."

Odds

at odds. In a state of disagreement; in a quarreling condition; at variance.

> "On this matter he is at odds with his own family."

> "The present translation is at odds with the first."

by all odds. In any way you consider it; by far; on all counts.

> "This is by all odds the best of his recent novels."

the odds are. It is most likely; the chances are.

> "The odds are that we will not get the contract, but let's bid anyway."

odds and ends. Things left over; various unrelated things; odd objects or pieces.

> "He constructed this cart from odds and ends he got at the junkyard."

Odor

be in bad odor. To have a bad reputation; to be lacking in esteem.

> "He is in bad odor with the community, and being seen with him will not help your career."

Off

be off. To leave; go; depart; to be absent; to be away on some enterprise.

> "It's time to be off, but we will see you soon."

> "He is off today because of illness in the family."

Offense

give offense. To create displeasure, resentment, or anger; to insult.

> "Such a mild statement could give offense to no one."

take offense. To feel displeasure, resentment, or anger because of something that is said or done; to have one's feelings hurt.

> "If you asked him the right way, I am sure he didn't take offense."

Oil

pour oil on troubled waters. To do something soothing in order to allay anger, mitigate resentment, or settle disputes.

> "Her charming presence seemed to pour oil on troubled waters. The tenseness definitely disappeared."

strike oil. To discover underground oil while drilling for it; to discover anything worthwhile; to do well financially; to get rich quickly.

> "After many years of frustration, he struck oil by discovering the new strain of virus."

> "Once in a while an amateur inventor strikes oil with a simple gadget, but this is the exception rather than the rule."

On

and so on. And continued in the manner of the preceding; and more like that mentioned.

> "They spent their time visiting friends, reading, watching television, and so on."

have something on someone. To know something about another person that, if revealed, would embarrass him or cause him harm.

> "She must have something on him, or he wouldn't obey her as he does."

on and off. Now and then; at times; intermittently.

> "He works on and off doing odd jobs. He has no steady work."

on and on. Without a stop; at length; of such duration as to become boring.

> "This is nothing new. The harassment went on and on for months."

> "Don't get her started on that subject! She will go on and on for hours."

on to. Aware of the real situation; finally cognizant of what goes on or of the ulterior motives of another.

> "I happen to know that she is on to your little tricks. She is not taking you seriously."

Once

all at once. 1. Suddenly; without notice or warning. 2. All at one time; simultaneously.

> 1. "All at once she decided she wasn't going. She didn't explain why."

> 2. "We do want them to come and visit with us, but not all at once."

at once. 1. Immediately; without delay. 2. Simultaneously; at one time.

> 1. "We don't mean that you must do this at once."

> 2. "It is impossible to solve all these problems at once. We will take one at a time."

for once. At least once; this or that one time at least.

> "I don't believe it! For once you are on time!"

once and again. Over and over; repeatedly; at one time and another.

> "I told him once and again to be sure to put out the lights before leaving."

once and for all. This or that time and for the last time; finally. finally.

> "This matter has to be decided once and for all."

> "Once and for all he spoke up to voice his opposition."

once in a while. Occasionally; not often; from time to time.

> "No, we don't see each other very often. He drops in once in a while when he is in the neighborhood, but that isn't very often."

once upon a time. Many years ago; at some time in the far past.

> "Once upon a time it was indeed an influential country, but not at present."

One

at one. 1. In a state of accord or agreement. 2. Joined together in feeling or spirit.

> 1. "They disagree on many issues, but on this matter they are at one."
>
> 2. "In the serenity of the chapel, he felt at one with his departed wife."

one and all. Every person present or listening; everybody.

> "One and all, from the cities and from the villages, came to see him off."

one another. With reference to a relation or function involving three or more persons, one person relating or doing something to another.

> "The members of the group were expected to help one another."

one by one. One person at a time; not all at once; one person following the other; one after the other.

> "One by one the residents of the neighborhood moved to the suburbs."

Oneself

be oneself. 1. To be in one's usual or normal condition physically and mentally. 2. To act the way one feels, without affectation.

> 1. "He wasn't himself when he made that statement. You know that."

> 2. "The best advice I can give you is to be yourself.
> I think you'll make out better this way."

by oneself. 1. Alone; without the company of other people. 2. Without the aid of others; by one's own efforts.

> 1. "She lives in that house by herself, and she likes it that way."
>
> 2. "It took him almost two years, but he built this house by himself."

come to oneself. 1. To regain one's senses, as after a fainting spell. 2. To regain one's self-control, as after an embarrassment.

> 1. "When he came to himself, he realized that he had been robbed."
>
> 2. "For a moment she was nonplused and didn't know what to say, but she soon came to herself."

Open

open to. 1. Vulnerable to; subject to. 2. Willing to accept or receive. 3. Suitable for; available to.

> 1. "Were he to do this, he would be open to criticism."
>
> 2. "Before he makes his decision, he is open to suggestions."
>
> 3. "This gadget is open to utilization in various ways."

open up. 1. To start; to begin doing something. 2. To become friendly and intimate in discussion; to reveal confidential information.

> 1. "As soon as we came in, she opened up with a torrent of questions and criticism."
>
> 2. "It took me a while to win her confidence, but then she opened up and told me the whole story."

Operation

in operation. 1. Functioning; working; in the act of doing. 2. In effect; exerting a force.

> 1. "The construction is finished, but the mill is not yet in operation."

> 2. "The new procedure will be in operation by the first of the month."

Order

a tall order. A task or demand difficult to fulfill; a formidable assignment.

> "Repairing this car in three hours is a tall order, but we can try."

a large order. Same as *a tall order*, which see.

by order of. By the authority of; in accordance with an order from.

> "This leaflet was distributed by order of the police commissioner."

call to order. 1. With reference to a meeting, to begin the activities. 2. To request the cessation of disorderly conduct or shouting and the resumption of normal activities.

> 1. "The meeting was called to order an hour late."

> 2. "Kids, the librarian is calling to order. Quiet down!"

in order. 1. As it should be; properly arranged; in a working condition. 2. Appropriate; right for the occasion; suitable. 3. According to the rules of procedure.

> 1. "Everything was checked and found in order for the extended trip."

> 2. "A coffee break would seem in order right now. We worked all night without a stop, you know."

> 3. "A discussion of the proposal would seem to be in order."

in order that. For the purpose or reason (specified); so that.

> "We are calling you now in order that you may be ready by the time we arrive."

in order to. For the purpose or reason (specified); for the accomplishment of goal (mentioned).

> "Let's walk faster in order to keep warm. I'm cold."

in short order. Before too long; right away; quickly.

> "He'll be here in short order. Watch my word."

on the order of. Similar to, or like, something specified.

> "The report is not complete by any means. It is on the order of a resume."

out of order. 1. Not in a condition to operate or function; broken down. 2. Not suitable for the occasion; not appropriate. 3. Not in accordance with the rules of procedure.

> 1. "There is only one telephone in this motel, and even that is out of order."
>
> 2. "Such attire is out of order for an occasion like this."
>
> 3. "The speaker was told emphatically that he was out of order."

to order. Following specifications made by a customer or buyer.

> "This suit was made to order, but it fits no better than the ready-made clothes I buy in the local stores."

Other

every other. Every first, third, fifth, etc., or every second, fourth, sixth, etc.; every alternate.

"We don't have the time to interview them all, so
let's see every other applicant."

"We go to Europe practically every other year."

of all others. With regard to, or in comparison with, all other
persons, things, or conditions.

"I chose him, of all others, because of his background."

the other day, evening, night, week, *etc.* A couple of days, eve-
nings, etc., ago; recently.

"Just the other day I happened to think of your
nephew. Have you heard from him lately?"

Out

all out. Applying the utmost effort; with all of one's energy or
will.

"There are no halfway measures for him. When he
wants something, he goes all out to get it."

on the outs. Having unfriendly relations; not on speaking terms
with; no longer in communication with.

"No, they no longer date. In fact, he has been on
the outs with her for nearly a year."

out and away. To an exceeding degree; by a wide margin; by
far.

"He is out and away the most popular candidate."

out and out. All the way through; no matter how you consider
it; completely.

"He is an out and out scoundrel, and you should
have nothing to do with him."

"That is an out and out lie, and you know it!"

out for. Aiming to get or accomplish; intending to do (something specified).

> "There can be only one explanation. He is out for revenge."

out from under. Free from a difficult situation; relieved of a burden.

> "Yes, he didn't do too well during the first couple of years, but he is out from under now."

out of. 1. From (a specified material). 2. Motivated by; because of. 3. Not available; not contained in stock; not in possession of. 4. From a specified quantity or number.

> 1. "No, it does look like plastic, but it is made out of paper."
>
> 2. "He had no reason. He did it out of sheer perversity."
>
> 3. "Are you out of this item, or don't you carry it at all?"
>
> 4. "Well, you might be able to use one out of three or four, but no more."

out to. Intent or determined to accomplish (something specified).

> "It is clear that he is out to embarrass his opponent."

Outside

at the outside. At the highest point or level; as a maximum; certainly no more.

> "It might cost ten dollars, or fifteen dollars at the outside."

outside of. Not counting; excepting; other than.

> "I saw no one outside of the three or four salespeople."

Over

all over. 1. Covering all of something; everywhere. 2. Completed; finished.

> 1. "The graffiti were all over the walls and even the ceiling."

> 2. "The fight was all over by the time the police arrived."

over again. One more time; once again.

> "I didn't quite get it. Would you please read it over again?"

over and above. In addition to something (specified); on the top of.

> "This amount is over and above his regular salary."

over and over again. Many or several times; repeatedly.

> "They talked about the same subject over and over again."

over there. 1. In that place. 2. In Europe, especially during World War I.

> 1. "He is standing over there. See?"

> 2. "He enlisted late in the war and was never sent over there."

Overreach

overreach oneself. To attempt to do something which is beyond one's capabilities or talents and, therefore, to fail.

> "He overreached himself when he accepted this project. He should have never undertaken it."

Own

come into one's own. To receive the recognition that one deserves; to begin to perform at one's best.

"He wrote successful novels before, but he really came into his own with the latest one. The critics unanimously acclaimed it."

of one's own. Actually belonging to oneself; that one may call his own.

"This is the first time that he has had a car of his own."

on one's own. Relying on one's own effort, ability, etc.; by one's own resources.

"I don't think he would have ever made it on his own. But he proved to be a useful member of the family business."

P

Pace

put one through one's paces. To make one demonstrate his best performance; to test one's talents or abilities.

> "Here is one chess player who will put our friend through his paces."

> "This golf course will put one through his paces."

set the pace. 1. To act in such a way as to be a good example for others. 2. In a race, to move at a speed that others accept as a guideline.

> 1. "This particular network sets the pace for the entire broadcasting industry."

> 2. "One of the older runners set the pace for most of the course in this year's marathon."

Packing

send packing. To send away or dismiss a person unceremoniously; to order out of one's way.

> "They wasted no time on this fellow. They sent him packing the day he came."

Paddle

paddle one's own canoe. To do one's own work; not to depend on another.

> "When his father died, he knew that he would have to paddle his own canoe."

Pain

on pain of. Subject to the penalty of; under the penalty of if a specified requirement is not fulfilled.

> "They are required to report escaped prisoners on pain of death."

under pain of. Same as *on pain of*, which see.

upon pain of. Same as *on pain of*, which see.

Paint

paint out. To hide or obliterate a symbol, sign, or painting by covering it with fresh paint.

> "One of the bilingual street signs was not painted out by mistake."

Pair

pair off. To cause people or things to be arranged in couples or pairs.

> "For the walk through the park, the guide paired off the boys and girls."

Palm

carry off the palm. To win a prize; to be the winner, as of a contest.

> "In tennis, the Australians invariably carry off the palm."

cross someone's palm. To pay someone, especially in advance; to bribe.

> "The gypsy asked her clients to cross her palm with silver."

grease someone's palm. To bribe; to pay someone, especially clandestinely.

> "You can hardly do anything in this town without greasing the mayor's palm."

have an itchy palm. To be excessively desirous of making money or of being paid for every minor service or favor; to want bribes.

> "The help in this motel have itchy palms."

> "I hate to have a waiter with an itchy palm."

have an itching palm. Same as *have an itchy palm,* which see.

palm off. To pass on, give, or sell something with intent to deceive, by misrepresenting it.

> "They palmed off the piece of junk as a genuine antique."

Pan

pan out. To yield a particular result; to turn out in one way or another; to succeed.

> "We had every reason to believe that the deal would go through without a hitch, but somehow it didn't pan out."

Paper

on paper. 1. By mere calculation and without actually doing or converting. 2. Existing only in the form of a design; not existing in reality.

> 1. "On paper, the stock certificates are worth about fifty thousand, but if you sell them and pay the tax, you will have much less."

2. "The shopping center exists only on paper at this time."

Part

for one's part. As far as one, or a particular person, is concerned; if one's opinion were to be taken.

"I can see his interest in the matter, but for my part, I would rather not participate."

for the most part. As far as the greatest part of something is concerned; on the whole; mostly.

"It has its flaws, but for the most part it is a smooth composition."

in good part. 1. In good humor; without resentment. 2. To a considerable extent; to some extent.

1. "Most people call him 'Shorty,' but being the nice guy he is, he takes it in good part."

2. "Success in show business depends in good part on luck, on being in the right place at the right time."

in part. To a certain, relatively small, extent; partly; in some degree.

"The unemployment is due in part to cutbacks in defense spending and the resulting massive layoffs."

on the part of. 1. So far as one, or a particular person, is concerned or involved. 2. As expressed or performed by.

1. "There was no open objection on the part of the neighbors, but the proposal may run into difficulties with the zoning board."

2. "Cooperation on the part of our allies could be reasonably expected."

part and parcel. An essential component of something; an inseparable part.

"Being available when someone needs you is part
and parcel of this profession."

play a part. To contribute to the performance or accomplishment of something.

"His ability to get along with people plays a part in
his successful career."

take someone's part. To support the cause of a particular individual; to lend moral or material support to one side in a dispute.

"Although I cannot fully agree with either him or
her, I would be inclined to take his part."

take part. To participate in some action or movement.

"Many people who are in favor of the movement do
not take part in the demonstrations for personal reasons."

Pass

bring to pass. To cause to occur or happen; make something take place.

"His marriage to this wonderful girl brought a remarkable change to pass in his attitude toward practically everything."

come to pass. To take place; occur; happen.

"It is a great pleasure to see him graduate. I never
thought it would come to pass."

make a pass. 1. To make an attempt, under the circumstances improper, to touch, hug, kiss, etc., a girl or woman; to indicate a desire for improper physical intimacy with a female. 2. To make a motion as if to strike someone; to hit someone, as with the fist.

1. "His practice of making passes at waitresses will
surely get him into trouble."

> 2. "The policeman hit the arrested man because he
>   thought the man was making a pass at him."

pass away. 1. To vanish; to disappear with time; to end. 2. To spend, as leisure time. 3. To die.

> 1. "These pains usually pass away in a few weeks."
>
> 2. "How do you pass away your time while you
>   have this cast on your leg?"
>
> 3. "The expression 'pass away' is a euphemism for
>   'die'."

pass current. To pass from mouth to mouth, as a rumor; to circulate or make the rounds.

> "There is always a rumor passing current in this
> town that the plant, on which its economy depends,
> is about to shut down."

pass for. Capable of being accepted as something else; be regarded as.

> "She is well preserved and can easily pass for a person much younger than she really is."

pass off. 1. To cause a person to be regarded or accepted as someone he is not. 2. To cause something to be regarded or accepted as what it is not. 3. To diminish and finally cease. 4. To take place; to go through from beginning to end.

> 1. "His was one of the classical cases of a layman
>   passing himself off as a physician."
>
> 2. "She tried to pass it off as a three-bedroom house,
>   but it was really a small duplex."
>
> 3. "The gusty winds finally passed off but not before
>   blowing down a few barns."
>
> 4. "We had our misgivings, but the festival passed
>   off without serious incidents."

pass on. 1. To transmit, as from one person to another; to give by inheritance. 2. To die.

> 1. "The patriarch of the family passed on to his children a deep-rooted esteem for linguistics."

> 2. "People who are squeamish about the word 'die' often substitute the term 'pass on'."

pass one's lips. 1. To be taken by mouth, as certain food or drink. 2. To be uttered; to be articulated or spoken.

> 1. "No alcoholic beverage ever passed his lips, or so he wants us to believe."

> 2. "He is a very delicate person, and I am sure that no four-letter words ever passed his lips."

pass out. 1. To faint; to lose consciousness. 2. To disappear; to go out of style or existence.

> 1. "She still passes out occasionally at the sight of blood."

> 2. "That style of dress passed out along with vaudeville."

pass over. To pay no attention to; to disregard; to skip in favor of another.

> "He passed over that part of the commentary without saying a word."

> "Most of the boys passed over the older sister in favor of Martha."

pass through. To live through; to go through; to experience.

> "He wasn't always affluent. Before he reached the top, he passed through several financial reversals."

pass up. To let go by without taking advantage, as an opportunity; to choose not to avail oneself of.

> "I think I'll pass up the offer to buy the securities and the rights this time."

Pat

have something pat. To know something very well; to have mastered thoroughly.

> "He has the whole manual pat, including the statistics."

stand pat. To retain an opinion, a plan, a course of action, etc., in spite of attempts by others to dissuade.

> "While some of his colleagues disagreed, he stood pat on his original diagnosis."

Patch

patch up. To bring a dispute or quarrel to a satisfactory conclusion; to correct; settle.

> "They patched up their tiff and they are together again."

Patient

patient of. 1. Tolerant of; capable of enduring or putting up with. 2. Subject to, as an interpretation; having the possibility of (as a meaning).

> 1. "He is particularly patient of the older people."

> 2. "Such a frank statement is patient of misunderstanding."

> "The opinion is patient of a dual interpretation."

Pave

pave the way to *or* for. Lead to; make the way to something more acceptable; prepare an approach to.

> "A phone call or a friendly letter may pave the way to a personal meeting later on."

Pay

in the pay of. On the payroll of; hired and paid by; a hired hand of.

> "He is obviously in the pay of the local gambling boss."

pay as you go. To pay expenses, a debt, etc., not in advance or in one lump sum but in installments or as the expenses arise; not on credit.

> "To buy this business you need only a small down payment. The rest you can pay as you go."

pay back. 1. To repay, as a debt. 2. To retaliate; to inflict a penalty for an injury.

> 1. "I am certain that he will pay back every cent he owes you."

> 2. "He is a kindly sort of fellow and will probably not try to pay back for the insult."

pay down. To pay a part of the total price of an article at the time of purchase, with the remaining part to be paid on the installment plan.

> "You pay down only ten dollars, and then you pay five dollars a month for eight months."

pay for. 1. To make a payment in money or its equivalent. 2. To suffer pain or anguish, as for some wrongdoing. 3. To make restitution; to atone for.

> 1. "You pay for it at the time you order it."

> 2. "I made a mistake and I am paying for it!"

> 3. "She knows she wasn't fair to him in the past, and now she is trying to pay for it with kindness."

pay off. 1. To pay someone all that is owed him; to repay a debt completely. 2. To redound in a favorable way; to result in a good yield. 3. To bribe. 4. To punish; to inflict vengeance.

1. "They fired him without notice, but they did pay him off."
2. "That small investment surely paid off better than anyone had expected."
3. "The inspector had to be paid off to let that go through!"
4. "He'll pay them off for their act! You'll see."

pay one's way. To pay one's own expenses, i.e. not to depend on someone else.

"He paid his way through college by working after hours."

pay its way. To yield enough profit to cover all expenses and return the investment.

"It may take some time, but this business will pay its way eventually, and then some!"

pay out. 1. To expend money by making payments. 2. To let out or supply rope (or similar line), especially from a coil.

1. "They pay out large sums of money, especially on Fridays."
2. "The rope should be kept taut by paying it out slowly."

pay up. To pay whatever is owed without delay and usually without quibbling.

"There is no reasoning with those people. You either pay up or else."

Peace

hold one's peace. Cease talking; be quiet; keep silent.

"I would appreciate it if you would hold your peace till it is your turn."

keep one's peace. Same as *hold one's peace*, which see.

keep the peace. To preserve a peaceful state of affairs; to prevent the creation of a disturbance; to maintain good order.

> "The belligerents agreed to keep the peace for the duration of the negotiations."

make one's peace with. 1. To accept something undesirable and cease objecting to it; to reconcile oneself to an unpleasant situation and make the best of it. 2. To bring about a reconciliation with.

> 1. "After opposing and fighting the construction project through the courts for several years, they finally decided to make their peace with it."
>
> 2. "Let's make our peace with the opposition and work together for the benefit of the community."

Pearl

cast pearls before swine. To offer something valuable or exquisite to those whose coarseness makes them incapable of appreciating it.

> "To present this architectural design to the city officials would be like casting pearls before swine."

Peck

peck at. 1. To eat only small portions of the food offered; to eat sparingly and without interest. 2. To attack someone with frequent criticisms on trivial grounds.

> 1. "No wonder he is losing weight. He hardly eats. He just pecks at the food."
>
> 2. "You had difficulty finding a secretary, and if you don't stop pecking at her she will surely quit."

Peel

keep one's eyes peeled. To look at or watch carefully; to be alert, as for a particular happening.

> "Keep your eyes peeled for the left side of the stage. That's where the action is."

peel off. To take off one's clothes; to undress; to do a strip tease.

"She peels off at stag parties, but that's as far as she goes."

Peer

peer of the realm. In Great Britain, any of a class of noblemen entitled to a seat in the House of Lords; a very important person.

"He may be an important person, but he is not exactly a peer of the realm."

Peg

round peg in a square hole. A person not suited for a particular task; a person out of his milieu; a person acting awkwardly in a given situation.

"He is certainly a man of diverse talents, but in this situation he proved to be a round peg in a square hole."

square peg in a round hole. Same as *round peg in a square hole*, which see.

take down a peg. To show someone that he is not so talented, intelligent, etc., as he thought he is; to reduce in self esteem; to humble.

"The loss of two matches in tennis took him down a peg."

"He didn't have a single winner that day, and that took him down a peg."

Penny

a bad penny. Something unpleasant or undesirable that keeps coming back to embarrass or discomfort.

"That kid seems to turn up like a bad penny at every game."

a pretty penny. A large amount of money; a considerable profit.

> "The redecorating job cost them a pretty penny."

> "They made a pretty penny from the sale of the old houses along the right of the way."

turn an honest penny. To make an honest living; to earn money in a fair and honest manner.

> "Maybe now that he is married he'll turn an honest penny. He never tried to before."

Perish

perish the thought. Let's not even regard this as a possibility; do not even think about it.

> "More rain after all we had? Perish the thought!"

Petard

hoist by *or* with one's own petard. Caught in one's own scheme; injured by one's own machination or device intended to harm another.

> "It was indeed a clever plan to entrap his opponent, but in the end he was hoist by his own petard."

Pick

pick and choose. To be fastidious in selecting what one wants; to choose with great care.

> "It takes her twice as long to shop for groceries as it does the average housewife because she likes to pick and choose."

pick apart. To examine with excessive thoroughness, especially in order to find faults.

> "He is always picking apart every girl he meets. Naturally, everyone has some faults."

pick at. 1. Same as *peck at*, which see. 2. To finger; touch; get a hold of.

> 2. "He has a habit of picking at his nose, especially when he is on edge."

pick off. 1. To remove, as small particles, with the fingers or a pointed instrument. 2. To hit with the bullet of a sharpshooter or sniper; to wound or kill by a selective shot.

> 1. "The insecticide might harm the flowers. Let's pick off the insects by hand."

> 2. "The sniper picked off several of our men before we finally got him."

pick on. 1. To criticize someone more frequently or more severely than the situation justifies; to harass without good reason; to annoy with puns or embarrassing remarks. 2. To select for a particular task or function.

> 1. "The kid has a persecution complex. He thinks everyone is picking on him."

> 2. "We usually pick on the bigger boys for guard duty."

pick one's way. To move along slowly, choosing each step with care; to proceed cautiously.

> "If you'll be careful, you can pick your way across the street without stepping into the slush."

> "It will obviously not be easy, but I believe we can pick our way through this Russian language text with the aid of a dictionary."

pick out. 1. To select or choose from a number of others that which one wants. 2. To recognize, as a hidden meaning. 3. To discern something or someone by distinguishing from the surroundings. 4. To pull out; extract.

> 1. "You may pick out any two books listed here."

> 2. "Can you pick out what he is driving at?"

3. "Because the hall is darkened, the performer on the stage is unable to pick out any celebrities that might be in the audience."

4. "For a while she attempted to pick out the offending gray hairs, but she gave it up."

pick over. To examine a number of items for the purpose of selecting the choicer ones, as at the counter of a store.

"By the time we get there, the merchandise will have been picked over. The store opens at eight, you know."

pick up. 1. To grasp and lift; to take a hold in the hand. 2. To obtain something by chance or an unexpected opportunity. 3. To regain, as a former status, good health, etc. 4. To stop for someone or something for the purpose of taking along, as in one's automobile. 5. To speed up; to proceed faster. 6. To receive, as by radio, television, or the ear. 7. To do better; to improve. 8. To arrest; apprehend. 9. To succeed in inviting someone, usually a girl, to be one's companion, especially for amorous purposes. 10. To assume the responsibility for payment.

1. "I picked it up three or four times, but it keeps on sliding off the table."

2. "He picked up several antique chairs on his last trip."

3. "He looked ill last time I saw him, but he picked up since then."

4. "She doesn't drive to work any more; one of the girls picks her up."

5. "Her typing is bound to pick up. She hasn't worked for more than a year."

6. "While turning the dial I picked up a European station."

7. "It's slow now, but business usually picks up during the winter months."

8. "The robber was picked up no more than two blocks from the bank he held up."

9. "I don't know where he picked her up, but she seems like a nice girl."

10. "Her father picked up the tab for this shindig."

Piece

a piece of one's mind. See under *give a person a piece of one's mind.*

go to pieces. To lose one's self-control; to become agitated and act irrationally.

> "He is a rather stable person, but this time he went to pieces."

speak one's piece. To express one's opinion with feeling or vehemence; to let loose with previously unexpressed thoughts.

> "She decided to speak her piece whatever the consequences might be."

Pig

pig in a poke. An obscure object; something not fully explained; a project or offer the details of which are not revealed.

> "While we are interested in this offer, we cannot buy a pig in a poke. We must have full details."

pig it. To rough it; to live in untidy surroundings; to live in a disorganized manner.

> "While his wife was away, he didn't do any housework. He just pigged it."

Pillar

from pillar to post. 1. From place to place, without a plan or purpose. 2. From one harassment or difficulty to another.

1. "Some people enjoy that kind of life, drifting from pillar to post."

2. "He would appreciate a quiet, peaceful life, as he had been knocked about from pillar to post."

Pin

on pins and needles. In a state of mind marked by restless anticipation; characterized by anxiety and suspense.

"Although he could have relieved her anxiety, he let her be on pins and needles for two days."

pin one down. To cause a person to reveal his opinion, stand on a particular matter, etc.; to cause a person to fulfill a promise, commitment, etc.

"We did try to pin him down on his plans for the swimming pool, but he remained evasive."

"If I can find the letter in which he promised to make a contribution, I'll pin him down to it."

pin something on one. To show or prove that the blame for a wrongful act belongs to a particular person.

"We know that he did it, but it would be difficult to pin it on him since there are no witnesses."

pin up. To attach something to a wall or any surface so that it may be easily observed.

"He liked to pin up the pictures of pretty girls that he clipped from various magazines."

Pipe

pipe down. To stop talking loudly; stop objecting; calm down; stop shouting.

"Will you fellows pipe down! I want to hear what he has to say."

pipe up. 1. To speak up loudly; to express one's opinion with determination; to shout so as to make oneself heard. 2. To accelerate; to increase in speed and force.

> 1. "If you want them to listen to you, you'll have to pipe up."

> 2. "By the time the game started the wind piped up to about thirty miles per hour."

Pitch

pitch in. 1. To join someone in his effort in order to help; to make a contribution. 2. To increase one's effort; to apply oneself more thoroughly.

> 1. "He wouldn't have finished the painting if his wife hadn't pitched in."

> "The neighbors pitched in and presented him with a nice homecoming gift."

> 2. "He was fooling around the first part of the day, but he pitched in later in the afternoon and got the work done."

pitch into. To assail someone physically or with words; to attack.

> "Some of the local citizens pitched into the visiting politician when he invited questions from the audience."

pitch on. To choose or select on the spur of the moment; to decide on haphazardly.

> "We can still change the date. We pitched on the tenth without a particular reason."

Pity

have pity on. To sympathize with; have compassion for; feel sorry for.

> "He said that he has no pity on people who do not try to help themselves."

take pity on. To develop a feeling of compassion for someone; to feel the beginnings of a sense of sorrow, as for the misfortune of another.

> "For a long time, he paid no attention to this poor soul. Then, suddenly, he noticed her and took pity on her. Since then he has helped her in many ways."

Place

give place to. 1. To give up a place or position, as for someone or something new. 2. To be ousted or replaced by.

> 1. "The old strictures against explicitness in sex are giving place to new interpretations."

> 2. "He has no intention to give place to the new-comer without a struggle."

go places. 1. To become successful financially or in any other way. 2. To visit various places of entertainment.

> 1. "Even when he was only a boy he gave the impression that he would go places some day."

> 2. "When he visits us, on his vacations, he doesn't want to stay home. He likes to go places."

in place. 1. In the proper position or location. 2. Appropriate, as for the time or place; fitting.

> 1. "One of the runners was not in place when the starter's gun went off."

> 2. "It was not in place to raise the issue at that time."

know one's place. To be aware of one's rank or social position, especially when inferior, and to act accordingly; to be modest.

> "Although she was accepted as one of the family, she knew her place."

out of place. 1. Not in the proper position or location. 2. Not appropriate, as for the time, place, or occasion; not fitting.

> 1. "One of the books in the case is still out of place."

> 2. "Brown shoes are definitely out of place for this occasion."

put someone in his place. To lower a person's self-esteem by proving him wrong or inferior in some way; to deflate an arrogant person.

> "I just had to win this game in order to put him in his place."

take place. To occur; to be performed or staged; to happen.

> "The contest takes place in this town every other year."

> "The ceremonies will take place on the fifth, as scheduled."

take the place of. To take over the position or role of someone; to act as a substitute or surrogate.

> "It will be difficult to find a political figure strong enough to take the place of the deceased."

Plank

plank down. 1. To lay something down with force, as an expression of resentment. 2. To make an immediate payment of money; to pay money in a demonstrative way.

> 1. "He planked down the book and walked out without saying a word."

> 2. "You can't buy this on installment. You'll have to plank down the whole amount when the set is delivered."

plunk down. Same as *plank down,* which see.

walk the plank. To be forced to do something to one's own detriment; to give up something under coercion.

> "The prisoner knew that it was extremely dangerous to climb the wall, but his buddies threatened him and made him walk the plank."

> "As soon as the new owner takes over this business, the manager will surely walk the plank."

> "Several of the bureau chiefs will walk the plank when the publication is absorbed by the parent company."

Play

bring into play. To introduce something that has some effect on a particular activity or process; to cause something to exert an influence; to take into consideration; set into motion.

> "The defense may be expected to bring into play the emotional factors of this spectacular case."

make a play for. 1. To make a concerted effort to attain or obtain something. 2. To attempt to become amorous with a person of the opposite sex; to try to become intimate with a girl.

> 1. "Everyone expected him to make a play for the chairmanship, but when the time came he showed no interest in it."

> 2. "He knows he is a handsome guy and he likes to make a play for every pretty girl in the office."

play at. 1. To give an impression of one's interest in something; to pretend having an interest. 2. To do something in a half-hearted manner.

> 1. "He played at stamp collecting to please his father who is a well-known philatelist."

> 2. "As I see it, he is merely playing at becoming his father's assistant. He is not interested in this kind of work."

play both ends against the middle. To manipulate opposing parties or factions against each other for one's own benefit.

> "Undoubtedly, some underdeveloped countries ma-neuver the two superpowers in a kind of selfish game which amounts to playing both ends against the middle."

play down. To regard or treat something as if it were of little importance; to minimize.

> "This time the President chose not to play down the danger of the military buildup."

played out. 1. Tired; exhausted. 2. No longer in use; out of style. 3. Used up; finished.

> 1. "You can't judge him by this performance, as he was played out when he started."
>
> 2. "Some fashions are quickly played out; others last for years."
>
> 3. "Our stock of canned goods was played out in a short time."

play fair. To act or behave in a just or honorable way.

> "He is a hard-nosed businessman, but you can be sure that he'll play fair with you."

play for time. To do what is necessary to delay something, as a decision; to extend or prolong an activity in order to gain more time for a particular purpose.

> "The delegate was instructed to play for time until the results of the test become available."

play into someone's hands. To do something, usually inadver-tently, that gives one's opponent an advantage or the upper hand.

> "By bringing up trivial objections which can be refuted, you are only playing into your opponent's hands."

play it by ear. To handle a situation without a predetermined plan, by improvisation; to meet and solve difficult problems as they come along and as the circumstances make advisable.

> "In dealing with that unpredictable man, you simply cannot follow a prearranged plan. You have to play it by ear."

play off. 1. In games, to break a tie by playing an additional or extra round. 2. To cause one person, group, or country to exert influence or power against another, for one's own advantage.

> 1. "The two teams will have to play off next Saturday."
>
> 2. "The practice of playing off one great power against another is not new."

play one off against another. Same as *play off,* definition 2.

play on *or* upon. To utilize the susceptibilities or weaknesses of another person for one's own advantage.

> "She knew how to get her way with him by playing on his sense of chivalry where women are concerned."

play one's cards right *or* well. To proceed wisely; to do the right thing; to utilize one's assets in the most advantageous way.

> "You have all the requirements for the position, and if you play your cards right I see no reason why you should not get the appointment."

play out. To become exhausted; to tire; to lose vigor or strength.

> "By the end of the week he was all played out."

play up. To give importance to; to cause to appear prominent; to publicize.

> "An attempt was made to play up the President's role in settling the crisis."

play up to. To try to please a person in order to gain his favor; to get into the good graces of someone by devious means, as by flattery.

> "His aunt paid no attention to him. She knew that he was playing up to her as his birthday was approaching."

Please

if you please. If you like to; if you will allow; if it is acceptable to you.

> "You can spend the night with us if you please."

> "We would rather settle this here and now, if you please."

Pledge

take the pledge. To promise solemnly not to drink alcoholic beverages.

> "Several of the fellows thought that by taking the pledge together they would provide a stronger commitment."

Plow

plow into. 1. To drive forcefully into something; ram into; barge into. 2. To intensify one's effort; to start an activity with great vigor.

> 1. "The car went out of control and plowed into the crowd."

> 2. "On his return to the office, he plowed into a backlog of orders and other work."

Plug

plug in. To make an electrical connection by inserting the prongs of a plug into the slots of a socket or other outlet.

"It is a good idea not to plug in too many appliances into a single electrical outlet."

Plumb

out of plumb. Not exactly perpendicular or vertical; not in agreement with a given standard; not according with.

"The new directive is out of plumb with the first one."

Plunge

take the plunge. To begin some enterprise after some hesitation; to decide to go ahead, especially with something involving some risk or uncertainty.

"After deliberating for nearly a month, we decided to take the plunge and buy the restaurant, although the price was rather high."

Pocket

in one's pocket. In one's control; under one's domination or influence; in one's actual possession.

"She is so pretty and clever that she has her boy-friends in her pocket."

"They haven't signed the contract yet, but he has the deal in his pocket."

line one's pockets. To make a great deal of money, especially in an unsavory manner, at the expense of others or during a time of public distress.

"During this war, as during any other war, some businessmen and profiteers were lining their pockets."

out of pocket. Poorer (by a specified amount of money); having lost (a certain amount of money).

> "On the hotel bills alone, he'll be a hundred dollars or so out of pocket."

> "He had to sell his securities during a bearish market which caused him to be about a thousand dollars out of pocket."

Point

at *or* on the point of. About to; near; on the verge of.

> "He was at the point of giving in when he remembered something his father had told him, and then he decided to fight it out."

beside the point. Not relevant to the matter at hand; unrelated to the subject; having no bearing on a particular issue.

> "What you say is undoubtedly true, but it is beside the point in this situation."

in point. Pertinent to the matter at hand; relevant; applicable; illustrative.

> "Talking about violence, the latest kidnaping is a case in point."

in point of. As far as something specified is concerned; with regard or reference to.

> "In point of the latest poll, I would be inclined to question the results."

make a point of. To regard as necessary or advisable; to set something up as an example to follow; to make it a rule.

> "We make it a point to stop by or call her at least once a week, to make sure she has everything she needs."

on the point of. See under *at the point of.*

point up. To emphasize; to give prominence, as by illustration, expansion, or repetition.

> "The frequency of mugging in the public parks points up the need for more guards and better lighting."

stretch a point. To make an exception by deviating from a rule or a standard procedure because of certain circumstances or because of favoritism.

> "Although the specifications called for a younger man, they hired him anyway, by stretching a point, because of his unusual qualifications."

strain a point. Same as *stretch a point,* which see.

to the point. Relating to an issue or subject; pertinent; apropos.

> "Your present discussion is more to the point."

> "His explanation was brief but to the point."

Poke

poke fun at. To ridicule; to direct humorous derision at; to mock.

> "The renowned comedian was fond of poking fun at politicians."

Pole

be poles apart. To have widely divergent views; to be in complete disagreement; to have opposite opinions, tendencies, etc.

> "They were in agreement on most world issues, but they were poles apart about the war."

Polish

polish off. 1. To consume speedily; to devour; to eat completely and quickly. 2. To dispose of; to beat easily; to overcome without much difficulty.

1. "He polished off a steak dinner and two pieces of cherry pie."

2. "My friend polished off the assailant with a left hook to the jaw."

polish up. To refine or improve; to make more acceptable or desirable by removing minor flaws.

"He has the speech written but he wants to polish it up a bit before he delivers it."

Pot

go to pot. To deteriorate; to fall into a state of ruin; to become dilapidated.

"After the old lady died, the stately mansion went to pot."

Pound

pound out. To play an instrument, especially the piano, with a heavy, unskilled hand; to type laboriously.

"The tired pianist pounded out the popular tune for the nth time."

"He pounded out the lengthy letter on an old typewriter, using two fingers."

Power

in power. In control; having authority; holding office.

"After thirty years, the general is still in power."

the powers that be. The persons who are in authority; the officials who are in control.

"The powers that be don't seem to think that the town needs a public library."

Praise

sing someone's praises. To praise someone frequently, enthusiastically, or publicly; praise highly.

"He is always singing the praises of someone. Now it's his son."

"As usual, he is singing his car's praises."

Premium

at a premium. 1. At an abnormally high price. 2. Scarce; hard to get; in demand.

1. "These prints are now sold at a premium because of the publicity received by the artist."

2. "In spite of all that has been written about the subject, nurses are still at a premium."

Present

by these presents. By means of these documents or this document.

"You shall know them by these presents."

for the present. As far as the present time is concerned; for a while at this time; for now.

"This apartment will have to do for the present, at least until we have the time to look for something better."

Press

go to press. Of a book, magazine, newspaper, etc., to go into the process of being printed.

"The last edition of this newspaper goes to press at six P.M."

Price

at any price. No matter how expensive; regardless of the cost; in spite of the sacrifice, effort, etc., required.

> "It isn't a question of cost. You can't get this kind of paper at any price."

> "He made up his mind to get to the top at any price."

beyond *or* without price. So valuable that it cannot be priced; of immense value.

> "These scrolls are undoubtedly beyond price."

Prick

prick up one's ears. To begin listening attentively; to become alert.

> "He was barely listening until the salary was mentioned. Then he pricked up his ears."

Pride

pride oneself on. To be delighted or very much satisfied about something; to feel pride because of.

> "He prides himself on being the only man in town to receive a personal letter from the President."

Principle

in principle. In essence, but not necessarily in every detail; on the basis of the principle involved.

> "The proposal seems to be acceptable in principle, but some of the provisions might have to be revised."

on principle. 1. In accordance with a plan or a customary procedure. 2. Following a moral standard; as a matter of principle.

> 1. "He takes a walk every night, when the weather permits, on principle."

> 2. "We cannot accept such an offer on principle, although we realize that it is financially sound."

Print

in print. Of a book, still available from the publisher; still being published.

> "Although the book was first published more than
> thirty years ago, it is still in print."

out of print. Of a book, no longer available from the publisher; no longer published.

> "The book you want is out of print, but you may get
> a copy from a dealer in used books."

Propriety

the proprieties. The accepted standards of proper behavior in polite society.

> "You'd better watch your step when the old lady is
> around. She is very strict about the proprieties."

Proud

do one proud. 1. To be the source or cause of pride to someone. 2. To do very well. 3. To receive or treat someone with kindness and generosity.

> 1. "His performance in this difficult situation did
>   him proud."
>
> 2. "In the final set he really did himself proud."
>
> 3. "We had a tough time getting there, but our host
>   did us proud when we arrived."

Pull

pull apart. To criticize, especially for the purpose of finding fault; to find fault with for the sake of discrediting.

> "The candidate did a good job of pulling apart his
> opponents' speech."

> "He seems to enjoy pulling apart everything we sug-
> gest."

pull down. 1. To destroy or demolish. 2. To lower, as in dignity; to humble. 3. To draw or receive as a salary.

> 1. "The old building will have to be pulled down to make room for the proposed parking lot."

> 2. "Such irresponsible behavior can only pull him down."

> 3. "He is pulling down about two hundred per week in this job alone."

pull for. To hope for the success of someone; to work or campaign in behalf of; to encourage.

> "We are obviously pulling for our local team."

pull in. 1. To come in; to arrive. 2. To take into custody; to arrest.

> 1. "The train pulled in two hours late."

> 2. "The police pulled in several suspects but had to let them go for lack of evidence."

pull off. To accomplish something requiring guile, daring, shrewdness, etc.

> "The spectacular holdup was pulled off by three masked men."

pull oneself together. To calm oneself; to regain one's composure; to recover command of one's emotions.

> "Now, pull yourself together and tell us what happened."

pull out. 1. To leave, as a train or ship. 2. To break an association with.

> 1. "The train pulled out to the cheers of the crowd."

> 2. "Two members of the group pulled out immediately, as soon as they heard of the incident."

pull over. To steer an automobile or other vehicle toward the curb.

> "When he heard the ambulance siren, he pulled over."

pull through. To come through successfully, as an illness, financial crisis, etc.

> "He was on the critical list for several days, but he pulled through."

> "The company is in financial difficulties but we expect it to pull through."

pull up. 1. To cause to come to a stop. 2. To pull out, especially with the roots. 3. To cause to move ahead for some distance.

> 1. "After such a long drive they were glad to pull up at the first restaurant they saw."

> 2. "We decided not to pull up the morning-glory plants this year."

> 3. "To get to the intersection, they had to pull up about fifty feet."

Punch

pull punches. 1. To diminish the force of one's punches or blows, as in order to spare one's opponent. 2. To restrain one's criticism; to weaken one's verbal attack deliberately.

> 1. "The champ was obviously pulling his punches to prolong the bout and give the customers a better show for their money."

> 2. "What a vitriolic denunciation! He surely didn't pull any punches."

Purple

born in *or* to the purple. Of noble, royal, or otherwise exalted birth; of high family origin.

"Those born to the purple are not necessarily heirs to a happy and prosperous life."

the purple. Royal, noble, or otherwise high rank.

"These are not the days of glory for members of the purple."

Purpose

of set purpose. Intentionally; with a purpose in mind; deliberately.

"The omission of his name from the list was not an oversight; it was of set purpose, to discredit him."

on purpose. With a definite intention; not by accident; deliberately.

"This might have happened accidentally, but I think it was done on purpose."

to good purpose. Usefully; with a desirable effect.

"This compost can be used to good purpose in your vegetable garden."

to little *or* no purpose. With little or no results; with little or no effect.

"We tried hot applications, as you suggested, to little purpose."

to the purpose. Relevant; applicable; suitable; pertinent.

"At least some of the objections are to the purpose."

Purse Strings

hold the purse strings. To be in control of the expenditure of money; to have the authority to determine when and how much money should be spent.

"Father likes to think that he holds the purse strings in this household."

loosen the purse strings. To allow more money to be spent; to become more lenient about spending money.

> "Now that he has gotten a raise, he may loosen the purse strings a little."

tighten the purse strings. To restrict expenditures; to become more concerned about spending money.

> "We'll make it all right. We will just have to tighten the purse strings for a while."

Push

push off. To make a start in a journey; to set out to go; to depart.

> "Just as we were getting ready to push off, we found out that the bridge was down."

> "Let's push off early so that we'll get there before nightfall."

push on. To continue, especially in face of obstacles or disappointments; to proceed in spite of difficulties.

> "We were discouraged by the difficulty of the terrain, but we pushed on anyway."

Put

put across. 1. To succeed in communicating; to make something understandable to someone. 2. To succeed in accomplishing; to cause to be successful. 3. To be successful in having a deceitful act accepted or a lie believed.

> 1. "He was able to put across his idea with the aid of diagrams and a crude model of the device."

> 2. "To put across your project, you will need a backer with a great deal of money."

> 3. "Only he with his glib tongue could put across such an obvious piece of chicanery."

put aside. 1. To save something for later use. 2. To put something out of one's way; of a task, or any work, to schedule for a later time.

> 1. "On your salary, you should be able to put aside at least twenty dollars a week."

> 2. "He was unwilling to put aside his present work in order to start on your job."

put away. 1. To eat a large amount of food; to consume voraciously. 2. To kill, especially in gangland style.

> 1. "He can put away more in one meal than you eat in two days."

> 2. "He was put away by the gang because they thought he was about to inform on them."

put down. 1. To suppress; to crush. 2. To record in writing; to write down. 3. To ascribe or attribute to. 4. To degrade or embarrass someone. 5. To land an airplane, helicopter, or other aircraft.

> 1. "The uprising was put down in a few days."

> 2. "Put this down in your notebook for future reference."

> 3. "He puts down his failure to the sudden change in weather."

> 4. "I don't mean to put him down, but he can do better than that."

> 5. "After circling the field for two hours, the plane finally put down without incident."

put forth. 1. To present or offer, as a proposal. 2. To sprout or grow, as leaves. 3. To make public; to publish. 4. To use; exert.

> 1. "Several proposals were put forth but none was practical."

> 2. "This year, our forsythia put forth its yellow flowers even earlier."

3. "The government is expected to put forth a clari-
fying statement."

4. "You may be sure that he will put forth his best
effort in your behalf.

put forward. To present or offer, as a proposal.

"No one put forward anything better than the plan
now under consideration."

put in. 1. To offer for consideration; to insert. 2. To devote time
in a specified way. 3. To make an application, as for a transfer.

1. "I am sure that he'll put in a few good words in
your behalf."

2. "He put in five years in that business, but he had
to give it up."

3. "She put in for a transfer to another office."

put it on. To make a show of something; to be pretentious; to
exaggerate in order to impress.

"He is a pretty good dancer, but he was putting it
on to impress his girl."

put it *or* something over on someone. To trick someone; to succeed in deceiving.

"I don't know exactly what it was, but he was trying
to put some kind of deal over on me."

put off. 1. To delay or postpone; to schedule for a later time. 2.
To turn away; to rebuff.

1. "Let's not put it off any longer than we have to."

2. "They put him off with some kind of silly explanation."

put on. 1. To pretend; to act in an ostentatious manner. 2. To
clothe oneself in a specified garment. 3. To kid; to tell little lies
or exaggerations.

1. "He is not that well-to-do. He likes to put on."

2. "Why not put on your sweater instead?"

3. "He was just putting him on about getting another job."

put oneself out. To make an effort; to go to some trouble or pains.

"He could help us if he would be willing to put himself out a little."

put out. 1. To extinguish or quench. 2. To disturb; confuse. 3. To inconvenience. 4. To issue or publish. 5. To make; produce; manufacture. 6. To expel. 7. Of a woman, to submit to coitus.

1. "We succeeded in putting out the fire ourselves."

2. "They were put out by the sudden turn of events."

3. "We would like you to do it for us if it won't put you out too much."

4. "In addition to the printing, they put out two weekly newspapers."

5. "This company puts out the best lawnmower we know."

6. "If you don't stop this noise, we will put you out."

7. "I am told this girl puts out, for a price."

put over. 1. To accomplish something against opposition or difficulty. 2. To schedule for a later time; to delay or postpone. 3. To trick or deceive.

1. "He is just the man to put over this difficult transaction."

2. "The weekly meeting was put over because of the bad weather."

3. "You'll have to get up early in the morning to put over this scheme on her."

put someone on. To deceive in a playful way by attempting to make someone believe that which is untrue.

> "I don't believe it. You must be putting me on."

put something over on. To take advantage of; to deceive; to succeed in making the victim of a dishonest act; to foist something upon.

> "You have to watch that guy, or he'll put something over on you before you know it."

put through. 1. To succeed in completing. 2. To cause to take place; to effect.

> 1. "There isn't enough time left for him to put through his plan."

> 2. "We have not had a chance so far to put through the required changes in the construction."

put to it. To place or be placed in a hazardous or difficult position; to be challenged by an unusual problem.

> "The mechanic was put to it to find a part for this very old car."

put up. 1. To provide, as money, material, etc. 2. To arrange, as the hair, in a particular style. 3. To preserve food in sealed cans or jars. 4. To erect or build; construct. 5. To provide lodging, especially on a temporary basis. 6. To wager or bet. 7. To name as a candidate. 8. To pack or place in a container. 9. To urge or incite to do something. 10. To raise or elevate.

> 1. "We still have to find an angel to put up the money for your play."

> 2. "I hate to see women put up their hair in curlers and go shopping."

> 3. "She puts up her own jams and jellies, much of it from berries grown in her own garden."

> 4. "The new library will be put up by a local contractor."

5. "I am sure my mother can put you up for at least a week."

6. "He is willing to put up money on the local team."

7. "Who will put up our candidate's name at the convention?"

8. "They usually put up six packs to a carton."

9. "I am sure it wasn't his idea. Somebody must have put him up to it."

10. "The holdup man instructed his victim to put up his hands."

put up with. To accept unwillingly; to endure; bear.

"If you want to live in the country, you will have to put up with certain inconveniences."

put upon. To take advantage of; to impose on.

"I would say that the boy has some justification for feeling put upon by you, because you frequently ask him to run errands for you on his time."

Puzzle

puzzle out. To figure out or solve by mental effort.

"I haven't yet puzzled out the meaning of the message."

puzzle over. To wonder about; to try to solve; to cogitate.

"He puzzled over it for weeks before he realized what it meant."

Q

Quarter

at close quarters. Near each other or one another; at close range.

"Most of the fighting took place at close quarters."

cry quarter. To beg to be spared; to cry for mercy.

"The stubborn enemy is not likely to cry quarter."

Queen

queen it. To behave in a haughty manner; to domineer.

"She won't be able to queen it with her new husband. He is not the uxorious type."

Question

beside the question. Outside the scope of what is being considered or discussed; not related to the issue at hand; irrelevant.

"What you say is true, but it is beside the question."

beyond question. So certain that there is no doubt whatever; that cannot be questioned.

"It is, beyond question, the best performance so far."

call in question. 1. To challenge, as the veracity of a statement. 2. To cast doubt or uncertainty upon.

> 1. "We do not mean to call his statement in question, but some proof would be in order."

> 2. "The latest report seems to call in question our previous conclusions."

in question. Being considered or debated; in dispute.

> "In question here is his alleged negligence, not his qualification."

out of question. So unlikely, so out of reach, etc., that it cannot even be considered; impossible.

> "Adding a new building at this time is out of question."

> "Paying that much for a used car is out of question."

> "This idea of yours is out of question. I won't discuss it any more."

R

Rack

on the rack. Subjected to pressure or strain; in a difficult situation; anxious.

> "In that type of job you are always on the rack."

> "We were on the rack for nearly two weeks, while waiting for their decision."

rack one's brains. To strain one's memory in trying to recall something; to try very hard to bring to memory.

> "Stop racking your brains about that phone number; it isn't that important."

Rag

chew the rag. To chat; to talk idly; to spend time in unimportant conversation.

> "No, you didn't disturb us. We were just chewing the rag."

> "Stop chewing the rag and get to work."

from rags to riches. From a state of poverty to wealth.

> "That man went from rags to riches in the short period of about five years."

Ragged Edge

on the ragged edge. In a dangerous situation; on the verge of something undesirable.

> "He was on the ragged edge of a mental breakdown when the good news arrived and rescued him."

Rail

ride someone on a rail. To punish and banish someone from a community or country; to tar and feather someone and remove from a community.

> "After several warnings which he did not heed, they rode him out on a rail."

Raise

raise Cain. To shout in anger; to create a disturbance; to cause trouble by behaving in a boisterous manner.

> "When they started raising Cain in the middle of the night, the neighbors called in the police."

raise the devil. Same as *raise Cain,* which see.

> "He started raising the devil because the store would not refund his money."

raise hell. Same as *raise Cain,* which see.

> "He took the refusal as a personal insult and started raising hell."

raise the roof. Same as *raise Cain,* which see.

> "There is no point in raising the roof. They are only following instructions."

Ran

also-ran. One who participated in a contest but did not win; competed but did not win.

"In this town he is the perennial also-ran. He never missed a race and he never won."

Rank

pull one's rank on someone. To make use of one's rank or high status in order to exact compliance, respect, etc., from one of lower rank or status.

"If your argumentative powers fail, you can still pull your rank on him!"

rank and file. The body of soldiers of a military force, as distinguished from the officers; the ordinary members of an organization, as distinguished from the officers or leaders.

"The agreement between the company and the union leaders must still be voted on by the rank and file."

Rat

smell a rat. To detect some evidence of deceit, trickery, etc.; to become suspicious of an ulterior motive.

"When they accepted our first offer, we smelled a rat. It turned out that the property was about to be condemned."

Rate

at any rate. Regardless of other factors; no matter what happens; anyway.

"At any rate, you can always get your money back, and perhaps even make some profit."

Raw

in the raw. 1. As it occurs in nature; not refined. 2. Unclothed; naked.

1. "Gold ore in the raw is very unimpressive to the eye."

2. "Most of the second scene finds the actors in the raw."

Read

read in. To ascribe a certain meaning to a text or statement; to interpret in a particular way.

"Perhaps because we hoped for it, we read in a stipulation that was not in the agreement."

read out of. To cause to be expelled from an organization, society, etc.

"We believe that he will be read out of the party at the next convention."

Real

for real. Actually; as a matter of fact; seriously; not as a jest.

"I heard that he bought a new home for her, but I wonder if it's for real."

"He said he was quitting his job, but I doubt that he meant it for real."

Reality

in reality. Existing in fact; actually; not fictitious or pretended.

"He tells everyone that his salary is ten thousand per year, but in reality he makes twice as much."

Rear

bring up the rear. To march or ride at the end, as of a procession.

"The men were at the head of the procession, the women came next, and the children brought up the rear."

Reason

bring someone to reason. To cause someone to think or reason rationally; to bring someone to a sensible or reasonable point of view or opinion.

> "We couldn't do anything with him while he was drunk, but when he sobered up we brought him to reason."

by reason of. Because of a specified condition or event; on account of.

> "He was one of the few not laid off, by reason of his being with the company for more than twenty years."

in reason. Reasonable; based on reason; proper; not outrageous or extravagant.

> "The union leader feels that the workers' demands are in reason; the company disagrees."

out of reason. Not reasonable; extravagant; outrageous; beyond the limits of good sense.

> "The company feels that the union demands are out of reason."

stand to reason. To be based on sound reasoning; to be a logical conclusion.

> "Since the demands are so outrageous, it stands to reason that they will reject them."

with reason. On the basis of a good reason; justifiable; by right.

> "No one expects a quick settlement, and with reason. The parties involved are poles apart in their demands."

within reason. Same as *in reason*, which see.

> "If your price is within reason, I think we can make a deal."

Reckon

reckon with. To recognize and take into consideration; to face; to deal with.

> "We didn't reckon with so many applicants. It will take us a month to interview them."

> "You will have to reckon not only with your neighbors but also with the zoning board."

Reckoning

day of reckoning. A day of judgment; a time when one must account for one's deeds; the time when one must pay for one's indiscretions.

> "People would use better sense if they would realize that there is a day of reckoning."

Record

break a record. To excel a previous record; to do better than the best done previously.

> "It isn't likely that anyone will break a record at this meet, because of the wet ground."

break the record. Same as *break a record,* which see.

> "He broke the record for the mile which was set about five years ago."

go on record. To make public one's stand or opinion with regard to a particular issue.

> "He went on record as opposing the bussing of students."

off the record. Not intended for making public; confidentially; not officially.

> "Officially, no one will talk, but off the record they admit that the mission has failed."

on record. 1. Known publicly; publicized. 2. Existing in a recorded form; published or filed.

1. "He is on record as opposing the bussing of students."

2. "Although he states that he applied formally, his application is not on record."

Red

in the red. Of a business, not making any profits; losing money; in debt.

"In this business you must expect to remain in the red for the first two or three years of operation."

"He is making more money, but his expenses have doubled. He is still in the red."

paint the town red. To have a boisterous good time by visiting many places of entertainment, as night clubs, bars, etc.

"He is painting the town red in celebration of his good luck at the track."

see red. To be very angry; to become enraged; to be so furious as to see a challenge or danger in practically everything.

"The mere mention of the war makes him see red."

Regard

as regards. About; concerning; with reference to.

"As regards the other matter, we can discuss that at the next meeting."

without regard. Not considering; paying no attention; disregarding.

"He made the statement without regard to the opinions of the other members of the board."

"He bought the car without regard to the high upkeep."

Rein

draw rein. To reduce speed; to diminish; to curtail an activity, expenditure, etc.

> "With our income sharply reduced, it is time to draw rein on our expenditures."

> "It would be a good idea to draw rein on your temper."

draw in the reins. Same as *draw rein,* which see.

> "To curb inflation, it may be necessary to draw in the reins with regard to certain types of construction work."

give free rein. Allow complete freedom; permit to function without restraint.

> "You must not give free rein to your ambitions."

> "When I give free rein to my dreams, I can see a rosy future, but not in reality."

keep a rein on. Exert a controlling influence; restrain; check.

> "The main office keeps a rein on the subsidiaries and branches."

Relief

on relief. Receiving financial assistance from a federal or municipal agency because of poverty.

> "Almost half of the families in this community are on relief."

Request

by request. In response to a request, as from a listener, an audience, etc.

> "On Saturdays, this station plays records by request."

Reserve

in reserve. Set aside and kept for some future use, or for some particular person.

"A certain amount of the assets is kept in reserve."

without reserve. With frankness; subject to no restraint; without reticence.

"We are willing to state our views on the subject without reserve."

Respect

in respect of. With regard to; with reference to.

"There is no objection in respect of the location of the proposed museum."

with respect to. Same as *in respect of,* which see.

"With respect to the latter the vote was unanimous."

Rest

at rest. Motionless; in a state of inactivity; in repose.

"He is a person who cannot remain at rest for a long time."

lay to rest. To bury a deceased person; inter.

"He was laid to rest in a national cemetery."

Return

in return. In response; as a reward or compensation; as an equivalent.

"We will use their garage, and in return they can use our back yard."

Rhyme

rhyme or reason. Order or logic; plan or sense.

"We looked for rhyme or reason, but found neither."

neither rhyme nor reason. Neither order nor logic; neither a logical plan nor sense.

> "The proposed method has neither rhyme nor reason."

Rid

be rid of. To be free from someone or something unpleasant; be relieved of.

> "Let's pay the man and be rid of him once and for all!"

get rid of. To cause to be free from someone or something undesirable; to dispose of.

> "I don't care how you do it, but get rid of him!"

> "Let's get rid of this old barn. It's of no use to us."

Ride

ride down. To catch up to; to overtake, as in a chase.

> "The motorcycle cop rode down the escaping youth."

ride for a fall. To be headed toward disaster; to misbehave in such a way as to make misfortune or downfall inevitable.

> "The way he was living and spending his money made one realize that he was riding for a fall."

ride herd on. Keep guard over; maintain order over; watch over.

> "It was her turn to ride herd on the children."

ride out. To sustain oneself successfully against an undesirable condition; to live through a hard or dangerous period.

> "By reducing expenses to the minimum we were able to ride out the period of recession."

take for a ride. 1. To take a person somewhere by force or guile and then kill him. 2. To victimize; to take advantage of; to deceive.

> 1. "The man disappeared, and it is assumed that he was taken for a ride by the gang."

> 2. "He had no experience in such transactions, and they took him for a ride."

Right

by right *or* rights. For the sake of justice; to be fair; properly.

> "He should by rights have been asked for his opinion."

in one's own right. By one's own effort, talents, etc.; in one's own name or ownership; not dependent on others.

> "He makes excellent copies of the masters, but he is also a talented painter in his own right."

in the right. Supported by facts, justice, the law, etc.; right; correct.

> "He is not likely to be intimidated, because he knows he is in the right."

Mr. Right. The man who is just the one for a particular girl to marry; a person who is especially suitable for a particular position, task, etc.

> "We believe that every girl knows when she meets her Mr. Right."

to rights. In good order; in the proper condition; straightened out; properly informed.

> "The house will be put to rights before you are ready to move in."

> "You talk to your serviceman. He'll put you to rights on how this machine works."

Ring

ring a bell. To sound familiar; to remind of something; to elicit a response.

"The name of the company rang a bell. One of my neighbors worked for them during the war."

ring down the curtain. To put an end to; to mark the end of something.

"The divorce most likely rang down the curtain on his political career."

ring in. 1. To mark officially the time of one's arrival at work, usually by punching a time clock which emits a ringing sound. 2. To introduce by fraud or artifice.

1. "He was fired for ringing in late once too often."

2. "They will surely try to ring in an unqualified delegate."

ring out. 1. To mark officially the time of one's departure from work, usually by punching a time clock. 2. To emit a ringing or booming sound.

1. "The company gave the men permission to ring out early so that they might have time to vote."

2. "Some witnesses said that two shots rang out."

ring the bell. To have a strong appeal; to supply exactly what is necessary or desired.

"The Vice President's speeches ring the bell with certain segments of middle America."

ring up. To punch in the amount of a sale (or the like) on a cash register.

"The salesgirl was instructed to ring up every sale, however small."

ring up the curtain. To mark the beginning of something; to initiate something.

> "The luncheon rang up the curtain on the fund-raising drive for a new library."

run rings around. To be able to do things much better or faster than another specified person.

> "He is a good all-around athlete, but in tennis she can run rings around him."

Riot

run riot. 1. To act without discipline or restraint; to run wild. 2. To grow in annoying profusion.

> 1. "Don't let these kids run riot. They'll tear the house down if you let them."
>
> 2. "Because of the frequent rains, the weeds are running riot in our vegetable garden this summer."

Riot Act

read the riot act to. To order someone to stop a specified activity under threat of punishment; to censure; to chastise severely.

> 1. "The principal read the riot act to the boisterous kids."
>
> 2. "You don't have to read the riot act to me. I know I was wrong and I apologize."

Rip

rip into. To assail viciously, physically or with words; castigate.

> "He does deserve some criticism, but you didn't have to rip into him like this."

rip out. To exclaim violently; to burst forth with anger.

> "He has a volatile temper and is likely to rip out with unseemly language. You would do well not to say anything at all."

Rise

get a rise out of. To elicit a desired response, as by a provocative statement; to incite to action.

> "It will be difficult to get a rise out of him no matter what you say or do."

> "We did get a rise out of her when we mentioned the possibility that he is ill and is unable to write."

give rise to. To produce; cause to come into being or existence; give origin to.

> "An innocent statement or inquiry may give rise to all sorts of undesirable rumors."

rise to. To exhibit a capability of meeting a situation; to produce the necessary talent or capability.

> "I have never seen this man fail to rise to the needs of a situation."

Risk

run a *or* the risk. To place oneself in a dangerous situation; to do something involving a hazard.

> "With this type of investment you also run the risk of losing a part of the principal. However, the dividends are substantially higher."

River

sell down the river. To betray; to desert someone in an emergency, especially for personal gain; to inform upon.

> "I just don't trust that man. He looks like one who would sell you down the river for fifty cents."

up the river. In a prison or penitentiary; to a prison or penitentiary.

> "He has been up the river for more than ten years."

> "He was sent up the river for armed robbery."

Road

burn up the road. To drive an automobile very fast; to move fast in any manner.

"He is not exactly burning up the road, but he'll get there."

hit the road. To begin a trip, especially on land; to resume a tour.

"The circus usually hits the road in early spring."

on the road. Traveling from place to place, as a performer or a salesman.

"They are on the road about eight months out of the year."

one for the road. An alcoholic drink taken just before one leaves the house and begins driving, usually as a bracer.

"If you are going to have one for the road, I'll do the driving."

take to the road. To begin traveling on a route or tour, as a salesman, theatrical troupe, etc.

"After playing in New York for about a year, the producer decided to take the play to the road."

Rock

on the rocks. 1. In or into a condition of destruction or desolation; in financial ruin. 2. Bankrupt; poverty stricken. 3. Of an alcoholic beverage, served with or over ice cubes.

1. "They say that the mutual fund you mentioned yesterday is on the rocks."

2. "Not having worked for more than a year, he is on the rocks at the moment."

3. "He usually takes vodka on the rocks."

Rod

spare the rod. To abstain from punishing (a child); to be lax in disciplining a child.

> "There is that old proverb about sparing the rod and spoiling the child."

Roland

a Roland for an Oliver. A retaliation in kind; a reprisal equal to the provocation.

> "You might say that for the attack they received a Roland for an Oliver."

Roll

roll back. 1. To reduce prices of merchandise or commodities to a previous level, usually in response to a government order. 2. To move backward, as weapons.

> 1. "No one believes that the current high prices will be rolled back."

> 2. "The United States insisted that the missiles be rolled back."

roll in. To come in abundantly; to arrive in large numbers or quantities.

> "After that, the money just rolled in."

> "The smoke rolled in through the open window."

roll out. To unroll; to spread something that is rolled.

> "He expected us to roll out the carpet when he came."

roll round. To come again, as a recurring event or condition; to recur.

> "Before you know it, Christmas will roll round again."

roll up. 1. To receive a large quantity or number. 2. To ride up to in a vehicle. 3. To form into a roll.

1. "He rolled up quite a vote in the northern part of the state."

2. "He rolled up to the theater in a vintage car."

3. "The material comes rolled up in lengths of a hundred feet."

strike off the rolls. To remove one's name from a list, as a membership list.

"As a result of the incident, I expect the membership committee to strike him off the rolls."

Roost

come home to roost. With regard to an action, to have unfavorable repercussions; to come back to haunt.

"That remark of his will come home to roost."

rule the roost. To be the dominant figure in a family or any group.

"The matriarch of the family rules the roost."

Root

root and branch. Completely; without leaving a trace; utterly.

"The tornado demolished the buildings root and branch."

take root. To become settled permanently; to establish oneself satisfactorily.

"He is a person who finds it difficult to take root anywhere."

Rope

at the end of one's rope. With no resources or alternatives left; at the end of one's ability to endure; as far as one can go.

> "He tried every possible way to salvage the business, and you might say that he is now at the end of his rope."

give one enough rope. To allow a person enough freedom to continue with a wrongful act, in the hope that he will overreach himself and be punished.

> "They decided to give the boy enough rope until he compounds his misdeeds and is punished adequately."

know the ropes. To be thoroughly familiar with the intricacies of a complex business or other enterprise.

> "They are looking for an experienced man who knows the ropes in this unpredictable business."

on the ropes. Near defeat or collapse; in a difficult or hopeless situation.

> "The small merchant who tries to compete with the chain stores soon finds himself on the ropes financially."

rope in. To entangle in an unpleasant situation; to inveigle.

> "He didn't want to get married, but she roped him in."

Rose

bed of roses. A job, position, or situation which is easy and comfortable; a state of pleasant idleness.

> "The new job isn't exactly a bed of roses either, but it is not nearly as arduous as the old one."

under the rose. Confidentially; not publicly; in private.

> "The details were given to him under the rose."

Rough

in the rough. In an unfinished or unpolished state; in the natural or crude form.

> "Even a diamond is not very attractive in the rough."

rough it. To live under rugged conditions; to get along without the usual conveniences of modern living.

> "He thought he was roughing it when the air conditioning was turned off for a few days."

Round

go the rounds. To circulate, as a rumor; to be told or talked about.

> "One of the rumors going the rounds is that the negotiations are still continuing but in secret."

in the round. In a theater having the stage surrounded by the audience, as in an arena.

> "Some performers cannot accustom themselves to play in the round; others like it very much."

make the rounds. To make a series of routine or scheduled stops; to go from place to place.

> "Our newspaper boy makes the rounds on a bicycle."

> "He is out of work again and is making the rounds of employment offices."

round off. To express as a round figure or number, i.e. to the nearest ten or hundred.

> "Let's round off these figures to the nearest hundred."

round out. 1. To make complete. 2. To make rounder or full; to become plumper.

> 1. "The new acquisition rounds out our collection."

2. "As she grew older, she rounded out in the right
places."

round up. To gather into a group; to assemble; to bring in, as
for questioning.

"We rounded up all available volunteer workers."

"The police rounded up more than a dozen sus-
pects."

Route

go the route. 1. To work at something till it is completed. 2. In
baseball, to pitch a complete game.

1. "Putting up that fence was a difficult job for one
man, but he went the route."

2. "In spite of a sore arm, the pitcher went the
route."

Row

hard row to hoe. Something difficult to accomplish; a difficult
chore or task.

"With prices being as high as they are, a man with a
big family often finds making ends meet a hard row
to hoe."

long row to hoe. Same as *hard row to hoe,* which see.

Rub

rub down. 1. To make smooth by rubbing; to polish. 2. To mas-
sage; to rub the surface of the body, especially with a medicinal
substance.

1. "We rubbed down the top of the desk with fine sand-
paper."

2. "Rubbing down with alcohol often relieves the
pain."

rub it in. To remind one repeatedly of a failure, error, etc. in order to tease or annoy.

"He delights in rubbing it in, but I don't mind."

rub out. 1. To obliterate by rubbing; to erase. 2. To murder.

1. "It would be impossible to rub out the inscription without marring the surface."

2. "The suspected informer was rubbed out in the typical gangland style."

rub the wrong way. To displease or antagonize, especially by saying or doing something contrary to good taste, manners, etc.

"Her appearance in a miniskirt at this stately function seemed to rub everyone the wrong way."

Rubicon

cross the Rubicon. To take a decisive step which commits one to a particular course; to make an irreversible decision.

"By bombing Pearl Harbor, the Japanese crossed the Rubicon and became participants in World War II."

pass the Rubicon. Same as *cross the Rubicon,* which see.

Rule

as a rule. Generally; more often than not; usually.

"As a rule, she retires by eleven, but that night she was up later waiting for the phone call."

rule out. To regard as impossible, unacceptable, etc.; to exclude.

"You can rule out robbery as a motive."

Run

a run for one's money. 1. Strong competition; powerful opposition. 2. A pleasant or profitable return for one's effort or expense.

1. "You will probably win, but she'll give you a run for your money."

2. "This touring company gives the audiences a run for their money."

in the long run. In the end; in the course of a long period of time; ultimately.

"In the long run, it is cheaper to use a better quality paint since it lasts much longer."

on the run. While moving about; while in a hurry. 2. Avoiding someone; running away. 3. Moving frequently from place to place; hurrying.

1. "He seldom sits down to eat lunch. Usually he eats on the run."

2. "He has been on the run from his wife for nearly a year."

3. "His peculiar job keeps him on the run most of the time."

run across. To meet someone, or to encounter something, accidentally.

"She had no idea he was in town. She just ran across him accidentally at the party."

run afoul of. To incur the ill will of someone; do something contrary to.

"He did not wish to run afoul of his wealthy uncle."

"The company ran afoul of the local zoning laws."

run after. To seek the friendship or company of someone; to try to be a part of, as of a certain group.

"He said he wouldn't run after any girl, but he is running after this one!"

"Both of them are running after the jet set."

run around. To philander; of a married man or woman, to consort with a member of the opposite sex; to be unfaithful to one's husband or wife.

> "Rumor has it that while his wife was in Europe, he
> was running around."

run around with. To keep company with; to be frequently with.

> "He runs around with some of the boys at the office."

> "She runs around with the long-haired set."

run away. To escape; to flee; to leave a place clandestinely without any intention to return.

> "Many youngsters run away from home these days."

run away with. 1. To cause to lose self-control, rationality, etc. 2. To win handily; to win a prize by outdoing others. 3. To leave with a lover; to elope. 4. To flee with, as stolen goods.

> 1. "Don't let your dreams run away with your good
>   sense."
>
>   "Her emotions often run away with her."
>
> 2. "As usual, he ran away with the highest honors."
>
> 3. "Knowing her father's opposition to the young
>   man, she decided to run away with him."
>
> 4. "The maid ran away with some jewelry and a fur
>   coat."

run down. 1. To pursue or run after and capture. 2. To knock down by running a vehicle into. 3. To inspect; to glance over. 4. Of a mechanism, to stop moving because of exhaustion of power. 5. To lose strength or vigor; to become enfeebled. 6. To speak of in such a way as to degrade or disparage. 7. To trace, as the origin of something. 8. To deteriorate; to become dilapidated. 9. To read rapidly, as a list of names or figures.

> 1. "The police were trying to run down the suspect
>   before he had a chance to leave the state."

2. "The car went out of control and ran down two pedestrians before it came to a stop."

3. "His alert eyes ran down the people standing in line, but the suspect wasn't there."

4. "The clock will soon run down if you don't replace the battery."

5. "This exhausting work is enough to run anyone down."

6. "Don't run yourself down. I think you are doing well."

7. "It may take a while, but I am sure we can run down the order and find out who issued it."

8. "The last tenant allowed the house to run down, but it can be quickly refurbished."

9. "You run down this list while I check the files."

run for it. To hurry or run away in order to avoid something undesirable.

"If you don't want to face this man, you had better run for it, as he'll be here any minute."

run in. 1. To arrest; to commit to jail; to take into custody. 2. To stop in for a short time; to visit briefly.

1. "The policeman told the boys that he'll run them in if they don't disperse and go home."

2. "If I get through early enough, I'll try to run in for a little while."

run into. 1. To meet or encounter someone accidentally. 2. To drive a vehicle into; to crash into. 3. To add up to; to total. 4. To follow closely. 5. To enter; to encounter; to meet with.

1. "I just happened to run into him at the bank."

2. "Try not to run into the curb. It isn't the best thing for the tires."

3. "It is only a little here and a little there, but it runs into more than a thousand dollars a year."

4. "One season runs into another without a sharp change."

5. "Here, take the topcoat. You may run into cold weather."

run off. 1. To depart quickly. 2. To create rapidly and without much effort. 3. To expel; to force to leave. 4. To print, duplicate, or typewrite.

1. "If you hadn't run off unexpectedly, you would have met her."

2. "He runs off an article a week during the winter months."

3. "If you don't quiet down, he'll run you off the premises."

4. "We expect to run off a thousand copies of the brochure."

run on. To continue at length; to talk without interruption.

"If she starts talking about her grandchildren, she may run on for hours."

run out. 1. To end or expire, as a time limit. 2. To force someone to leave a particular place.

1. "The time limit on a claim like this runs out in two years."

2. "If you carry on like this much longer, they'll run you out of here."

run out of. To become depleted of; to be exhausted of; to have no more.

"We ran out of this item two weeks ago."

"Try not to run out of patience with her. She has enough reason to complain."

run out on. To abandon or desert; to cease giving support without a good reason.

> "He is not known for his loyalty. He may run out on you."

run over. 1. To ride over something with a vehicle. 2. To flow over, as the edge of a container. 3. To read or rehearse quickly.

> 1. "Running over the garden hose doesn't do it any good."
>
> 2. "The sink somehow got stopped up and the water ran over."
>
> 3. "Let's run over the instructions once more."

run through. 1. To spend quickly; to exhaust recklessly. 2. To read, review, or rehearse quickly. 3. To pierce; to cut through.

> 1. "He runs through his monthly allowance in a few days."
>
> 2. "I would like to run through this manual once more."
>
> 3. "He ran through the tablecloth with the carving knife."

run up. 1. To cause to be higher; to increase. 2. To cause to accumulate; to incur.

> 1. "The special packaging will run up the price of the item."
>
> 2. "His wife ran up quite a debt unbeknown to him."

Running

in the running. In the contest or competition; still having a chance to succeed.

> "He isn't as popular as he used to be, but I would say that he is still in the running."

out of the running. Out of competition; not in a contest; no longer having a chance to win or succeed.

> "That unfortunate incident put him out of the running."

> "She is definitely out of the running now."

Rustle

rustle up. To prepare; to improvise; to collect from various, often unusual, sources.

> "My wife is visiting her mother, but I think I can rustle up some dinner for the three of us."

S

Sackcloth

in sackcloth and ashes. Feeling remorse; in a state of penitence; contrite.

> "It is a pity that you didn't win, but I wouldn't be in sackcloth and ashes over it."

Saddle

in the saddle. In a position of power; in control; in command or authority.

> "He was out of favor with his company for a few years, but the new president reinstated him, and you might say that he is in the saddle again."

Sail

sail against the wind. To proceed in face of difficulties; to labor against opposition.

> "You may try to put your plan in operation, but you'll be sailing against the wind."

sail into. 1. To attack severely, especially with words; to castigate; reprimand. 2. To begin work with great vigor. 3. To enter with fanfare; to rush in.

1. "When he got home, his wife sailed into him for being late."

2. "Having been idle for some time, he sailed into the new project with enthusiasm."

3. "She sailed into the lobby of the hotel like a supertanker."

set sail. To begin a voyage by ship; to begin a journey or trip.

"I think we'll be setting sail rather early, perhaps by six in the morning."

Salt

salt away. To put aside for future use; to save, especially money; to store.

"He is able to salt away most of his weekly salary."

salt of the earth. The best there is; the noblest or finest person or persons.

"In this town, at least, they are regarded as the salt of the earth."

with a grain of salt. With some skepticism; with an allowance for exaggeration.

"Knowing her flair for dramatics, I am inclined to take her estimate of the situation with a grain of salt."

worth one's salt. Worth the cost of upkeep; deserving one's salary or wages.

"You can hardly find a repairman these days worth his salt."

Satisfaction

give satisfaction. To respond in a satisfying manner; to recompense.

"We asked him several times, but he gave us no satisfaction."

Say

have the say. To have the authority to decide; to have the final word.

> "Let's face it, in his household, the wife has the say."

> "The local office doesn't have the say about such matters."

that is to say. Putting it in other words; the meaning or significance is.

> "He has no motive for concealing the truth; that is to say that I accept his version of the incident."

Saying

go without saying. To be so obvious as to need no particular mention; to be self-evident or understood without explanation.

> "It goes without saying that the more you produce the more you will earn."

> "It goes without saying that we will miss him, but he can't stay with us for the rest of his life."

Scales

tip the scales. 1. To be of a specified weight; to weigh. 2. To direct a trend; to decide in favor of someone or something.

> 1. "He used to tip the scales at two hundred pounds, but he went on a diet recently."

> 2. "The President's visit tipped the scales in favor of our candidate."

turn the scales. 1. Same as *tip the scales,* definition 2. 2. To reverse an existing trend.

> 2. "It would be difficult to turn the political scales so late in the campaign."

Scarce

make oneself scarce. 1. To leave suddenly; to depart, especially by request. 2. To make it a habit to stay away from a particular place; to avoid habitually.

1. "Father motioned to Jim to make himself scarce."

2. "He doesn't really like crowds and so he makes himself scarce at parties."

Scare

scare up. To produce or obtain somehow; to gather or collect, especially by unconventional means.

"I think I can scare up enough food for both of us."

Scratch

from scratch. 1. From the beginning of something; from the time of origin. 2. From a humble origin; without the advantage of resources; without funds.

1. "He joined this company when it was founded, you might say from scratch."

2. "When his father died, the business was in poor shape and in debt. He had to start from scratch, and look at it now!"

up to scratch. 1. Well-informed; ready to start or to meet any emergency; prepared. 2. Fulfilling requirements; meeting standards; at top form.

1. "He is an avid reader, and you may be sure that he is up to scratch on the latest developments."

2. "Even with the new recruits, the force is not up to scratch."

Screw

have a screw loose. To have something wrong with one's mind; to be somewhat eccentric or odd.

> "I don't know, sometimes I think he has a screw loose in his head, or he wouldn't do such crazy things."

> "She must have a screw loose to quit such a good job."

put the screws on. To cause to do something, or not to do, by coercion; to exert pressure upon, as by threats.

> "They can put the screws on us for payment any time they want to, and you know it."

> "You will have to put the screws on; otherwise he won't do it."

put on the screws. Same as *put the screws on,* which see.

screw around. To spend time in childish or foolish activities; waste time in foolishness; fool around.

> "No wonder he didn't finish the homework. He screwed around most of the evening."

screw up. To frustrate by bungling or interference; to cause to fail; to complicate matters.

> "You can congratulate yourself. You screwed things up for us with that silly remark."

to screw. To have sexual intercourse; to inflict coitus on a female.

> "He is just out to screw any female that comes his way."

Sea

at sea. Puzzled; bewildered; confused; perplexed.

> "In spite of the instructions, I am still at sea at the moment as to how to put this together."

follow the sea. To make a living as a sailor; to make service on seagoing ships one's life's work.

"Following the sea is the tradition of his family."

half seas over. Partly intoxicated; drunk; completely inebriated.

"More likely than not, he'll be half seas over by tonight."

Seal

set one's seal to. Approve; give one's endorsement to.

"I am sure that he'll set his seal to this proposal."

Search

in search of. In the process of trying to find; attempting to attain or reach.

"Some people are always in search of something un-attainable."

"They are still out in search of the lost cat."

search me! I have no idea; I don't know and don't care; how would I know?

"You are asking me where she went? Search me! She never tells me."

search out. To find by diligent search; to uncover by patient scrutiny.

"We are trying to search out the few remaining errors in the script."

Season

for a season. For a short time; for a certain length of time; for a while.

"She did live in Los Angeles for a season some years ago."

in good season. Early enough to allow sufficient time for something; sufficiently in advance.

> "If he decides to come, he'll let you know in good season."

in season. 1. Of certain foods, as fruits or vegetables, available during the time when they ripen and can be eaten fresh, i.e. without being preserved by freezing or canning. 2. Designating a time of the year when the hunting of certain animals is permitted by law.

> 1. "This restaurant has the best strawberry pie when the berries are in season."

> 2. "Deer will soon be in season in this locality."

in season and out of season. At all times; without respite; always.

> "He is always interested in girls, in season and out of season."

out of season. The opposite of *in season,* which see.

> "Strawberries are now out of season, but you can use the canned berries."

> "These animals seem to know that they are out of season and, therefore, quite safe."

Seated

be seated. To be in a sitting position; to be settled in a chair; to sit down.

> "All who are standing now will be seated in the next thirty minutes."

> "Won't you be seated, please?"

See

see about. 1. To make an investigation about someone or something. 2. To attend to or take care of.

1. "As for the second applicant, we will have to see about him. We'll check his past experience."

2. "Don't worry about the bill. She said she'll see about paying it, on her lunch hour."

see after. To take care of; keep an eye on; watch over; look after.

"Our neighbor promised to see after the cats while we are on vacation."

see double. 1. To be very angry; to be so upset as to be unable to see or observe properly. 2. To be intoxicated; to be on a drinking binge.

1. "When he was told that he would not be allowed to board the plane, he saw double and uttered some harsh words for which he later apologized."

2. "He had a spat with his girl and is seeing double again."

see into. 1. To make an inquiry about something; to investigate. 2. To comprehend the deeper meaning of something; to understand the true nature of.

1. "I called them and they promised to see into this, as they had previously stated there would be no charge for the adjustment."

2. "Frankly, I was unable to see into their problem at that time."

see off. To accompany someone to a place of departure, as an airport; to say good-by to someone setting out on a relatively long journey.

"He had a cold and was unable to see her off at the pier."

see out. To continue with something until it is finished; to remain with a project or task until it is completed.

"It may take a long time, perhaps five years, but we will see it out."

see through. 1. Same as *see out*, which see. 2. To be able to comprehend something not easily understood; to understand the true nature of something by penetrating the superficialities. 3. To give sufficient aid to pass through a crisis; to suffice for a particular length of time; to carry through.

> 1. "We feel committed to this project, and you may be sure that we will see it through."
>
> 2. "Although she is a clever deceiver, he was able to see through her guile."
>
> 3. "His brother gave him enough financial aid to see him through the first two years of college."
>
>   "I am sure this is enough firewood to see us through the winter."

see to. Make sure that; do what is necessary to accomplish something.

> "I'll see to it that he gets your message on time."

Seed

go to seed. To become dilapidated; to deteriorate; to grow weak; to become unprofitable or run-down.

> "The business went to seed when the old man retired."
>
> "He went to seed physically and mentally after his wife ran off with another man."

Seize

seize on. To grab, figuratively, as a reason or as an excuse; to choose something and dwell upon it.

> "She seized on his failure to send her a gift as a reason for breaking off with him."
>
> "He seized on this minor setback as a major worry."

seize upon. Same as *seize on*, which see.

Sell

sell off. To dispose of a portion of something, especially by selling at reduced prices; to sell something for the purpose of becoming rid of it.

> "He decided to sell off some of the less promising stocks."

> "We decided to sell off the bottom land of the farm."

sell oneself. 1. To sacrifice one's leisure, comforts, or freedom for the sake of some reward, usually financial. 2. To submit sexually for money. 3. To succeed in convincing someone about one's qualifications, talents, or other desirable features, especially by guile or deceit.

> 1. "He sold himself completely to his business. He even gave up his one evening out with the boys."

> 2. "Some of the younger women were able to survive by selling themselves."

> 3. "I don't know how she did it, but apparently she succeeded in selling herself to her new employer. She got the job."

sell out. 1. To free oneself from something, as a failing business, by selling it completely, i.e. by selling all of it. 2. To betray someone (as a friend) or something (as a principle or cause) for the sake of financial gain.

> 1. "The long hours at the service station finally got him down. I think he decided to sell out."

> 2. "It takes a stout heart not to sell out when the price is right."

Send

send down. 1. To deliver; to dispatch. 2. To cause to move or flow downward.

> 1. "Mother sent down some fried chicken which was delicious."

2. "The sudden thaw sent down a torrent of water which flooded the lower parts of the town."

send flying. 1. To cause someone to leave in a hurry. 2. To repel violently, as with a punch. 3. To cause to scatter or fly in many directions. 4. To put to flight, as by force, threats, etc.

1. "My mere mention that she might come in any minute sent him flying. He didn't want to face her."

2. "The would-be victim sent the assailant flying with a blow to the jaw."

3. "The explosion shattered the window and sent the pieces flying."

4. "The enemy was sent flying by a vigorous counterattack."

send for. To request the coming of; to order, as a piece of merchandise; to request the delivery of.

"They sent for a doctor at once, but he hasn't arrived yet."

"The store didn't have the part in stock. They had to send for it."

send forth. 1. To emit; to produce; cause to issue. 2. To cause to form or unfold.

1. "That plant sends forth billows of smoke and steam."

"The flowers send forth a subtle and pleasant aroma."

2. "The warm spell caused some of the shrubs to send forth an early bloom."

send in. To dispatch or send to a particular place; to cause to be delivered to.

"All entries must be sent in by the fifteenth of the month."

"I would advise you to send in your name and address."

send off. To send something by mail; to cause something to be carried to a particular place; to instruct someone to go to a specified place or person; to dismiss.

"We sent off a number of entries but none won anything."

"I sent off a protest to the manager of the station."

"The foreman sent him off to see the doctor at once."

"The teacher sent him off without a satisfactory explanation."

send out. To distribute something to various places, especially from a central point.

"The company sends out thousands of circulars every month."

send packing. To dismiss someone unceremoniously; to instruct someone to leave immediately.

"He was obviously intoxicated, so the manager had no choice but to send him packing."

send up. To send to jail; to sentence someone to prison for a specified time.

"Since this was his second offense, he was sent up for twenty years."

Sense

in a sense. From one point of view or aspect; to a certain degree or extent.

"In a sense he was right. It took longer than he predicted, but she did get tired of it eventually."

make sense. To be logical or reasonable; to behave in a normal or sensible way.

"The suggested solution makes sense to me."

"His reaction to the news just doesn't seem to make sense."

Serve

serve one right. To mete out just punishment; to get the kind of poor treatment one deserves.

"It will serve him right if he finds himself out of a job. There is no reason why he should come in late every morning."

Service

at someone's service. At the disposal of some person; ready and willing to help someone.

"At that hospital, there was always a nurse at his service."

"My secretary can be at your service, if you so desire."

be of service. To assist; to be useful or helpful in some way.

"If you feel that I may be of service to you in this case, all you have to do is call me."

Set

all set. Fully prepared; ready for some task or activity; having one's mind made up.

"I am all set to go but I don't think you are."

"He was all set to accept the offer, but his wife changed his mind almost in the last minute."

get set. To make oneself ready for some activity; to prepare one-self for.

> "He wants to know how long it will take you to get set for this trip."

> "One of the runners jumped the gun when the starter said 'Get set!' "

set about. To begin, as a task; to start doing something; to try or attempt.

> "They set about to paint the barn early in the morn-ing."

> "Before you set about to conquer the world, you might help me with the dishes!"

set against. 1. To cause someone to become unfriendly toward another person. 2. To compare, as in order to note or show dif-ferences. 3. To place in contrast.

> 1. "She tried to set her brother against his old friend, but he saw through her."

> 2. "You have to set the higher price of this paint against its superior quality and durability."

> 3. "These flowers were set against a rather dull background."

set apart. 1. To put away for a particular purpose; to separate and keep away from others or another. 2. To distinguish; to emphasize the difference from another or others.

> 1. "We set these children apart from the others be-cause they require more personal supervision."

> 2. "His very appearance sets him apart from the other kids. He is a head taller than the others."

set aside. 1. Same as *set apart,* definition 1. 2. To reject as un-worthy; to rebuff; to dismiss, as from the mind. 3. To declare null and void.

1. "Let's set aside one hour a day for review purposes."

2. "She found it difficult to set aside a vague feeling of anxiety caused by his failure to call or write."

3. "The higher court is expected to set aside the verdict."

set back. 1. To impede the progress of; to put a person or a process back on a lower level of progress; to reverse. 2. To turn back; to move the hands of a clock or watch to an earlier time.

1. "The breakdown of the equipment will set us back at least two months."

2. "Tonight is the night. Don't forget to set back your clock."

set down. 1. To attribute to someone or something; to ascribe. 2. To regard as; to consider. 3. To make a printed or written record. 4. To humiliate or disparage; to belittle. 5. To place an object on the surface of something; to put something down, as on a table. 6. To cause a plane or other aircraft to land in a particular manner or a specified place.

1. "I am willing to set down his failure to lack of experience rather than lack of interest."

2. "You'll be making a mistake if you'll set him down as an aimless drifter. He knows where he's going."

3. "It would be best to set it down on paper so there will be no questions later."

4. "Why are you always trying to set him down! He may not have a formal education, but he is well-read and remarkably informed about most subjects."

5. "Please set this vase down on the television set in the living room."

6. "The pilot tried to set the plane down in a cornfield."

set forth. 1. To begin a journey. 2. To propound, as a theory; to state in words.

1. "They set forth to the West Coast with high hopes."

2. "He set forth his objections in a short, well-written statement."

set forward. To move the hands of a clock or watch to show a later time.

"It is easier to set a clock forward than it is to set it back. In fact, some clocks and watches cannot be set back."

set in. To begin to manifest itself; to assume a certain condition; to come on.

"You better hurry; darkness will soon set in."

"Rigor mortis set in before the body was discovered."

set off. 1. To cause to detonate or explode; to ignite. 2. To incite; to get a person started. 3. To accentuate, as by contrast; to make more prominent. 4. To begin, as a trip.

1. "It is believed that static electricity set off the stored powder."

2. "What really set him off was her remark about his speech impediment."

3. "The green foliage sets off the red blossoms."

"His dullness sets off her brilliance and charm."

4. "He expects to set off on his fishing trip at five in the morning."

set on. 1. To urge or cause to attack someone. 2. To instigate, as to a riot.

> 1. "He threatened to set his dog on the children if they did not leave."
>
> 2. "The radicals were accused of setting on the students to riot."

set upon. Same as *set on*, definition 1, which see.

set out. 1. To start, as a journey; to begin, as upon a course. 2. To undertake a specified task; to mark as one's goal. 3. To set in the ground; to plant. 4. To formulate, as a plan or design. 5. To explain or describe. 6. To put on display.

> 1. "He set out on foot but will ride a bicycle part of the way."
>
> 2. "He set out to complete the course in three years and to win top honors."
>
> 3. "He plants the seeds indoors during the last part of the winter and sets out the young plants when the danger of frost is gone."
>
> 4. "She set out the rough sketch of the pattern in pencil."
>
> 5. "He expects to have an opportunity to set out his plan at the next meeting."
>
> 6. "He set out his baskets of tomatoes at the roadside."

set to. To begin something with vigor and enthusiasm; to make a determined beginning.

> "He set to the accomplishment of the task with the enthusiasm of a beginner, which he was not."

set up. 1. To place in a high position; to elevate, as in rank; to put in power. 2. To put in an upright or vertical position. 3. To

construct from disassembled parts; to erect. 4. To provide someone with money or any other means necessary to begin something, as a business. 5. To found or establish. 6. To enliven;
stimulate; cheer up. 7. To treat, especially to drinks; to place
free drinks before guests or customers, as in a bar.

1. "We set up these cartons on the top shelf, where
   it is warmer."

   "They set him up in a high position, but whether
   he has the corresponding power I do not know."

2. "Before we do anything else, let us set up the
   center post for the tent."

3. "Setting up this knocked down tool shed is not
   that simple."

4. "He expects his father-in-law to set him up in
   business."

   "His aunt set him up in a nice apartment and
   found him a job."

5. "The businessmen of the town set up a fund to
   take care of such emergencies."

6. "A few sincere compliments will set him up for
   the occasion."

   "He was set up by her cheerful smile and genuine
   interest."

7. "The visitor asked the bartender to set up drinks
   for everyone present."

set upon. To assail physically; to attack suddenly and violently;
to harass.

   "As he turned the corner, he was set upon by two
   youths."

Settle

settle down. 1. To apply oneself efficiently to a given task. 2. To calm oneself; to quiet down. 3. To begin leading a more temperate form of life; to change from an irresponsible way of life to an orderly life; to stop running around or seeking pleasure and start living a purposeful life; to abandon an aimless or dissolute life in favor of a meaningful life.

> 1. "With so much on his mind, he was unable to settle down to the demands of his new job."
>
> 2. "She was so upset by the accident that she couldn't settle down long enough to explain just what happened."
>
> 3. "He was such a swinger that we thought he would never settle down. But he married a very nice girl and is now an exemplary husband."

settle upon. To decide on something; to make a choice; to make up one's mind, as to what to do.

> "We finally settled upon the house near the highway."
>
> "Let's settle upon a course of action and follow it."

settle on. Same as *settle upon,* which see.

> "I don't know that this is the best or only solution to our problem, but we settled on it anyway."

Sew

sew up. 1. To make certain of; to obtain and regard as one's own. 2. To gain exclusive control of; to monopolize. 3. To succeed in bringing something to a desirable conclusion. 4. To close an incision, laceration, etc., by means of sutures; to suture.

> 1. "He sewed up at least a dozen pledges during the half hour that he was here."

2. "He and his family have the local market for this product sewed up."

3. "You leave it to me. I'll have the deal sewed up in less than an hour."

4. "The boy wanted to know if the cut will have to be sewed up."

Sex

sex it up. To indulge in ardent necking; to engage in passionate contrectation.

"They haven't enough privacy here to really sex it up as they would like to."

sex up. 1. To arouse the libido; to excite sexually. 2. To heighten the interest, as of a book or motion picture, by introducing sex-oriented material. 3. To make more interesting or exciting in any way.

1. "He is easily sexed up by a girl in a mini, no matter how homely she may be."

2. "The movie was sexed up for the European market."

3. "The novel is sexed up by means of excessive violence."

the fair *or* **weaker** *or* **gentle sex.** The female sex; women or girls, collectively.

"He says that the fair sex is showing its claws."

"The women's liberation movement shattered his concept of the gentle sex."

"The weaker sex is not so weak as far as longevity is concerned."

the stronger sex. The male sex; males or men, collectively.

"In the United States, at least, the stronger sex is generally dominated by the weaker sex."

Shack

shack up. 1. To spend the night with; to live or reside at a particular place. 2. To have sexual intercourse, especially out of wedlock. 3. Of a man and woman, to live together without being married. 4. Of a woman, to consent to submit to coitus.

1. "It's too late to start looking for a hotel, so why don't you shack up with us for the night?"

2. "He was looking for a dame to shack up with when the police picked him up."

3. "I hear that they are not married, just shacking up."

4. "She'll probably shack up with him after a while."

Shade

put someone *or* something in the shade. To make someone or something seem unimportant by comparison with someone or something else.

"Her new novel puts the others in the shade."

"The new manager puts his predecessor in the shade."

Shake

give someone the shake. To run away from, or avoid, someone; to get away from; to get rid of.

"It was obvious that she was trying to give him the shake."

"I don't mean to give you the shake, but I do have to leave you. I have another appointment."

no great shakes. Nothing to brag about; no great bargain; not of great importance; not remarkable or outstanding.

"Her present boyfriend is better than the other one but still no great shakes."

"Even with the raise, his job is no great shakes."

shake down. 1. To obtain money from someone by blackmail or other threats. 2. To frisk or search someone, usually for concealed weapons.

> 1. "They tried to shake down the local business community, but they came up against a stone wall."

> 2. "He didn't like the idea of being shaken down at the police station, but he realized it would be foolish to resist."

shake hands. Of two persons, to grip each other's hand, as an expression of greeting, parting, or agreement.

"He feels that the custom of shaking hands is much overdone."

shake off. 1. To dispose of a feeling, mood, worry, etc. 2. To rid oneself of someone; to leave someone behind; to lose someone advisedly.

> 1. "In spite of all her reasoning and her attempts to reassure herself, she could not shake off the feeling of anxiety and frustration."

> 2. "We tried to shake him off, but he stuck like a leech."

shake one's head. 1. To indicate negation or disapproval by turning one's head several times from one side to the other. 2. To indicate affirmation, acceptance, or approval by moving one's head up and down several times.

> 1. "He indicated his disapproval by shaking his head."

> 2. "As she shook her head in acceptance, the auctioneer lowered his gavel."

shake out. To remove water, dust, or other particles from an object by shaking it.

> "He broke the handle of the mop while shaking it out."

shake the dust from one's feet. To leave in anger; to depart from a place with an obvious intention never to return.

> "He disliked his home town for a long time and finally shook its dust from his feet."

shake up. 1. To mix the contents of something by shaking. 2. To disturb or agitate; to disconcert. 3. To rearrange or redistribute.

> 1. "The label should state that you must shake it up before pouring."
>
> 2. "The news that his former wife remarried shook him up."
>
> 3. "The new president promised to shake up the organization."

the shakes. A nervous trembling; agitation accompanied by trembling; extreme restlessness.

> "He was out drinking last night, and now he has the shakes."

two shakes of a lamb's tail. An instant or moment; a very short period of time.

> "Hold your horses; I'll be there in two shakes of a lamb's tail."

Shame

for shame! You should be ashamed of yourself! Here is a reason for being ashamed.

> "For shame! A big boy like you and afraid of the dark!"

put to shame. To surpass someone; to show someone to be inferior; to outdo.

"His excellent sketches put the others to shame."

"He can surely put you to shame in chess."

shame on. One should feel ashamed; something specified should be a source of shame for someone.

"Shame on him for behaving in such an asinine manner."

Shank

shank of the evening. The best part of the evening, usually the last part of it.

"Are you leaving already? This is the shank of the evening."

Shape

shape up. 1. To assume a definite form; to develop into a particular condition. 2. To develop satisfactorily.

1. "His project is now beginning to shape up."

2. "The new department is not shaping up as expected."

take shape. To assume a recognizable form; to develop into a definite shape or condition.

"The shopping center is beginning to take shape at last."

Shed

shed blood. To kill deliberately, especially by cutting, stabbing, or shooting.

"The gang isn't averse to shedding blood in order to attain its goal."

Sheep

separate the sheep from the goats. To separate the good from the bad; to separate people on the basis of their qualifications for a particular purpose.

> "The need for workers was so keen that the employer did not take the time to separate the sheep from the goats."

make sheep's eyes at. To look at someone with loving tenderness; to look at meekly; to look amorously but shyly at.

> "The young man was making sheep's eyes at the nurse."

Sheet

be three sheets to the wind. To be very drunk; intoxicated.

> "He was three sheets to the wind when we arrived, and he wasn't about to quit drinking even then."

Shell

come out of one's shell. To start mingling with people; to become less reserved and more sociable; to become more of an extrovert.

> "I hope that this girl will make him come out of his shell."

> "He started coming out of his shell when he joined our bowling team."

retire into one's shell. To become more reserved and less interested in mingling with people; to become less sociable; to become more of an introvert.

> "After her mother died, she retired into her shell and you can't get her to attend anything."

shell out. To pay out; to part with a large amount of money, especially for an unworthy cause or under duress.

> "The manager expected the men to shell out ten dollars each for the slush fund."

> "Some people don't mind shelling out fifty dollars for a good seat at a championship fight."

Shine

come rain or shine. 1. No matter what the weather is or may be; whether the weather is good or bad. 2. Regardless of the circumstances; no matter what the situation is or may be.

> 1. "A football game is played come rain or shine."

> "He takes his daily walk come rain or shine."

> 2. "Don't worry. He'll get you there on time come rain or shine."

rain or shine. Same as *come rain or shine,* which see.

shine up to. To make an effort to become friendly with someone; to make overtures to.

> "He tried to shine up to her, but she gave him the cold shoulder."

take a shine to. To become fond of; to take a liking to; to become interested in.

> "Generally he is not interested in girls, but he took a shine to this one."

Shingle

hang out one's shingle. To open an office for the practice of medicine or law.

> "He won't think of marriage until he hangs out his shingle and makes a go of it."

Ship

when one's ship comes in. When one succeeds in one's undertaking; when one makes his fortune; when one's goal has been attained.

> "He said that when his ship comes in he'll buy her a mink coat."

Shirt

in one's shirt sleeves. Wearing a shirt but no jacket or coat over it.

> "He preferred to work in his shirt sleeves even when it was rather cool in the office."

> "In this bank the tellers are not allowed to work in their shirt sleeves."

keep one's shirt on. To refrain from losing one's temper; to remain calm or cool.

> "I advise you to keep your shirt on no matter what he says."

lose one's shirt. To sustain a severe financial loss; to lose all of one's money or possessions.

> "In a business like this you can make a lot of money, but you can also lose your shirt."

Shoe

fill someone's shoes. To replace someone or do someone's work in a satisfactory manner.

> "It will be difficult to find someone to fill the old professor's shoes."

in another's shoes. In another person's situation; facing a problem similar to that of another person.

> "You really don't know what you would do were you in his shoes."

the shoe is on the other foot. The conditions or the circumstances are reversed.

> "Now that he is working nights and you are working during the day, the shoe is on the other foot and he will understand why you complained."

where the shoe pinches. Where the trouble really is; the cause of the difficulty; the source of the annoyance.

> "You can help him with his homework, but where the shoe pinches is that he will have to pass the exams by himself."

> "We can lend him some more money, but that will not help where the shoe pinches, which is his lack of interest in the business."

Shoot

shoot at. To attempt to attain; to aim at; strive for; try to accomplish.

> "He is shooting at a new record for the mile."

shoot down. To cause to come down or fall from a height by hitting with a bullet or the like.

> "One of the attacking planes was believed shot down."

shoot for. Same as *shoot at,* which see.

shoot off one's mouth. 1. To speak thoughtlessly; to blab; to reveal confidential matters through careless talk. 2. To brag; to exaggerate one's own virtues.

> 1. "I wouldn't tell him about the deal just yet. He is likely to shoot off his mouth. He always does."

> 2. "His earnings are probably not that high. He's always shooting off his mouth."

shoot the breeze. To chat; to talk for the sake of talking, i.e. aimlessly; to exaggerate; brag.

"No, you are not interrupting anything. We are just shooting the breeze. Come right in."

"I take everything he says with a grain of salt, as he is prone to shoot the breeze about his achievements, earnings, just about everything."

shoot up. 1. To rise rapidly through vigorous growth. 2. To hit an object with many shots; to shoot at repeatedly. 3. To terrorize, as the inhabitants of a town, by aimless or wanton shooting.

1. "It seems that the weeds shot up almost overnight."

2. "He got drunk and he shot up the entire front of the house."

3. "It was not unusual in those days for roving bands to shoot up a town, just for kicks."

shot through with. Mingled profusely with; interspersed with, especially something undesirable.

"I noticed that his hair became shot through with gray after the ordeal."

Shop

set up shop. To open a business; to start a practice; to begin in any endeavor.

"He expects to set up shop in his home town after he completes his training."

shut up shop. 1. To close for the night; to close a shop or business temporarily. 2. To close a business for good; to go out of business.

1. "We usually shut up shop at five, but that night we worked till nearly eight."

2. "Business is getting worse, not better. We'll have to shut up shop, I'm afraid."

talk shop. To talk about one's work, whether trade, profession, or business.

> "She told him that she was sick and tired listening to him talk shop every time he takes her out. She wasn't that interested in how many cars he sold."

Shore

off shore. On the water or in the water not far from the shore; away from the shore, inland.

> "The people go out for an evening of fun on the ship which is moored off shore."

> "The property I have in mind is off shore, but it's a good investment."

Short

fall short. To be insufficient; to turn out to be not enough; to prove inadequate.

> "We fully expect our stocks and supplies not to fall short, but we have ordered more anyway."

fall short of. To fail to reach a specified or expected level or standard.

> "It wasn't a bad performance, but it fell short of our expectations, perhaps because of his fame."

for short. For the convenience derived from making something shorter, as a name.

> "He calls her 'Doll' for short, although she doesn't like it."

in short. Stated briefly; by way of a summary; putting it in a few words.

> "In short, we are not convinced that we know all about the case."

> "He said, in short, that more research is needed before a definite decision can be reached."

make short work of. To handle and dispose of quickly; to accomplish without delay.

"He'll make short work of cleaning up the place."

run short of. To become depleted of; to have less than enough; to have no more.

"We will probably run short of bandages before the week is over."

"We are running short of certain parts but we have plenty of others."

short and sweet. Brief; consisting of few words; concise but adequate or clear; brief and not so pleasant (when expressed with irony).

"We didn't have too much time, so we asked him to make it short and sweet."

"She made it short and sweet. She simply told him to look for another girl."

short for. An abbreviated form of or for; being a shortened version of; a nickname for.

"In these parts, Jeff is short for Jeffersonville."

short of. 1. Not sufficiently supplied with something specified; lacking. 2. Somewhat less than; not equal to. 3. Not going as far as something specified; excluding. 4. Not good or far enough to reach a specified point or objective.

1. "He is somewhat short of cash at the moment."

2. "He is a good mathematician but short of the genius they said he is."

3. "Short of moving to another city, he would do anything to advance himself in his work."

4. "For the second year in a row they fell short of reaching the goal they had set for themselves."

Shot

a long shot. Someone regarded as having a small chance to win; a horse that has very little chance of winning; something not likely to succeed.

> "He likes to live dangerously and always puts his money on a long shot."

call one's shots. To reveal one's plans beforehand; to indicate ahead of time how one is going to do something.

> "You can hardly expect so adroit a politician to call his shots."

call the shots. To give the orders; to control; to be in authority or power.

> "He prefers to remain in this smaller organization where he can call the shots."

have a shot at. To have an opportunity to try one's luck or talents at something.

> "He knew that the business had been unsuccessful under several previous owners, but he wanted to have a shot at it anyway."

like a shot. Very quickly; figuratively, with the speed of a bullet.

> "The minute I mentioned her name he jumped up and was out of here like a shot."

not by a long shot. Not in the least; not at all; not even by a stretch of the imagination.

> "He is not a fool, not by a long shot."

> "He is not as clever as his brother, not by a long shot."

shot in the arm. Something that invigorates; a stimulus; a booster.

> "The encouraging letter was like a shot in the arm."

shot in the dark. A mere guess; a wild conjecture; a random choice; an accidental selection.

> "We had nothing to go by. It was a shot in the dark, but it turned out right."

Shoulder

cry one someone's shoulder. To relate one's troubles to someone in order to unburden oneself or to receive sympathy.

> "He was always a source of comfort to her when she needed to cry on someone's shoulder."

> "I don't mind his crying on my shoulder if it helps him."

put one's shoulder to the wheel. To work hard toward a particular goal; to apply oneself vigorously to a particular task; to increase one's effort.

> "I think there is still enough time left to prepare for the exams, if he will put his shoulder to the wheel."

rub shoulders with. To have a close association with; to mingle with; to be frequently in the company of; to be on familiar terms with.

> "In his work he must often rub shoulders with notorious characters."

> "He enjoys rubbing shoulders with the more prominent members of the entertainment world."

straight from the shoulder. With candor; frankly; without ulterior motives.

> "He is a person who speaks without evasion, straight from the shoulder."

> "I want you to tell me straight from the shoulder whether I am right or wrong."

give a cold shoulder. To be aloof toward someone; to show no interest in; disdain; show contempt toward.

> "We expected to be received with open arms, but they gave us a cold shoulder instead."

Shove

shove off. To leave; to start leaving; to begin one's departure from.

> "I think I should shove off now, before it gets dark."

Show

for show. Just in order to make a visual impression; for appearance only; to attract attention.

> "The grille is for show only; it is not functional."

give away the whole show. To reveal confidential information or details.

> "That careless remark of yours probably gave away the whole show."

run the show. To be in command; to manage, as a business; to have control over.

> "The son is actually the one who runs the show."

show in. To lead in; to guide into a place; to usher into, as an office.

> "I asked my receptionist to show him in."

show off. 1. To accentuate; to show to better advantage. 2. To display with ostentation; to exhibit in a manner designed to attract attention. 3. To behave in a manner that calls attention to one's talents or accomplishments.

> 1. "The white gold setting shows off the beauty of the sapphires."

2. "As usual, they showed off their latest weapons during the three-hour parade."

3. "He is showing off again in the hope of impressing his boss who is also attending this party."

show out. To show the way in leaving a place; to usher out; to conduct or lead out of a place.

"Would you please show the gentleman out? Thank you."

show up. 1. To appear prominently; to be obvious or apparent. 2. To make visible or noticeable; to bring to public attention; to expose. 3. To arrive, especially early or late; to come, especially unexpectedly. 4. To demonstrate that a specified person is inferior; to show that one is superior to another. 5. To make a prominent or favorable appearance, especially with respect to someone or something.

1. "The imperfection shows up even more on a polished surface."

2. "The trial showed up his underworld dealings."

3. "He did show up, but he was two hours late."

4. "Try not to show up the other girl at the office who happens to be the boss's niece."

5. "He shows up even better against a tougher opponent."

stand a show. To have at least a remote chance; to enjoy some likelihood at succeeding; to be likely to.

"With regard to the forthcoming match, does he have what it takes? Does he stand a show?"

"He hardly stands a show to get that job when there are so many other applicants with better qualifications."

steal the show. To divert public attention from another to oneself; to outdo someone and thus become the focus of attention; to get the applause properly deserved by another.

> "They say that a child or an animal is likely to steal the show even from a star performer."

> "She did all the work behind the scenes, but he stole the show with a five-minute appearance."

stop the show. To give such an excellent performance that the applause stops the continuity of the show; to disrupt a conversation, game, etc., by a clever remark, impressive entrance, etc.

> "Her stunning appearance stops the show whenever she enters."

> "This isn't exactly an act that is likely to stop the show."

Shuffle

shuffle off. To depart clumsily or hesitatingly; to take leave and start moving toward.

> "I had to do a great deal of talking and persuading before he finally shuffled off to help his father at the store."

Shut

shut down. 1. To settle over or upon; to cover. 2. To close; to stop the operation of. 3. To hinder or restrict. 4. To close an opening or an entrance.

1. "In this part of the world, darkness seems to shut down more rapidly."

2. "In another year the plant will shut down for good."

> "The factory shuts down for two weeks every summer so that the employees may have their vacations at the same time."

3. "The government shut down on the export of certain strategic materials."

4. "I think we should shut down the windows before we go."

shut in. 1. To surround or enclose. 2. To confine to a place; to cause to remain in a particular place.

1. "We decided not to put up the fence because it would make her feel shut in."

2. "Without the use of his car, he felt shut in, and he didn't like the feeling."

"Even the cast on her leg didn't shut her in. She managed to attend the convention in spite of it."

shut off. 1. To discontinue the flow of. 2. To block the access to or passage through. 3. To separate; to sever communication with.

1. "The flow of gas was shut off at the intersection of the two highways."

"The electricity will have to be shut off at the substation."

2. "The main highway was shut off because of resurfacing work."

3. "The capital was shut off from the rest of the world for nearly a week."

shut out. 1. To keep out; to deny admission. 2. To prevent from being seen; to obscure. 3. In a game, to keep an opposing team or contestant from scoring.

1. "He was obviously intoxicated, but we were unable to shut him out from the clubhouse."

2. "These tall shade trees shut out the sun most of the day."

"The bush does not completely shut out the entrance."

3. "They not only won the game but also shut out the visiting team."

shut up. 1. To confine; to restrict the movement of; to place in an enclosure. 2. To stop talking; to become silent; to silence. 3. To limit access to; to close all the roads or entrances to.

1. "This man should be shut up in some kind of institution."

2. "He didn't have a chance to say anything because she wouldn't shut up."

"We tried to shut him up, but he paid no attention."

3. "The prolonged rain flooded the roads and shut up the old farmhouse."

Side

on the side. 1. In addition to one's main occupation or work. 2. As an adjunct to the main topic or issue. 3. Inclined or tending toward something specified.

1. "He does a little painting and minor repair work on the side."

2. "The conferees agreed to consider the pension proposal on the side."

3. "I would judge him to be on the liberal side."

"This paint is a little on the dark side. I would prefer something lighter."

side by side. 1. Close together; in association. 2. Situated or moving next to each other or one another.

1. "Although sharply divided ideologically, the two factions learned to live peacefully side by side."

2. "They left the house walking side by side, as if nothing happened."

side with. To be in favor of, or to support, one group or party in a dispute.

> "He always sides with his older sister in matters of household management."

take sides. To feel or express sympathy with one party in a dispute; to align oneself with one or the other side in a controversy.

> "I do not wish to express my opinion in this matter because it would give the impression that I am taking sides."

Sight

a sight for sore eyes. Something so pleasing to see that it cheers or inspires; a handsome or beautiful person; something one wishes to see.

> "The new house of worship was a sight for sore eyes."

> "That girl is certainly a sight for sore eyes."

at first sight. When first seen or noticed; on the first impression and without further consideration; from the very beginning.

> "At first sight, he seemed like the right man for the job, but that was before we received the report on him."

> "He believes that love at first sight is for kids only."

at sight. 1. At once, or as soon as seen. 2. On demand; when presented.

> 1. "He can add a column of figures at sight."

> 2. "I can assure you that this I.O.U. will be paid at sight."

by sight. Only by appearance; not by name or by personal acquaintance.

> "I know the man you are describing by sight, but I never met him and I don't know his name."

catch sight of. To get a glimpse of; to notice briefly; to espy.

"I caught sight of him in the crowd for a moment,
but I soon lost him. I don't know if he saw me."

know by sight. To be able to recognize someone or something on the basis of a previous visual experience. See entry *by sight.*

lose sight of. 1. To be unable to follow someone with the eye; to lose someone from one's field of vision. 2. To cease knowing about someone's activities or whereabouts.

1. "I saw him briefly in the crowd but then lost sight of him."

2. "After he resigned from this company, we corresponded for a while but after a while I lost sight of him."

not by a long sight. Certainly not; not by far; not at all.

"We haven't given up hope, not by a long sight."

"He hasn't got us fooled at all, not by a long sight."

on sight. As soon as one sees someone or something; as soon as noticed.

"If he returned to the States, he would be arrested on sight."

out of sight. 1. Not within the range of one's vision; so far removed that one or it cannot be seen. 2. Far removed; remote. 3. Beyond normal limits; out of reach; excessively high.

1. "By the time I got to the door, he was out of sight."

2. "There is that old saying that out of sight is out of mind; that is, if one is away or far removed, one is forgotten."

3. "This expensive house is clearly out of sight for a man with his income."

sight unseen. Without previous sight of; without having a chance to see or examine.

> "He had heard so much about the property in question that he was willing to buy it sight unseen."

Sign

sign away. To give away or transfer the ownership of something by signing an appropriate document; to dispose of by signing or by a similar procedure.

> "He later regretted that he signed away his right to his mother's estate."

sign off. 1. In radio and television, to stop broadcasting, usually at the end of the broadcast day. 2. To cease talking.

> 1. "The station usually signs off at midnight, but that night, because of a tornado alert, it stayed on all night."
>
> 2. "When he takes a drink, it is difficult to get him to sign off. He talks for hours."

sign on. To commit oneself to a particular job, usually by signing an agreement.

> "After finishing his internship, he signed on as a ship's doctor for a year."

sign up. To sign on (which see); to join an organization or a service; to enlist; to engage someone.

> "Her brother signed up with the Air Force, something he always wanted to do."

Silk

hit the silk. To parachute from an airplane or other aircraft.

> "The engine began to act up and he thought he would have to hit the silk."

Simmer

simmer down. To cease being agitated; to quiet down emotionally; to calm oneself.

> "I didn't even try to reason with him until he had a chance to simmer down."

> "Now, simmer down and let's talk this over quietly."

Sing

sing out. To utter in a loud voice; to call out for all to hear; to reveal, as one's opinion.

> "If you want them to come back, you'd better sing out here and now."

> "It isn't always advisable to sing out one's thoughts, especially about a controversial subject."

Sink

sink in. To make an impression upon the mind; to be comprehended or understood.

> "My impression is that your admonition didn't quite sink in. You may have to talk to him again."

Sit

sit down. To occupy a seat; to put oneself in a sitting position; to lower oneself into a chair or onto a bench.

> "He rarely sits down when he talks to me. He likes to pace around the room."

> "All right, let's sit down and talk about it."

sit in. To sit with others, as in attendance of a conference; to participate in some function which involves sitting.

> "Several foreign correspondents were allowed to sit in on the hearings."

sit on. 1. To keep certain information from becoming public; to suppress the publication or dissemination of news. 2. To rebuke; scold; reprimand. 3. To be in conference about something; to investigate.

> 1. "Although the inquiry was completed in September, the chairman of the committee decided to sit on the report until after the elections."
>
> 2. "She really sat on him for coming half an hour late."
>
> 3. "Several local, state, and federal investigating groups sat on the case, but the conclusions were neither unanimous nor convincing."

sit upon. Same as *sit on*, which see.

sit out. 1. To endure or stay till the end. 2. To abstain from taking part in some activity, as a dance, often by remaining seated. 3. To excel in endurance; to outdo or outlast.

> 1. "Although he soon realized that he had seen the picture before, he decided to say nothing and to sit it out because his girl friend seemed to be enjoying it."
>
> 2. "She did go to the dance but sat out most of the dances because of her sprained ankle."
>
> 3. "It must have been his clear conscience that enabled him to sit out three interrogators."

sit pretty. To be in a good financial or economic condition; to have an easy and well-paying job; to receive and be assured of a comfortable income.

> "Yes, he did have a rough time in the beginning, but I am told that he is sitting pretty now."

sit tight. 1. To refrain from action, pending some development. 2. To maintain one's stand or attitude; to be or remain firm.

1. "The best thing is to do nothing at this time.
   Let's just sit tight and see what the market does
   in the next week or two."

2. "I was unable to dissuade him. He is still sitting
   tight with regard to his opinion that he ought to
   leave his present job."

sit up. 1. To move up from a reclining position to a sitting position. 2. To refrain from going to bed; to remain up and about
instead of retiring for the night. 3. To take notice of something;
to show a response of interest to something said or done by a
change in one's position or by some motion, as a movement of
the head. 4. To sit upright or erect; to straighten one's spine
while sitting, to eliminate a slouch.

1. "He spends most of his time in bed in a recum-
   bent position, but he does sit up to take his
   meals."

2. "Young man! This girl sat up till three in the
   morning waiting for your call."

3. "All present surely sat up when another layoff of
   workers at the plant was announced."

4. "How many times have I told you to sit up when
   you read! You slouch like an old man."

Six

at sixes and sevens. 1. In a state of disagreement; in dispute; at
odds. 2. In a state of confusion; in disorder.

1. "I thought that they had decided what to do, but
   I see now that they are still at sixes and sevens."

2. "Although the lawyers have worked on his estate
   for more than a year, the fiscal situation is still
   at sixes and sevens."

Size

of a size. Of the same or nearly the same size, extent, or magnitude.

> "The two estates are of a size, although the land of
> one is much more valuable than that of the other."

size up. 1. To inspect or examine in order to form a judgment of; to make a mental estimate of a thing, situation, or person. 2. To meet certain requirements.

> 1. "It didn't take her long to size him up as a philanderer."
>
> 2. "He made a good personal impression on us, but when we inquired about his past, he didn't quite size up."

Skate

skate on thin ice. To put oneself, or to be, in a dangerous or precarious situation; to continue doing something in the face of danger; to be engaged in a risky project.

> "When a bank allows itself to remain with so little
> cash on hand, it is skating on thin ice."

> "A politician would be skating on thin ice if he took
> a stand in opposition of a popular cause."

Skeleton

skeleton at the feast. A person, thing, or occurrence that causes a joyous occasion to turn into one of sadness or sorrow.

> "As far as she was concerned, his presence at the
> birthday party was a skeleton at the feast."

skeleton in the closet. A shameful secret about a member of a family, or the family as a whole, which, if revealed, would be a source of disgrace or great embarrassment.

"We don't know exactly what it is, but they obviously have a skeleton in the closet."

"Their daughter had a child out of wedlock, and I suppose this is their skeleton in the closet."

Skids

on the skids. On the way down from a position of power, prestige, rank, etc.; headed in the direction of calamity or disgrace; becoming impoverished.

"Until a few years ago he had a good business and was a respected member of the community. Then he started drinking, experimenting with drugs, etc., and now he is on the skids."

put the skids under. To do something that will cause someone to fail or be frustrated; to cause someone to suffer a defeat.

"He was attending night classes and doing fine until he met this girl. She really put the skids under him."

Skin

be no skin off one's back. To be of no interest or concern to one; to have no effect whatever (on someone).

"You can sell the car or keep it. That is no skin off my back."

by the skin of one's teeth. By a very small margin; narrowly; just barely.

"Yes, he passed, but by the skin of his teeth."

"I would like to see him win decisively, not by the skin of his teeth."

get under one's skin. 1. To annoy painfully; to irritate so as to leave a lasting sense of discomfort; to anger. 2. To affect amorously; to make an indelible impression, usually in a favorable sense.

    1. "His constant picking at his necktie gets under her skin, but he doesn't know about it."

    2. "Her tearful face and pathetic appeal really got under his skin."

    "For some reason, this girl, who is not particularly pretty, got under his skin."

have a thick skin. To be indifferent to the opinions of others, especially with regard to criticism, insults, etc.; to be callous.

    "He is one of the few actors I know who have a thick skin. He is absolutely unmoved by the critical reviews."

have a thin skin. To be excessively sensitive to the opinions of others, especially with regard to criticism, insults, etc.; to have a tendency to be hurt or offended by unfriendly or critical remarks.

    "He has a thin skin and doesn't take kidding very well, so let's talk to him in a serious tone."

in *or* with a whole skin. Without being harmed; without bodily harm; unscathed.

    "In spite of his big mouth, he got out of the altercation with a whole skin."

    "He took part in many brawls, but he is still in a whole skin. He must be a better slugger than we think."

save one's skin. To save one's life; to avoid being killed; to escape injury or harm.

    "Some people will do just about anything to save their skin; others are more stalwart."

skin alive. 1. To censure or scold vehemently; to reprimand violently. 2. To defeat an enemy or an opponent in a decisive manner; to subdue overwhelmingly.

1. "He is a very difficult man to work for. He'll skin you alive for being late five minutes."

2. "That's hardly a fair match. The champ will skin the challenger alive."

Skittles

beer and skittles. Nothing but pleasure; easy or relaxed enjoyment.

"The job looks a great deal more attractive than it really is. It is certainly not all beer and skittles."

not all beer and skittles. See under *beer and skittles.*

Sky

out of a clear sky. Unexpectedly; without warning; suddenly; without notice.

"No, I had no idea he was in Florida. The call came out of a clear sky."

out of a clear blue sky. Same as *out of a clear sky,* which see.

to the skies. To the highest level; to the utmost; lavishly; extravagantly.

"I was disappointed in him, perhaps because you had praised him to the skies and he didn't quite live up to it."

Slate

a clean slate. 1. A record of a person free from misconduct, discredit, etc. 2. A beginning unburdened by past experiences; a condition of not being handicapped by debts, previous errors, etc.

1. "We don't hire employees without checking. He has a clean slate."

2. "He sold his old business, moved to another location, and started with a clean slate."

Sleep

sleep away. 1. To waste something, as a particular time or period, in sleeping. 2. To cure of some disorder by sleeping.

> 1. "By getting up so late you sleep away the best part of the day, in my opinion."

> 2. "It seems that nothing she does relieves her headache, but she usually sleeps it away."

sleep in. To sleep at the place where one works or is employed, as a domestic servant.

> "We would like her to sleep in, but she prefers to go home every night except when the weather is bad."

sleep off. To cure oneself of some discomfort by sleeping; to get rid of, as a headache, by sleeping.

> "He is in a bad humor today, but he'll sleep it off."

> "Go to bed and sleep it off. That's the best medicine."

sleep out. To sleep away from the place where one works or is employed, as a domestic servant; to sleep outside the place of one's employment.

> "Two or three of the girls sleep in, but the others sleep out; There isn't enough room for them."

Sleeve

laugh up *or* in one's sleeve. To laugh invisibly or inwardly at something or someone while remaining serious or indifferent outwardly.

> "She used to laugh up her sleeve when he would engage in his spirited dissertations about the alleged brilliant business deals he had pulled off."

up one's sleeve. Held in secret reserve but ready for use; designating something concealed that is advantageous to its possessor in an argument or contest.

> "He must have something up his sleeve to take this reversal so calmly."

> "His confident attitude makes me think that he has something up his sleeve."

Slide

let slide. To let something remain unattended; to fail to take care of; to let go without challenging, opposing, arguing against, etc.

> "We were so busy with the rebuilding of the house that we let the flower garden slide."

> "She hasn't been feeling well lately and she let the housework slide, but otherwise she is a very meticulous housekeeper."

> "I advised him to let it slide. The attorney's fee would amount to more than he could possibly collect."

Slip

give someone the slip. To escape from someone's custody or company; to elude or manage not to meet.

> "While we were jostling through the crowd, the boy gave me the slip."

> "I saw him coming, but I managed to give him the slip, pretending that I was in a hurry to catch the bus."

let slip. To say something inadvertently thus revealing a secret or intimacy.

"She didn't mean to, of course, but she did let it slip that they are not living together and that she plans to sue for divorce."

"Be careful. Don't let slip that you know anything about it."

slip a cog. To make a mistake in judgment; to do something unreasonable; to err.

"Once in a while he slips a cog, but generally he is a level-headed individual who does the right thing at the right time."

slip into. To don a garment that is easy to put on; to clothe oneself with something comfortable, as pajamas.

"This formal clothing I have had on all day is most uncomfortable. Let me slip into something else."

slip off. To remove a garment; to divest oneself of a piece of clothing, especially something easily removed.

"You don't have to get undressed for this examination. Just slip off your blouse."

slip on. To put on a garment, especially something comfortable and easily donned.

"The nurse instructed the patient to slip on a gown and lie down on the table."

slip out of. To take off a piece of clothing, especially with ease and dexterity.

"She stepped into the other room to slip out of her dress."

slip one over. To deceive; to trick; to succeed in cheating someone, especially by diverting the person's attention from the real issue.

"I really didn't notice the defect in the material until I got home. He slipped one over on me this time."

slip over. To examine superficially; to read quickly, without sufficient attention.

> "I must admit that I just slipped over this matter,
> but I will read it more carefully tomorrow."

slip someone's mind. To escape from one's mind; to forget; fail to recall or remember, especially to do something.

> "I did mean to call her, but it slipped my mind."

slip something over on. To succeed in perpetrating a deceitful act upon a person; to fool or cheat.

> "This is not the blanket we picked out at the store.
> They are trying to slip something over on the customers."

slip up. To make a mistake in judgment, action, etc.; to err; to forget to do something.

> "I slipped up on that one. I shouldn't have told her
> I intended to make a change in the office personnel."

> "It is a good piece of property and we intended to
> bid on it, but somehow we slipped up."

Slop

slop over. 1. To be excessively sentimental over someone or something. 2. To cause a liquid to spill over the edge of a container; to overflow.

> 1. "They love each other, but she objects to his slopping over her in public."

> 2. "He slopped over some of the punch while carrying the bowl to the table."

Small

feel small. To feel unimportant; to experience humiliation; to regard oneself as not coming up to a particular standard.

"He said that he feels small in the company of this illustrious man."

"Such courage makes some people feel rather small."

sing small. To behave in a humble manner, especially after being supercilious.

"Having lost his good job he sings small nowadays, but he used to be quite arrogant."

Smell

smell out. To look for something by smelling or as if by smelling; to search carefully; to find or discover by smelling (or as if by smelling).

"If there is an informer among them, they'll smell him out."

smell up. To cause a room or similar place to have a bad odor; to impart, or fill with, an unpleasant odor.

"We like the taste of cabbage, but the cooking smells up the whole apartment."

Smile

smile at. 1. To bear patiently; to endure. 2. To treat with kindness or benevolence.

1. "Some people can smile at their misfortunes, but she is not one of them."

2. "After many years of hardship fortune smiled at him. He is doing very well."

smile away. To dismiss with a smile or by smiling; to cover up or disguise with a smile.

"She tried to smile away her anxiety, but it was clear that she was deeply concerned."

smile on *or* **upon.** 1. To regard favorably; to encourage. 2. Same as *smile at,* definition 2.

> 1. "While he didn't exactly smile on my proposal, he wasn't vehemently against it."

Smoke

smoke out. To drive someone out of hiding; to cause a secret to be revealed.

> "The object is to smoke out the instigators of the riots."

go up in smoke. To be consumed by fire; to fail; to end unsuccessfully.

> "Before the firemen could get to the scene, the house went up in smoke."

> "When the higher court refused to consider the case, his last hope went up in smoke."

Smooth

smooth away. To make smooth by removing irregularities; to do away with obstacles, opposition, difficulties, etc.

> "Before we submit the proposal, let's smooth away some of the provisions that are likely to cause resentment."

smooth over. To treat something as if it were unimportant; to minimize the gravity of something; to pass over lightly.

> "She tried to smooth over her typographical errors, but he didn't buy it."

Snap

a snap. Something very easy to accomplish; an assured success; something one can count on.

> "With this power saw, cutting down the tree will be a snap."

> "Swimming the English Channel isn't exactly a snap."

snap one's fingers at. To regard something with indifference or contempt; to look upon as unimportant.

> "I did suggest that he stay over because of the expected heavy weather, but he snapped his fingers at the suggestion."

snap out of it. To succeed in putting aside a worry or anxiety; to recover from a particular state of mind, as a mental depression.

> "She has had several frustrating love affairs and she always snaps out of it. She will this time."

snap someone's head off. To criticize harshly and impatiently; to bark at; to subject to a burst of anger.

> "All right, he is wrong, but you didn't have to snap his head off."

not give a snap. To be indifferent; not care; to regard lightly; not give a damn.

> "They don't give a snap about what others think."

> "I know he doesn't like the idea, but I don't give a snap."

Sneak

sneak out of. To depart stealthily; to leave furtively; to escape doing something in an underhand manner.

> "She usually manages to sneak out of washing the dishes by making a phone call or some other subterfuge."

Sneeze

not to be sneezed at. Not unimportant; not insignificant; to be taken seriously; not to be taken lightly.

> "The quarterly bonus is not to be sneezed at. It amounts to about a thousand dollars a year."

nothing to be sneezed at. Not something that should be taken lightly or disregarded.

> "The free housing that goes with the job is nothing to be sneezed at."

Sniffles

the sniffles. 1. The common cold, especially as it affects the nose. 2. The sniffing which accompanies a crying spell; a bout of crying and sniffling.

> 1. "I was chilled last night and I think I am coming down with the sniffles."

> 2. "She became so emotional that she had to ask for his handkerchief to control her crying and the sniffles."

Snuff

up to snuff. Up to a specified or expected standard; up to one's best, as in health, performance, etc.

> "He is a good man, but his performance hasn't been up to snuff lately. I think he has some domestic trouble."

> "She took a rain check, saying she didn't feel up to snuff."

So

and so on *or* forth. And more of the same kind or in like manner; and continued in a similar way.

"She spends her day doing housework, watching television, reading, and so on."

"She told her doctor about her headaches, nervousness, and so forth, but she did not mention the fact that her husband had left her."

so as. For the purpose of; in order that; having as a goal or aim.

"We stamped 'Special Delivery' all over the carton so as to make sure that it will be noticed at the post office."

so to speak. To use a figurative expression; in a manner of speaking; putting it in a somewhat unusual way.

"I would suggest that we don't put all our eggs in one basket, so to speak."

so what? Assuming that it is so, what difference does it make? Even if so, it makes no difference.

"All right, they don't believe us. So what?"

"Granted that we might have offended them, so what?"

Soap

no soap. Not accepted; to no avail; rejected; nothing doing!

"If I told you once, I told you a dozen times, no soap! I am not going."

Song

for a song. At a bargain price; for almost nothing; for very little money.

"In that economically depressed region, with so many people out of work, you can get a house for a song."

song and dance. An evasive account or explanation; a story intended to cover up or mislead.

> "Don't give me that song and dance again about a headache. If you'd be interested in seeing me you wouldn't have a headache!"

Sorts

of sorts. Of some kind, but not of a superior kind; of poor quality; of a mediocre sort.

> "He is a television repairman of sorts, but I wouldn't depend on his opinion that you need another receiver."

out of sorts. 1. Not feeling well physically; somewhat ill. 2. In a bad humor; depressed; irritable.

> 1. "He isn't coming tonight. His wife phoned and said that he has a cold and is out of sorts."
>
> 2. "I don't know what was the matter with her last night. She was blue and out of sorts."

sort of. To a certain extent; in a small way; somewhat.

> "She says that she feels sort of nauseated and dizzy."

Sound

sound off. 1. To express one's opinion freely, especially in order to complain. 2. To speak in a boastful way; to brag.

> 1. "Whenever the subject comes up, he sounds off in opposition although he knows it won't do a bit of good."
>
> 2. "There he goes again, sounding off about his marksmanship."

Soup

in the soup. In difficulties; in an unpleasant situation; in deep trouble.

> "He'll be in the soup when he gets home. His wife
> is jealous and very suspicious."

soup up. 1. With reference to an automobile, to increase the
capacity for speed. 2. To enliven; to pep up; to add spirit.

> 1. "These kids tear down the road at eighty miles
> per hour in their souped-up cars."

> 2. "His anecdotes and witticisms souped up the
> otherwise dull party."

Speak

speak by the book. To state something with authority, quoting
or as if quoting from a source book.

> "With regard to electronics, you can depend on what
> he says. He speaks by the book."

speak for. 1. To speak in behalf of someone or something. 2. To
reserve for someone; to preempt.

> 1. "I am not speaking for the group; I am speaking
> only for myself."

> 2. "Sorry, young man, but this girl is spoken for."

speak of. To speak about a particular person or subject; to talk
about.

> "It is difficult to avoid speaking of something that
> one worries about."

> "Neither he nor his wife spoke of the accident until
> I brought it up."

speak out. To express one's opinions frankly; to speak without
hesitation, especially about a controversial subject.

> "He spoke out at a time when dissent was not popu-
> lar."

> "In this country you can at least speak out, some-
> thing you are not allowed in totalitarian countries."

speak up. 1. To speak in a loud voice; to speak louder or more clearly. 2. Same as *speak out,* which see.

> 1. "We can't hear you in the back. Please speak up."
>
> 2. "He doesn't mind speaking up even if it does get him into trouble at times."

speak well for. To indicate a favorable condition with regard to someone or something; to be to the credit of.

> "Their modest home speaks well for their sense of values. His salary is relatively small."

to speak of. Worthy of consideration or mention; deserving an evaluation.

> "There were some minerals in the sample, but not enough to speak of."

Speaking

be (*or* not be) on speaking terms. To be, or not be, sufficiently familar with someone to make conversation logical; to be, or not be, on good terms with someone.

> "I am on speaking terms with him, but I don't know that much about him."
>
> "They had an argument one day recently and haven't been on speaking terms since."

Speed

at full speed. 1. As fast as possible; at the utmost speed. 2. As diligently as possible; with one's maximum effort.

> 1. "We have never driven it at full speed, but it would no doubt go over a hundred."
>
> 2. "He is working at it at full speed, but I doubt that he can finish the job by tomorrow night."

at top speed. Same as *at full speed,* which see.

speed up. To increase the speed of something in motion; to do faster; to increase one's effort.

"When the voltage is increased, the fan speeds up."

"The new and improved equipment will undoubtedly speed up production."

Spell

cast a spell on. To win someone's affection or love, as if by enchantment or a spell.

"He paid little attention to girls before, but this one must have cast a spell on him. He acts like a fellow in love."

spell out. 1. To explain in simple terms; to make something perfectly clear. 2. To name or write each letter of a word.

1. "Well, if you don't get the message, let me spell it out for you. You are too old for this job!"

2. "In this office we like to spell out the title 'Dr.', namely, 'Doctor'."

Spirit

out of spirits. In a depressed mood; gloomy; unhappy; mournful.

"Whenever it rains you will find her out of spirits."

Spit

spit and image. An almost exact likeness; a perfect counterpart or image of a person.

"They are not twins, but she is the spit and image of her sister."

spitting image. Same as *spit and image,* which see.

spit on. To express defiance or contempt by spitting or ejecting saliva upon.

> "He said that he wouldn't even bother to spit on his opponent, that's how little he thinks of him."

Spite

in spite of. Notwithstanding (the fact that); regardless of a specified phenomenon.

> "In spite of the many interruptions he completed the job on time."

Splash

make a splash. To become suddenly popular, especially by a spectacular exploit, successful venture, etc.

> "He made a splash in the 50's with a very successful record, but we have not heard about him since."

Sponge

throw in the sponge. To acknowledge one's defeat; to admit that one has lost to an opponent; give up.

> "Although he was on the losing end of the match, he wasn't ready to throw in the sponge."

toss in the sponge. Same as *throw in the sponge,* which see.

Spoon

born with a silver spoon in one's mouth. Born to riches or other advantages or opportunities.

> "He comes to the office, but he doesn't really have to work. He was born with a silver spoon in his mouth."

Sport

in sport. As a joke; not seriously or in earnest; to cause mirth or laughter.

> "I hope you are not taking his remark seriously. I am sure he said it in sport."

make sport of. To make fun of; to belittle with ridicule; to mock.

> "He is not a good subject to make sport of. He is very sensitive."

Spot

hit the high spots. To consider or mention the most important points or parts of some topic or matter.

> "In so short a summary we were able to hit only the high spots."

hit the spot. To satisfy a particular need very specifically; to quench a desire in an effective way.

> "Sometimes, a sweet drink hits the spot, but at other times something tangy or bitter, like beer, does it."

in a spot. In an unpleasant situation; in some kind of difficulty.

> "He is in a spot. He promised to referee the game, but now he finds that he has to work overtime."

on the spot. 1. Immediately; without delay. 2. In an unpleasant or difficult situation; in a spot. 3. At the place talked about or described. 4. In a situation in which one has to say or do something which he would rather not.

> 1. "This matter will have to be settled on the spot. It cannot wait another day."
>
> 2. "While he was traveling abroad, the dollar was devalued and he found himself on the spot."
>
> 3. "They set off the burglar alarm and were apprehended on the spot."

4. "I had not intended to reveal that the property was actually sold, but her question about the matter put me on the spot."

touch one's *or* a sore spot. To mention or bring up a subject about which one is sensitive or which one would rather not discuss or be reminded of.

"When she said something about liking a tall man, she touched his sore spot because he is rather short."

Spread

spread oneself. To make an effort to create a good impression; to try to ingratiate oneself.

"It was quite obvious to everyone present that the girl was spreading herself in order to impress the handsome visitor."

spread oneself thin. To divide one's attention among several projects so that none is adequately attended to; to do so many things at one time that one's mental or physical health is endangered.

"He is a good craftsman, but he spreads himself thin by taking on too many jobs at one time."

Spur

on the spur of the moment. Without previous thought or deliberation; on the basis of a sudden impulse.

"Our decision to take this trip was made on the spur of the moment, therefore we had no time to make the necessary preparations."

win one's spurs. To do something that establishes one's reputation or proves one's ability.

"He is reputedly a brilliant lawyer, but he hasn't won his spurs yet. He has yet to handle a difficult case."

Square

on the square. Honest; sincere; just; fair.

> "As far as our experience with them is concerned, they have always been on the square."

out of square. Not in agreement or harmony; not correct; irregular.

> "Both reports are from supposedly reliable sources, but they are out of square."

square away. To prepare for something; to get ready, especially by disposing of obstacles.

> "It was ten o'clock before we squared away for breakfast."

square off. To assume a posture or position suitable for defense or offense; to take a position suitable for a particular purpose.

> "They squared off for a fight, but their buddies separated them before any harm was done."

> "We squared off for a long and hard winter by laying in supplies, etc., but it wasn't really all that cold."

square oneself. To make amends for a wrong that one has done to another; to restore cordial relations with a person that one has wronged.

> "I don't know how successful he is, but I know that he is trying to square himself with his girl for something he had done."

square peg in a round hole. See under *peg*.

square the circle. To attempt to do something that seems or is impossible.

> "Trying to reason with him is like trying to square the circle; it's impossible."

square up. To settle an obligation or debt; to pay or satisfy a claim.

> "His father will no doubt square up his debt. The boy certainly has no money."

Squeak

narrow squeak. An escape, as from a danger, by a narrow margin; a bare avoidance of death, injury, etc.

> "That was surely a narrow squeak when they skidded on the icy road and almost hit another car head-on."

close squeak. Same as *narrow squeak,* which see.

squeak through. To succeed in winning, passing, beating, etc., by a narrow margin.

> "He passed the examination but barely squeaked through."

squeak by. Same as *squeak through,* which see.

Stack

blow one's stack. To lose one's self-control and become abusive, physically or verbally; to become uncontrollably angry.

> "I never saw him so angry. He blew his stack when I mentioned his former girl friend."

stack the cards. To prearrange things unfairly for the benefit of a particular person.

> "The poor fellow didn't have a chance as far as the job was concerned. The manager stacked the cards in favor of his nephew."

Stage

by easy stages. Proceeding in an unhurried manner; marked by frequent periods of rest or by pauses.

"Our trip to California was pleasant because we drove by easy stages, spending as much as two or three days in some towns along the way."

hold the stage. To attract attention more than others; to be the center of interest or social attraction.

"Her beauty and personality enable her to hold the stage wherever she goes."

Stake

at stake. In a position of risk, as of losing, injuring, etc.; placed in a situation of hazard.

"Not only is his reputation at stake, but he stands to lose a few thousand dollars."

pull up stakes. To move from a place where one has lived for a substantial length of time.

"When you have lived as many years in a small town as we have, it is not easy to pull up stakes."

stake out. To maintain a place or a person under surveillance; to assign a person, as a detective or policeman, to maintain watch over a particular place or person.

"Hundreds of plainclothes men were staked out along the route of the President's scheduled visit."

Stand

make a stand. To assume a position suitable for resistance or defense; to assert one's position or opinion.

"They delayed as long as they could, but finally they had to make a stand on the sales tax issue."

stand a chance. To have a chance or likelihood, as of succeeding, surviving, etc.

"The challenger is a good boxer, but he doesn't stand a chance in the forthcoming bout with the champ."

stand by. 1. To remain faithful to an agreement, commitment, etc. 2. To be of help; to give aid; to uphold. 3. To keep oneself ready for a particular action; to await one's turn. 4. In broadcasting, to remain tuned in to a particular station during a break in transmission.

1. "He stood by his promise to help with the work although he no longer shared in the possible benefits of the project."

2. "He could always depend on her standing by him when he had a disagreement with his employer."

3. "The firemen stood by while the wreckers attempted to extricate the victims from the collapsed building."

4. "The radio announcer asked the listeners to stand by for a few minutes to clear up some technical difficulties."

stand down. To leave, or step down from, the witness stand in a court of law.

"The witness refused to stand down and continued with his harangue."

stand for. 1. To allow to occur or continue; to tolerate. 2. To represent; to symbolize. 3. To be in favor of; to promote.

1. "You may be sure that she won't stand for this kind of abusive language directed at her child."

2. "The emblem stands for an accomplishment beyond the call of duty."

3. "The organization stands for the attainment of justice for the little man and for minority groups."

stand in with. To have a friendly relationship with someone; to be in a position of influence with somebody.

"If any man can help you in this siutation, he is the one. He stands in with several members of the zoning board."

stand off. To keep at a distance; to discourage friendliness or intimacy.

> "She was an expert in standing off fellows with her icy look of aloofness."

stand on. 1. To rely or depend on; to rest or be based on. 2. To be demanding or fastidious about something.

> 1. "The entire project stands on the results of one survey which might not have been accurate."

> 2. "If I were you, I wouldn't stand on formality. I would call him."

stand one's ground. To hold on to one's opinion, position, etc., especially against opposition.

> "Although several members of the board denounced his action and his motives, he stood his ground."

stand out. 1. To attract attention; to be prominent or conspicuous. 2. To protrude. 3. To refuse to comply; to maintain a stand of resistance.

> 1. "His handsome appearance causes him to stand out in any group or crowd."

> 2. "The chimney was built to stand out from the side of the house."

> 3. "The national leadership signed the agreement, but several local unions are still standing out."

stand over. 1. To schedule for a later time; to postpone; to delay. 2. To watch closely; to monitor or supervise.

> 1. "The illness of his wife caused him to stand over the completion of the manuscript until the end of the summer."

> 2. "The child will not study unless you stand over her."

stand to. 1. To continue with something without interruption; 2. To maintain; to persist.

1. "The outside noise did disturb him, but he stood to his studies."

2. "In spite of all logic she stands to her childish accusation."

stand up. 1. To be durable; to be capable of resisting attack; to withstand denunciation. 2. To disappoint someone by not keeping an appointment.

1. "This paint will stand up much better than the other kind in the sun."

"In the final analysis this sort of proof will not stand up. We need something more substantial."

2. "She still insists that he stood her up, but he claims that they had no date that evening."

stand up for. To make an effort in defending someone; to lend support; to take up the cause of someone.

"He stands up for her every time, even when he knows she is wrong."

stand up to. To oppose courageously; to confront without fear; to face bravely.

"He is a tough little fellow. He'll stand up to anybody."

Star

see stars. To have a sensation of flashing lights before the eyes, especially when caused by a blow on the head or any severe pain.

"When the brick fell on his toes he saw stars and could not refrain from crying out."

thank one's lucky stars. To be grateful for one's good luck; to appreciate one's good fortune.

> "You can thank your lucky stars that the car didn't quit on you while you were on that side road. You would have never gotten any help there."

Stare

stare down. To disconcert someone by staring at him intently; to gaze at someone so steadily as to cause him to look away in discomfort.

> "She tried to stare him down, but he was too impudent and she had to give up."

stare one in the face. To be imminent or about to happen; to be unavoidable; to confront.

> "Eviction stared them in the face when the higher court finally ruled in their favor."

Start

start out. 1. To begin a journey. 2. To make a start in some activity.

> 1. "They plan to start out on the trip before dawn."
>
> 2. "He is a pharmacist now but he started out as an optometrist when he was a young man."

start up. 1. To initiate, or be initiated, suddenly; to form or be formed. 2. To cause a motor, as of an automobile, to begin running.

> 1. "Many restaurants and novelty shops started up around the new park."
>
> 2. "He had difficulty starting up the car this morning."

State

in a state. In a condition of excitement or agitation; in a difficult or unpleasant situation.

> "Having had a row with his business partner, he was in a state when we arrived, but he soon calmed down."

> "Last year, he was in a state, financially, but things have improved since."

lie in state. Of a deceased person, to be displayed publicly, with honors, before burial.

> "Thousands of people filed by the coffin as the President lay in state."

the States. The United States (usually so called by people outside this country).

> "Many Europeans regard the States as a latter-day Utopia."

State's Evidence

turn state's evidence. Of a participant in a crime, to give evidence for the prosecution, in a criminal case, against the other participants.

> "One of the arrested men promised to turn state's evidence."

Stave

stave off. To cause not to happen; to ward off; to keep off by some means.

> "He feels that by taking massive doses of vitamin C, he can stave off the colds that he usually gets during the winter."

Steady

go steady. To keep company with or date only one person of the opposite sex; to be on the level of sweethearts.

> "Neither of these kids has ever dated anyone but each other. They have been going steady since their high school days."

Steam

blow off steam. To release emotional tension or anger by talking or acting in an excited manner.

> "He is usually much more restrained. I do believe he was blowing off steam."

let off steam. Same as *blow off steam,* which see.

Steep

steeped in. Imbued with; saturated or permeated with; inured to, as cruelty.

> "These children are brought up in a tradition steeped in respect for one's elders."

Steer

steer clear of. To avoid becoming involved with; to keep away from.

> "I advised him to steer clear of that crowd for fear he might become tainted by the association."

Stem

from stem to stern. The entire length of a ship; from one end of something to the other end; throughout.

> "We searched the place from stem to stern but couldn't find the jewel box."

Step

in step. In rhythm with the movement of another; in harmony, conformity, or agreement.

> "The new methods of merchandising are in step with the changing habits of the consumers."

keep step. To keep up with; to follow with the proper speed so as not to fall behind.

> "Housing construction generally fails to keep step with the population growth of a community."

out of step. Not in rhythm with the movement of another; not in harmony, conformity, or agreement.

> "Their old-fashioned merchandising methods are out of step with the demands of the younger generation."

step by step. From one stage (as of production) to the following; gradually or slowly.

> "In order to find out where the trouble lies, we will have to go through the entire procedure step by step."

step down. To relinquish an office; to resign from a position of leadership.

> "On the basis of age, he could have continued as chairman, but he stepped down because of ill health."

step in. To enter as participant; to intervene, as in a conflict or dispute.

> "Neither the company nor the labor union wanted the government to step in."

step on it. To proceed, or cause to proceed, faster; to accelerate; hasten.

> "If we don't step on it, we'll never finish the job by five o'clock."

step out. 1. To leave a room for a short time. 2. To go out on a date; to go out in order to have a good time.

> 1. "He'll be back in a few minutes. He stepped out to make a phone call."

> 2. "He is trying to make up for lost time by stepping out practically every night."

step up. To increase the rate of; to speed up; accelerate.

> "They did step up production but even then it wasn't enough to meet the increased demand."

step up to. To come near something; to approach; to walk up to.

> "One by one the students stepped up to the podium."

take steps. To initiate the necessary measures for the accomplishment of something.

> "The President will undoubtedly take steps to see that such an incident is not repeated."

watch one's step. 1. To be careful in walking. 2. To be cautious about anything.

> 1. "Watch your step on that driveway; it's kinda slick."

> 2. "With the stock market being what it is, he should watch his step about additional investments."

Stew

stew in one's own juice. To suffer from, or be afflicted with, the consequences of one's own action.

> "We advised him not to put off the repairs till winter, but he did. Now let him stew in his own juice."

Stick

stick around. To remain near someone; to continue to be in the vicinity of something.

> "If you want to hear some high-level conversation, you better stick around."

> "Stick around for a while longer. She may still show up."

stick by. To hold on, as to an opinion; to remain loyal to someone or something.

> "He is still sticking by his story that his car was stolen and later returned."

stick to. Same as *stick by,* which see.

stick up. To rob or hold up, especially at the point of a gun or other weapon.

> "The owner of that store was stuck up three times in the last six months."

stick up for. In an argument, to take the side of someone; to come to the defense of; to speak in justification of something or someone.

> "I don't mean to stick up for him, but I do think that in this particular case he is right."

the sticks. The country, as opposed to the city; the rural areas of a country.

> "Yes, you might say that we live in the sticks, but we like it. Anyway, the air is cleaner."

Stink

raise a stink. To start an argument, as by bringing up a controversial subject; to complain, especially about a trivial subject.

> "We advised him not to raise a stink over the short wait, but he was not to be restrained."

Stock

in stock. Among the things available for sale, at a particular time, in a store.

> "We do not have a shirt of this size in stock now, but we can order it for you."

on the stocks. In the process of being built; in preparation.

> "This is one of his latest productions, but he has another model on the stocks."

out of stock. Of merchandise, etc., not immediately available for sale; not present on the shelves or in the warehouse of a store, shop, etc.

> "We do carry this item, but it is out of stock at the moment."

take stock. To determine how much merchandise, supplies, etc., one has on hand; to appraise one's chances, situation, etc.

> "This is the day on which they take stock at the store, so he'll probably be late for dinner."

> "Every person should take stock of himself now and then to see if he is on the right course."

take stock in. To believe in; to have confidence in; to regard as important.

> "Well, I don't take stock in this report. I regard it as just another rumor."

put stock in. Same as *take stock in,* which see.

Stone

cast the first stone. To be the first to criticize, propose punishment, etc.

> "With his personal record, he shouldn't be the one to cast the first stone at her."

leave no stone unturned. To avoid nothing, however difficult, in search of something; to do everything possible in the pursuit of a goal.

> "In searching for their missing son, they left no stone unturned, but he was not found."

Stop

put a stop to. To cause to discontinue; to bring about a cessation; bring to an end.

> "She was in the habit of playing records while doing her homework, but her mother put a stop to that."

stop by. To pay a short visit to someone or some place, usually on one's way elsewhere.

> "She said she would stop by here on her way to the supermarket."

stop in. To come to someone's home for a short social visit; to visit any place for a short while.

> "Her son stops in at least once a week to see if she is all right."

stop off. To interrupt a trip or journey and visit a particular place along the way, usually for a short time.

> "He stopped off to visit his mother on the way to New York and Europe."

stop over. To interrupt a trip or journey for the purpose of remaining at a place along the way, usually for a limited time, as overnight.

> "Because the car broke down we had to stop over for the night in the nearest small town."

Store

in store. 1. In reserve; ready for use. 2. Ready to befall; imminent; waiting for.

1. "They have a large supply of firewood in store just in case the power fails."

2. "There are a great many difficulties in store for you if you want to go through college on your own, but it may not be a bad idea."

set store by. To value; to have high regard or esteem for someone or something.

"I wouldn't set store by the reports coming from that source."

Stow

stow away. 1. To hide aboard a ship or aircraft in order to obtain free transportation or to escape from pursuit. 2. To put away something for future use; to conceal something; to amass.

1. "He was unable to save enough money for a trip to South America, so he decided to stow away."

2. "He stowed away a considerable amount of money while he worked for his uncle."

Strain

strain at. 1. To exert oneself physically, as in moving a heavy object. 2. To aim at; to strive for.

1. "He felt the pain in the back when he strained at moving the heavy bookcase."

2. "He is straining at the medal which is awarded for the highest grades achieved during the entire four-year course."

Straw

grasp at a straw. To reach out for anything that offers even the slimmest hope, as in a case of extreme danger.

"We knew that appealing to him was not likely to bring any useful response, but at a time like this one grasps at a straw."

clutch at a straw. Same as *grasp at a straw,* which see.

catch at a straw. Same as *grasp at a straw,* which see.

Stride

hit one's stride. To achieve one's normal or customary efficiency, speed, etc.; to reach one's highest level of performance.

> "He was an excellent salesman right from the start, but he really hit his stride after the second year."

take something in one's stride. To handle a difficult situation without much change in one's attitude; to cope with something calmly.

> "The additional responsibilities did not upset him. As usual, he took matters in his stride."

Strike

be struck by *or* with. To be impressed or amazed by something; to be puzzled by.

> "He was struck by the fact that the bed had not been slept in."

have two strikes against one. To have a handicap; to have a bad record; to be at a disadvantage.

> "The applicant had two strikes against him mainly because of his dishonorable discharge from the service."

strike down. 1. To knock someone down with a blow. 2. To disable, as by illness or injury.

> 1. "As we saw it, he was struck down by a left to the jaw."
>
> 2. "The fatal illness struck him down in the prime of life."

strike home. 1. To affect in a desired manner; to bring about the intended result. 2. To deliver a disabling or otherwise effective blow.

> 1. "The movie depicting the battles and bloodshed is bound to strike home."

> 2. "The challenger struck home with a left hook."

strike it rich. To become rich rather unexpectedly; to have an unexpected financial success.

> "He opened a store in the small town, and when the munitions plant was reactivated, he struck it rich."

strike off. To remove, as a name, from a list or a record.

> "The correspondent requested that his name be stricken off the mailing list."

strike out. To fail in an effort or enterprise; to lose favor with someone.

> "He tried to go in business on his own twice before, but struck out each time."

> "I think he kinda struck out with his lady friend."

strike up. 1. To start playing or singing; to begin. 2. To initiate, as an acquaintanceship.

> 1. "The band attempted to stop the brawl by striking up a patriotic tune."

> 2. "He struck up a friendship with one of the girls at the office."

String

have two strings to one's bow. To have two resorts; to have two sources of aid or comfort; to have two alternatives.

> "Being both a pharmacist and a chemist, he has two strings to his bow."

on a string. On a leash; subject to one's power; under one's control; in a position to keep someone from leaving.

> "He seems to have two girls on a string, but he can't make up his mind which one he really wants."

pull strings. To use the influence of one's friends in order to gain some objective.

> "He believes that to get ahead these days you have to pull strings. He feels it isn't enough to be qualified."

string along with. To continue to keep company with; to remain loyal or faithful to; to be a follower of.

> "As the saying goes, till something better comes along, I'll string along with you."

> "Most of the employees decided to string along with the older firm."

string out. To extend in time or geographically; to stretch out.

> "The procession was strung out for many blocks along Fifth Avenue."

> "The five months, in which he expected to finish the manuscript, strung out to nearly a year."

string up. To put to death by hanging.

> "In those days a man was usually strung up for stealing a horse."

Stump

up a stump. Puzzled; perplexed; unable to understand; at a loss (as to what to do).

> "Economists are up a stump over the issue of inflation."

Substance

in substance. As regards to the essentials or essential parts; in reality; actually.

> "The present report is in substance better than the previous one."

> "With regard to buying power, the current wages are in substance lower."

Such

as such. 1. In the capacity named or indicated; when considered as suggested. 2. Regarded in itself, without others or other considerations.

> 1. "An insurance agent, as such, is regarded as an arm of the company he represents."

> 2. "The television set, as such, is not of the highest grade, but the cabinet is exceptionally attractive."

such as. 1. Similar to the matter or thing discussed or specified. 2. As the following; like; for example.

> 1. "A house such as his would cost more than you are willing to spend."

> 2. "Light exercises, such as walking, are recommended in such cases."

Suck

suck in. To involve in an illegal adventure; to deceive; swindle.

> "He was sucked in as a partner in this venture against his better judgment."

suck up to. To act in a servile or fawning manner toward someone; to ingratiate oneself to.

> "In his quest for a transfer, he sucked up to his superiors in the hope that they would intervene."

Sufferance

on sufferance. With passive permission but no encouragement; allowed to exist or proceed but not assisted.

> "He functions in the campaign headquarters on suf-
> ferance; they are not really anxious to have him."

Suit

bring suit. To initiate action to secure justice in a court of law; to sue.

> "The company finally decided to pay off but only
> after the customer threatened to bring suit."

follow suit. The follow the example of others or another; to do the same as others have done.

> "When his neighbors on both sides built carports,
> he soon followed suit."

suit oneself. To do as one feels inclined to do; to follow one's own wishes.

> "You can have either one of these lots. Suit your-
> self."

Sum

sum up. 1. To condense into a few words; to present in brief form. 2. To formulate a quick impression of someone or something.

> 1. "It was necessary to sum up the lengthy article in
>   two or three paragraphs."
> 2. "It didn't take him long to sum up the situation,
>   that the bank was about to be held up."

Sun

place in the sun. A comfortable position in life; a position of prominence; the condition of being recognized or esteemed.

> "In the late sixties, the small independent movie
> producer gained his place in the sun."

under the sun. Anywhere on earth; any place in the world.

> "In his opinion, California has the best climate under the sun."

Sure

be sure. To be certain that something is as it should be or that something is done or accomplished.

> "Be sure to stop the mail delivery before you leave on your vacation."

for sure. Certainly; surely; without any doubt.

> "He'll be at the party, for sure. I'll bet on it."

make sure. To make certain; to remove all doubt; to determine.

> "I told him of my acceptance over the telephone, but to make sure I will also write him a letter."

sure enough. Certainly; as was to be expected; as might have been anticipated.

> "We never thought he would stick to his new job, and sure enough, after only two months he quit."

to be sure. Without any doubt; without the possibility of contradicting; certainly.

> "A provisional commitment was made, to be sure, but the circumstances have changed."

> "She is an experienced worker, to be sure, but consider her age."

Suspicion

above suspicion. So reliable or honorable as not to be suspected of any or of a specified offense.

> "There is only one person in this office who knew about the proposed sale, and she is above suspicion."

on suspicion. On the ground of suspecting; because a suspicion exists; because it is presumed or surmised.

> "Our action is based not on known facts but on suspicion."

> "He was picked up by the police on suspicion of murder."

under suspicion. Subject to suspicion; regarded as the object of suspicion about a particular offense.

> "A local man is under suspicion, but there isn't enough evidence to justify an arrest at this time."

Swath

cut a swath. To produce an ostentatious or pompous display; to do something which attracts attention.

> "The handsome visitor cut a swath in the social circles of our town."

Swear

swear by. 1. To have great confidence in someone or something. 2. To be absolutely sure of something.

> 1. "He has so much confidence in the efficacy of vitamin C that you might say he swears by it."

> 2. "I do believe he paid me, but I wouldn't swear by it."

swear in. To recite an oath in the process of admitting a person to an office, witness stand, etc.

> "The new President was sworn in by a local federal judge."

swear off. To make a solemn promise to oneself or to others to cease doing something.

> "He swore off smoking cigarettes at least twice before."

swear out. To get a warrant for someone's arrest by making an accusation under oath.

> "It would not be difficult to swear out a warrant for the arrest of the youth, but getting a conviction is something else."

Sweat

sweat something out. To await something with fear or anxiety; to live through a period of uncertainty.

> "They were forced to sweat out the long period of uncertainty about the fate of their missing husbands."

Sweet

sweet on. In love with; very fond of; infatuated with.

> "The assistant manager is said to be sweet on one of the checkers at the supermarket."

Swim

in the swim. Participating in a specified activity; still taking part; active.

> "Although he is not the leading contender any more, he is still in the swim."

Swing

in full swing. Going on at full speed; proceeding at the highest rate; actively in operation.

> "The plant had some initial operational difficulties, but it is now in full swing."

Sword

at swords' points. Ready to do battle or to quarrel; opposed to each other.

"The two sisters were usually in agreement on most issues, but they were at swords' points on the matter of abortion."

cross swords. To engage in a violent argument; to battle or fight.

"The president and the chairman cross swords frequently over company policy."

put to the sword. To slay or kill, especially in large numbers.

"In the Ukraine, especially, many civilians were put to the sword."

T

Table

turn the tables. To reverse the advantage or disadvantage of a situation as it affects two or more persons or groups.

> "We let our competitors believe that they were underbidding us, then we turned the tables on them and submitted the lowest bid."

under the table. Secretly; underhandedly; to serve as an illegal inducement or bribe.

> "To get these scarce materials, one would surely have to pay something under the table."

Tail

turn tail. To turn away from difficulty, danger, etc.; to turn and run from a hazardous or threatening situation.

> "Like all bullies, he turned tail when his would-be victim put up a fight."

with one's tail between one's legs. With an acknowledgment of defeat; in a state of utter humiliation.

> "He left the manager's office with his tail between his legs."

Take

take after. 1. To resemble someone in some way. 2. To follow or run after someone in order to capture.

> 1. "Temperamentally, the child takes after her mother."

> 2. "One of the customers took after the holdup man."

take off after. Same as *take after,* definition 2, which see.

take amiss. 1. To become offended by something. 2. To misinterpret the motive for a particular act by someone.

> 1. "She was apparently impressed by what we said, or perhaps she took it amiss."

> 2. "Our gesture was obviously taken amiss, but we meant well."

take at one's word. To accept someone as being sincere; to believe what one says; to regard as true or correct.

> "I have no proof that what he said is the truth, but I take him at his word."

take back. 1. To accept someone who has left but wishes to return. 2. To retract a statement, promise etc. 3. To go mentally to a period in one's past; to relive a past experience. 4. To return a piece of merchandise to the store from which it was bought. 5. To regain control or possession of something.

> 1. "She took him back once, but I doubt that she will take him back again after this caper."

> 2. "Since you explain it this way, I'll take back what I said."

> 3. "This television play took me back to my own childhood."

> 4. "We took the shoes back. They were the wrong size."

    5. "I took back our typewriter when I visited him last week."

take down. 1. To move something from a higher place to a lower place. 2. To record in writing, as a dictation. 3. To humble someone; to reduce someone's arrogance or conceit.

    1. "I suggested that she take down the most frequently used dishes to a lower shelf."

    2. "She was there to take down the more important parts of the lecture."

    3. "He was taken down a notch by the two losses he sustained in his recent bouts."

take for. 1. To regard as (something); to think of as. 2. To mistake someone or something for. 3. To defraud or cheat of.

    1. "Make no mistake. Don't take him for a fool; he is anything but that."

    2. "The commercials have the recurring theme of a mother who is so slim that she is taken for her daughter."

    3. "We lost two hundred dollars. How much were you taken for?"

take in. 1. To allow to enter; to provide a home or lodging. 2. To encompass; include. 3. To cheat or deceive. 4. To observe. 5. To visit. 6. To understand.

    1. "His neighbors will surely take him in for a few nights while the furnace is being repaired."

    2. "The area described takes in a number of small farms."

    3. "I am afraid you have been taken in by the glib tongue of the salesman."

    4. "He was watching the game intently, taking in every movement of the pitcher."

5. "There was nothing of interest on television, so we decided to take in a movie."

6. "It was obvious that many students fail to take in the importance of this course."

take it. 1. To assume; to understand something in a certain way. 2. To accept hardship, criticism, etc., usually without retaliation.

1. "I take it that you will try to be present."

2. "She has been nagging him for years and he has been taking it, but the worm may turn."

take it lying down. To submit to abuse, criticism, etc. without resistance or retaliation.

"He won't take it lying down forever. He is bound to react sooner or later."

take it on the chin. To suffer punishment, privation, pain, etc.; to have financial reverses.

"When the munitions plant was closed, the local merchants took it on the chin."

take it out of. 1. To deprive of vitality; to exhaust. 2. To obtain payment or financial satisfaction from; to deduct from.

1. "The hot, humid summers really take it out of them."

2. "They take a certain amount out of his salary every month to satisfy the debt."

take it out on. To let another person suffer the consequences of one's own anger, frustration, etc.; to relieve one's irritation or bad temper by chiding or blaming someone else.

"He always takes it out on his subordinates, no matter what bothers him or whose fault it is."

take off. 1. To remove. 2. To leave. 3. To rise from the ground, as an aircraft. 4. To remove from an assignment. 5. To deduct or subtract. 6. To imitate.

1. "He took off his jacket before he entered the car."

   "This will cook better if you take off the lid."

2. "He was in such a hurry that he took off without saying good-by."

3. "A number of dignitaries watched the President's plane take off for the Asian trip."

4. "He asked his superiors to take him off the swing shift."

5. "You may take off the amount I owe you from the price of the article."

6. "Now and then he likes to take off on Ed Sullivan."

take on. 1. To hire a worker or employee. 2. To acquire; assume. 3. To undertake. 4. To accept a challenge; to engage in a fight or battle. 5. To become very angry; to show sorrow.

1. "They are not taking on any new employees at this time."

2. "With this new explanation, his response takes on a new meaning."

3. "He cannot take on any new jobs at this time. He already has more than he can do."

4. "He travels with a small circus and takes on all local strongmen."

5. "I had no idea he would take on so because of a casual remark."

take one's time. To proceed slowly; to be in no hurry about something.

"Take your time and think it over carefully before making a decision."

take out. 1. To move something from one place to another; to remove. 2. To obtain security, coverage, etc., by application. 3. To escort a person, especially a girl, to a place of entertainment.

> 1. "Take out this chair so that we will have more room."

> 2. "We took out an insurance policy on the valuable documents."

> 3. "He told me he would like to take out my secretary but he hasn't the nerve to ask her."

take over. To take the office of manager, director, etc., from another person.

> "The manager from Madison took over here when our man got sick."

take to. 1. To become habituated or addicted to something. 2. To become friendly with or fond of. 3. To go to. 4. To resort to.

> 1. "When he is under a strain such as this, he takes to biting his nails."

> 2. "He doesn't take to strangers very often, but he surely took to you."

> 3. "When he is in a bad mood, he takes to his room after dinner."

> 4. "To get away from his morbid thoughts, he took to reading detective stories."

take up. 1. To engage in or occupy oneself with. 2. To occupy in space or time. 3. To absorb; pick up. 4. To advocate; support; espouse. 5. To continue after an interruption. 6. To accept, as a bet or challenge.

> 1. "He took up ice skating as a form of exercise."

> 2. "The discussion of this subject will take up most of the evening."

> "The draperies take up most of the wall space."

3. "This brush is supposed to take up most of the lint."

   "This brand of paper towel will take up a great deal of moisture."

4. "He is always busy, taking up one cause or another."

5. "Let's stop here for the present and take it up again tomorrow."

6. "I'll take you up on this one. I don't think it can be done."

take upon oneself. To assume as a duty or obligation; to proceed with something without consulting a superior.

"In the absence of his boss, he took it upon himself to order the necessary parts."

take up with. To associate with; to become a companion of; to be friendly with someone.

"It was probably his loneliness that forced him to take up with that woman and her friends."

Talk

big talk. Boastful talk; braggadocio; empty talk intended to impress.

"He is given to a lot of big talk. I don't believe a word of it."

make talk. To force conversation or talk merely to break an awkward silence or to pass time.

"No, you are not interrupting anything. We were just making talk."

talk around. To persuade a person to a particular point of view, to change his mind, etc.

"You may be able to talk him around with logic but not with harsh words or threats."

talk away. To spend or pass time by talking; to while away time in conversation.

> "Instead of watching television or talking away your
> evenings you could be studying or reading books."

talk back. To respond in a disrespectful manner; to answer defiantly.

> "His parents taught him never to talk back to his
> elders."

talk big. To brag; to exaggerate one's achievements; to use boastful language.

> "He usually talks big, probably to cover up his sense
> of inferiority."

talk down. To overcome or defeat a person by loud and continued talking; to shout down.

> "If he can't persuade you with logic, he'll try to talk
> you down."

talk down to. To talk to a person in a manner which assumes that he is on a lower intellectual or educational level than the speaker; to talk to in simple words or expressions.

> "He is sensitive about his lack of formal education,
> so be sure not to talk down to him."

talk of. To discuss, or speak about, a particular subject; to discuss an intention.

> "She talks of nothing else but her forthcoming trip."

> "They are talking of a possible change in location."

talk one's head off. To talk to such excess as to weary or bore the listener.

> "I tried to avoid his company, as he is prone to talk
> his head off, especially about his financial ventures."

> "He'll talk your head off if you give him a chance."

talk out. To discuss a subject at such length as to exhaust it; to talk excessively about something so as to leave nothing further to be said.

> "I think that the various radio and television shows have just about talked out the women's liberation movement."

talk over. 1. To discuss or debate a subject. 2. To cause someone to change his point of view by talking to him.

> 1. "We would like to talk it over with you before you make the announcement."
>
> 2. "If you give him a chance, he'll talk you over to his side. He always does!"

talk to death. To bore or weary someone by excessive talk; to talk about a subject to excess so as to make it dull.

> "Watch out! If you let her, she'll talk you to death."
>
> "Well, that subject has been talked to death. Let's drop it."

talk up. 1. To discuss something in a laudatory manner so as to enhance interest. 2. To speak frankly; speak without hesitation; speak without restraint.

> 1. "They are trying to talk up the importance of this farmland, but nobody is being fooled."
>
> 2. "They won't like you for talking up, but I think you should go ahead anyway."

Tan

tan one's hide. To give a beating; to thrash; to punish, as by whipping.

> "She'll tan your hide if you don't get off the roof at once!"

Tangent

go off on a tangent. To depart suddenly from one line of thought or course of action and to engage in another.

"It seems to me that the question disturbed the speaker, as he went off on a tangent right after that."

"Now, let's stick to the point. Let's not go off on a tangent, as we did last week."

Tap

on tap. 1. Ready to be drawn, as beer from a cask. 2. Available for immediate use; ready for action.

1. "There was plenty of food and beer on tap. You should have been there."

2. "Aside from the main force, several smaller units are on tap."

Taper

taper off. To diminish or decrease gradually; to cease slowly, by degrees.

"The demand for certain materials will taper off after the war is over."

"The severity of the hurricane is tapering off at last."

Tar

knock the tar out of. To give a sound beating; to defeat thoroughly.

"The challenger is a good man, but I still say the champ will knock the tar out of him."

tar and feather. To smear a person's skin with tar and then cause feathers to adhere; to criticize or punish severely.

"He said that anyone who desecrates the flag should be tarred and feathered."

tarred with the same brush. Having the same undesirable characteristics (as someone specified).

> "She and her brother are tarred with the same brush.
> Both are rather eccentric."

Tartar

catch a tartar. To find oneself confronted with someone much stronger or troublesome than one expected; to engage someone or something unexpectedly difficult to handle.

> "The champ caught a tartar in the plucky challenger."

Task

take to task. To require someone to explain or justify an action, stand, etc.; chide; reprove.

> "Don't take her to task for her husband's mistakes."

Taste

in bad taste. Not fit or proper for a particular occasion; not appealing to those having a sense or feeling for beauty.

> "Most of those present at the reception considered
> her appearance in a miniskirt to be in bad taste."

in good taste. Fit or proper for a particular occasion; appealing to those who have an appreciation for beauty.

> "I thought that the decoration was in good taste, but
> others may disagree."

to one's taste. Complying with one's expectations or liking; to one's satisfaction.

> "Those wide, striped ties are not to my taste."

> "A little painting might make the room more to his
> taste."

Tear

tear at. To attempt to remove by tearing; to pull at; to make pulling motions.

> "Strong gusts of wind tore at the flag atop the courthouse."

tear down. 1. To demolish; to take apart. 2. To prove to be wrong; to discredit; to lower or disparage.

> 1. "The city will tear down these building to make room for the new highway."

> 2. "The defense tore down the arguments of the prosecution point by point."

tear into. 1. To begin doing something with great energy; to start vehemently. 2. To make a violent physical or verbal attack.

> 1. "He tore into the project with the energy of a novice."

> 2. "As soon as she entered the room he tore into her for being late."

tear up. 1. To tear or pull apart into small pieces. 2. To make void; to annul.

> 1. "The dogs tore up the newspaper into shreds."

> 2. "They decided to tear up the agreement and part on a friendly basis."

Tears

in tears. In the act of crying; shedding tears; weeping.

> "We found her agitated and in tears because of the automobile accident."

Tell

tell off. To reprove sharply; to reprimand; to face and rebuke, as a critic.

"He always acted as if he owned the place, and I am glad somebody told him off."

tell on. 1. To affect in a certain, usually undesirable, way; to be visible on. 2. To inform about or against; to reveal some secret about someone.

1. "This hard work is beginning to tell on him."

"The years eventually begin to tell on you."

2. "She said she would not tell on him if he promised not to do it again."

Term

bring to terms. To cause someone to accept certain demands or conditions, usually by force or threats; to force into submission.

"Only the threat of cutting off all aid could bring them to terms."

come to terms. To succeed in reaching an agreement; to accept certain conditions.

"Union leaders and management came to terms after a strike of only one day."

"After a while he came to terms with his disability."

Tether

at the end of one's tether. Near the end of one's resources, endurance, ability to continue, etc.

"With all the work yet to be done and with all the interruptions, she was at the end of her tether."

Thank

have oneself to thank. To have only oneself to blame; to be personally responsible.

"He has himself to thank for the poor condition of his health. He was warned to slow down."

That

at that. 1. In spite of something specified; notwithstanding. 2. Besides; in addition. 3. At that time or point.

> 1. "Although the speech was a bit too flowery, it contained some good points at that."
>
> 2. "It was a difficult book to read, and a long one at that."
>
> 3. "There was very little enthusiasm after the announcement was made, and the meeting broke up at that."

in that. Because; by the very fact that; on account of.

> "Although the dividends are the same, this is the better investment in that it is a safer stock."

that is. More specifically; as an example; to illustrate; in other words.

> "We are not interested, that is, not at the present time."

> "He is here now, that is, he is in town."

that's that! It is finished; there is nothing more to be done or said.

> "We have torn up the contract, and that's that!"

Then

but then. But one has to remember that; but on the other hand.

> "He doesn't do as well as his brother, but then he is five years younger."

then and there. Without delay; at once; at the time and place designated or discussed.

> "They decided to terminate their partnership then and there."

what then? What would one do, or what would be the situation, in such a case.

> "But if they refuse to accept your proposal, what then?"

Thick

lay it on thick. To denounce or blame someone excessively; to praise effusively.

> "You may show him your displeasure with his conduct, but don't lay it on thick."

> "She is a pretty girl, and it was quite easy to lay it on thick."

through thick and thin. In good times and in bad; during pleasant and unpleasant conditions.

> "They have been together through thick and thin for more than thirty years."

Thing

make a good thing of. To turn an unpleasant situation into a profitable one; to put to good use; to make beneficial.

> "Though he was immobilized by the cast, he made a good thing of it by reading the many books he always wanted to read but had no time for."

> "She made a good thing of her secretarial training by getting a job while her husband was ill."

not get a thing out of. 1. To fail to get information from. 2. To be unable to derive pleasure from. 3. To fail to understand; to be unable to appreciate or benefit from.

> 1. "Although they interrogated him for hours, they did not get a thing out of him."

> 2. "I do not get a thing out of this kind of music."

> 3. "I did not get a thing out of his entire speech. What was he talking about?"

see things. To have the impression of seeing things that in reality are not present; to have hallucinations.

> "I am sure he wasn't there last night or the night before. You must be seeing things!"

the thing. 1. Something that is fashionable or regarded as correct at a particular time or place. 2. That which is applicable, effective, essential, etc. for a given situation or problem.

> 1. "The wide, striped ties were the thing at that time."
>
> 2. "Under the circumstances, the thing to do was to call the police."

Think

think better of. To reconsider and not do what one originally intended to do; to adopt a new and wiser course.

> "His first impulse was to reply in anger, but then he thought better of it."

think fit. To regard as proper or advisable; to consider suitable or appropriate.

> "He apparently thought fit to take the day off."

think nothing of. 1. To regard as unimportant. 2. To consider as easy to accomplish.

> 1. "He did hear the dog barking, but he thought nothing of it."
>
> 2. "He thought nothing of lifting a 200-pound crate."

think of. 1. To form a mental concept or image. 2. To have an opinion of something. 3. To regard or consider. 4. To remember; recall.

> 1. "I cannot think of anything that would have this shape."

2. "He hardly knew what to think of the latest development."

3. "In connection with the environment, one must think of the future as well as of the present."

4. "I know the man but I can't think of his name."

think out. 1. To think about something in order to understand or reach a conclusion. 2. To invent or contrive; to formulate by thinking.

1. "Let's think this out together. There must be a way to solve this without legal action."

2. "It is usually possible to think out a new method, but whether it is economical is another matter."

think out loud. To express one's thoughts in words as the thoughts come to mind.

"This is not my final opinion of the matter; I am merely thinking out loud."

think over. To think carefully about a particular matter; to ponder alternatives.

"You don't have to make up your mind immediately. You can think over the matter for a few days."

"Let me think this over for a while before I give you my answer."

think through. To think about something for the purpose of understanding it or reaching a conclusion.

"It was difficult to think through this maze of contradictory facts and statistics."

think twice. To consider carefully; to think about something more than once before acting or reaching a conclusion.

"Having been beaten by this boy, he'll now think twice before challenging him again."

think up. To devise, contrive, or invent, especially something odd or fanciful.

> "Look at this contraption. What will they think up next?"

Thorn

thorn in one's (*or* the) flesh. A source of irritation, embarrassment, or annoyance, especially a persistent one.

> "His mother-in-law is the thorn in his flesh."

thorn in one's (*or* the) side. Same as *thorn in one's flesh,* which see.

Though

as though. As the case would be if (a specified condition prevailed).

> "I don't understand it. He acted as though he hadn't met me before."

Throat

cut each other's (*or* one another's) throats. To do harm to each other (or one another).

> "The oil companies are cutting one another's throats in this gasoline price war."

cut one's own throat. To do harm to oneself through one's own action.

> "You'll be cutting your own throat if you continue to disregard the complaints of your customers."

cut someone's throat. To do someone serious harm; to ruin financially.

> "By opening a branch store here, the food chain cut his throat. He couldn't compete with their prices and their immense stock."

jump down someone's throat. To scold severely; to attack verbally with excessive vehemence.

> "All right, he was wrong, but did you have to jump down his throat in front of everybody?"

lump in one's throat. A feeling of tenseness or constriction in the throat resulting from a strong emotion, as sympathy, compassion, etc.

> "The scene in which the son parted from his father raised a lump in her throat."

ram something down one's throat. To impose undesirable terms upon someone; to force someone to accept or to agree to something.

> "I think this is a good deal for him, and I did try to persuade him to accept it. On the other hand, I did not attempt to ram it down his throat, as you say."

stick in one's throat. To be hesitant about saying; to be unable to express in spoken words.

> "He wanted to say that he was sorry, but the words stuck in his throat."

Throw

throw away. 1. To discard, as a useless article. 2. To fail to utilize; fail to make use of an opportunity. 3. To waste or squander.

1. "He asked me not to throw away the old magazines but to save them for him."

2. "He had an excellent chance to get the contract but he threw it away by not submitting his bid on time."

   "He threw away three years of college education by quitting in his senior year."

3. "He thinks nothing of throwing away two or three hundred dollars at the crap table."

throw a monkey wrench into. To check or hinder a procedure by objections, criticism, the creation of obstacles, etc.

"We were ready to proceed with the construction, but a neighbor threw a monkey wrench into the project by raising some legal questions."

throw back. 1. To slow or check the progress or development of something. 2. To cause to become dependent on something or someone. 3. To take one back, in thought, to a past experience or time.

1. "The bad weather threw us back at least a month in the construction of the supermarket."

2. "You see, her television set being on the blink, she was thrown back to reading books and magazines."

3. "That late-show movie threw her back to the days when she was a young girl and was being courted by her present husband."

throw cold water on. To do or say something that discourages someone or cools his enthusiasm.

"You can depend on that guy to throw cold water on anything you propose!"

throw in. To add as an extra or bonus; to add something by way of information, diversion, fun, etc.

"If you'll be a good boy, she'll throw in a few of your favorite cookies."

"In his reading of the poems, he is fond of throwing in some explanatory remarks and, occasionally, witticisms."

throw off. 1. To manage to evade a pursuer. 2. To free oneself from something or somebody. 3. To emanate; emit; discharge. 4. To produce or say something quickly, in an offhand manner. 5. To bewilder or confuse.

1. "By plunging into the stream and swimming underwater, he was able to throw off his pursuers."
2. "The girl felt that the only way to throw off her mother's domination was to leave town and to get an apartment of her own."
3. "In hot weather, this plastic cover throws off an unpleasant odor."
4. "He is quick-witted and able to throw off a few cogent anecdotes for any occasion."
5. "Her unexpected appearance threw him off for a few moments, but he soon regained his composure."

throw on. To put on or apply hastily and without care; to don a garment in a hurry.

"He seems to have been in a great hurry, as he threw on the paint in a careless manner."

"When she heard the siren, she just threw on her house coat and ran out of the house."

throw oneself at. To use every means, however degrading, in order to win someone's affection or love.

"She was generally aloof, but she really threw herself at this boy."

throw oneself into. To enter into some activity with the utmost enthusiasm.

"To forget her sorrow, she threw herself into various social activities."

throw oneself upon. To depend completely on the aid or support of someone; to put one's fate into the hands of someone.

"During her crisis, she threw herself upon him for both financial and moral support."

"The accused threw himself on the mercy of the court."

throw open. To make access or entry easy by removing all restrictions.

> "The college threw open its doors to students belonging to minority groups."

throw out. 1. To propose; to propound; to offer for consideration. 2. To put outside; to remove from a place by force. 3. To discard. 4. To discard as useless or unworthy of consideration. 5. In baseball, to dispose of a runner by throwing a ball to a fielder before the runner reaches base safely.

> 1. "During the course of the speech, he threw out a few hints about the future of the company."

> 2. "When the dissidents refused to remain silent, they were ordered out and finally thrown out."

> 3. "I asked him not to throw out the old copies of his medical journals."

> 4. "The proposal was not really thrown out; it is still under consideration."

> 5. "We saw the infielder throw out the runner at second."

throw over. To give up or abandon, as a project; to forsake, as a friend, husband, etc.

> "He started several businesses in the past ten years, but he threw them over."

> "They kept company for several years, but she threw him over for a younger man whom she later married."

throw the bull. To talk ostentatiously; to speak insincerely.

> "Don't take him seriously. I happen to know that he likes to throw the bull."

throw together. 1. To make, prepare, or construct hurriedly. 2. To cause to live together or in close proximity; to make it necessary to associate.

1. "She can throw together a good meal in a matter of minutes."

2. "When people of such diverse origins are thrown together, there is bound to be some friction."

throw up. 1. To build or construct hurriedly. 2. To mention something repeatedly in an accusatory way. 3. To vomit.

1. "We can throw up a shed for the tools in an hour."

2. "There is no point in throwing up his one mistake. He knows he made it and he is sorry."

3. "The sight of blood causes some people to throw up."

Thumb

all thumbs. Awkward with one's hands; clumsy; not dextrous.

"When he is around, she is nervous and seems to be all thumbs. At other times she is quite agile."

thumb one's nose. To put one's thumb to the nose with the other fingers of the hand extended, as an expression of derision or defiance.

"He didn't mind her at all. In fact, he thumbed his nose at her."

thumb through. To examine the contents of a magazine or book by, or as if by, releasing the pages rapidly along their edges with the thumb.

"In the short time that he had available, he could only thumb through the book."

turn thumbs down. To indicate disapproval by extending the thumb downward from a clenched fist; to express rejection or disapproval in any manner.

"They turned thumbs down to our proposal of a merger."

under one's thumb. Subordinated to someone; under someone's control or domination.

"She was a stern mother who kept her children under her thumb at all times."

Thunder

steal someone's thunder. To use the ideas or methods of another without permission, often to the disadvantage of the originator; to diminish the effectiveness of another's statement by anticipating it.

"He stole his opponent's thunder by proposing a toast for the distinguished visitor."

Ticket

that's the ticket. Now, this is right! That's the correct thing! That's what I want, meant, etc.

"Move it just a little to the right. Now, that's the ticket!"

Tide

tide over. To help overcome or endure a transient period of difficulty; to help survive.

"I asked him if the amount would be sufficient to tide him over, and he said that it would."

turn the tide. To reverse the direction of a particular process or course of events.

"The tank battle at Kursk turned the tide of the German invasion of Russia."

Tie

tie down. To restrain or limit one's activities; to confine to a particular place.

"His job tied him down so that he could not participate in any social activities."

tie off. To constrict a collapsible tube, as a blood vessel, by means of a suture, in order to check the flow of fluid within.

> "The surgeon tied off each bleeding vessel individually."

tie up. 1. To immobilize by tying with a cord, rope, etc. 2. To surround and fasten with a string, etc. 3. To hinder; to check or stop. 4. To make something unavailable by committing to a particular use. 5. To fasten a boat, ship, etc. 6. To occupy completely.

> 1. "The intruder tied up the old lady with a drapery cord."
>
> 2. "The package wasn't tied up securely and came apart while in the mail."
>
> 3. "The repair work on the road ties up the traffic, especially during the afternoon rush."
>
> 4. "Her money is tied up in securities and is not available to her at present."
>
> 5. "The rowboat was tied up as usual, but somebody cut it loose during the night."
>
> 6. "The secretary told us that the doctor will be tied up for at least two hours."

Tilt

at full tilt. With the greatest speed; with full force.

> "In spite of the holidays, production at the local plant continued at full tilt."

tilt at windmills. To battle with imaginary opponents; to attack nonexisting problems or hazards.

> "Like a typical paranoiac, he is always tilting at windmills."

Time

abreast of the times. 1. Informed about topical matters and current events. 2. Modern in thought, ways, etc.

> 1. "He reads a great deal to keep abreast of the times."

> 2. "His dress and even his manners show that he is abreast of the times."

against time. In an attempt to complete something by a certain time or within a specified time.

> "They worked against time to install the furnace before nightfall."

ahead of time. Before a specified or expected time; earlier than expected.

> "He likes to arrive ahead of time rather than late."

at one time. 1. At the same time; simultaneously. 2. At some time in the past.

> 1. "Several persons were injured when so many tried to get through the door at one time."

> 2. "The two continents were connected by a land mass at one time."

at the same time. 1. Simultaneously. 2. Yet; also; nevertheless.

> 1. "It isn't a good idea for all of us to go there at the same time."

> 2. "It is a safe investment, but at the same time, you must remember that the dividends are rather small."

at times. Sometimes; on certain occasions; now and then.

> "At times, he says, he does miss the big city, but most of the time he is happier in this rural environment."

beat someone's time. To win the love of a girl courted by someone else; to beat a rival for the attention or love of a woman.

> "John was beginning to suspect that his best friend
> was trying to beat his time and that Betty seemed
> to like the idea."

behind the times. Not informed about topical matters or current events; outdated; old-fashioned.

> "He is so busy with his work that he doesn't have
> the time to read even the daily newspaper. He is
> behind the times."

> "He is behind the times in everything, including
> his business methods."

for the time being. For the present time only; for now; temporarily.

> "This will have to do for the time being, but we
> will certainly look for a better apartment."

from time to time. Occasionally; at intervals but not too frequently.

> "He drops us a card from time to time, but we are
> not really in touch with him."

gain time. 1. To prolong or postpone an action in order to gain an advantage or until something can take place. 2. Of a clock or watch, to run too fast.

> 1. "By refusing to sign the sales contract, he hoped
>   to gain time and get a better price for the property."

> 2. "This battery clock seems to gain time during
>   cold weather."

in good time. 1. At the proper time. 2. Right on time; punctually. 3. Earlier than expected; in a relatively short time.

1. "Don't rush us, boy. You'll hear all about it in good time."

2. "Even if you drive only at forty miles per hour, you'll arrive in good time."

3. "With talents like his and his energy, he'll make a success of the business in good time."

in no time. Almost immediately; without consuming much time; practically instantly.

"Well, you see, we got here in no time, as I promised."

in time. 1. In the end; ultimately; in the future. 2. Not late; at the proper time. 3. Early enough to do good. 4. In the correct tempo or rhythm.

1. "In time, the investment will pay off, but for an immediate return you should try something else."

2. "We arrived in time to see the important part of the play. The first act is not really important."

3. "If treated in time, it is certainly curable."

4. "If you keep in time with the other musicians, no one will know how poorly you play!"

keep time. 1. To observe a tempo or rhythm. 2. To record or indicate time, or the passage of time.

1. "In learning how to dance, it is important to keep time with the music."

2. "A timepiece that doesn't keep time accurately is worthless."

kill time. To occupy oneself with some trivial activity in order to make time pass more pleasantly or quickly.

"You can kill a lot of time watching television if you let yourself in for it."

lose time. 1. To let time pass by without doing what one sets out to do in order to gain a certain objective. 2. Of a clock or watch, to run too slowly.

> 1. "While going to college he lost an entire year because of his mother's illness, then he lost more time when she passed away."

> 2. "This clock loses time during the summer months."

make time. 1. To recover lost time by moving, working, etc. faster. 2. To travel at a specified speed, usually fast. 3. To be doing well in a love affair; to be romantically successful with a girl.

> 1. "Now that the entire staff is back at work we are making time."

> 2. "The train had some engine trouble, but it is making good time now."

> 3. "He must have something, as he is surely making time with the girls at the office."

many a time. Many times; frequently; often; on many occasions.

> "Many a time she felt like scolding him, but she restrained herself."

on one's own time. (Performed) during a time other than one's working hours; not (done) during the time of one's regular employment.

> "He repairs radios and television sets on his own time."

on time. 1. At the time specified or expected. 2. On a plan which provides for a payment to be made over a period of time, in installments.

> 1. "In spite of our late start, we managed to arrive on time."

> 2. "The more expensive items are usually bought on time."

out of time. Not in keeping with a given tempo or rhythm; not consonant.

> "His steps and lip movements are out of time with the music and picture."

take one's time. To do something in a leisurely manner; to let time pass before taking action.

> "He'll be here, but as usual, he is taking his time about it."

time after time. Numerous times; continually; repeatedly.

> "Time after time he applied for a job, but he never succeeded in getting one."

time and time again. Same as *time after time,* which see.

> "Time and time again we told him to keep up with his homework, but his mind wasn't on school."

time and again. Same as *time after time,* which see.

> "He came late time and again, until he was fired."

time of life. A particular period in one's life; the age or age bracket of a person.

> "They say that at this time of life men begin to look at younger women."

time of one's life. A very pleasant experience; a most enjoyable time.

> "She had the time of her life on her trip to the Bahamas."

Tiptoe

on tiptoe. 1. Cautiously; quietly. 2. Eager; anxious; desirous.

> 1. "They did not hear him come in, as he entered on tiptoe."
>
> 2. "The kids were on tiptoe to see their favorite movie idol."

Tire

tire of. To become bored with; to lose interest in; to become annoyed with.

> "Mark my word, she'll tire of him in two or three months."

> "After a while, he tired of reading detective stories."

> "Finally, he tired of listening to their cavils and complaints."

tire out. To cause someone to become tired; to become tired or exhausted.

> "Her unceasing chatter will surely tire you out."

> "I could tell that the long walk tired him out."

To

to and fro. Toward and away from; back and forth; (moving) first in one direction and then in the opposite direction.

> "The rocking chair still moved to and fro when we entered the room, but she was gone."

Toe

on one's toes. Ready for any eventuality or opportunity; alert; watchful.

> "You can't put anything past him; he's always on his toes."

> "If you'll be on your toes with regard to the market, you'll know when and what to buy."

step on one's toes. To encroach on someone's rights or sphere of authority; to annoy; to offend.

> "When you are making decisions affecting so many people, you are bound to step on someone's toes now and then."

tread on someone's toes. Same as *step on one's toes,* which see.

toe the line. To obey; to follow another's wishes meekly or without protest.

> "In this case, he'll have to toe the line, because his job depends on it."

Token

by the same token. 1. For the same reason. 2. In addition; furthermore; moreover.

> 1. "It is true that we should help the starving in any country, but by the same token we should also help the needy in our own country."

> 2. "He comes from a poor family, and by the same token, he was unable to acquire an education."

in token of. As an indication of; as proof or evidence of.

> "He gave the man a deposit in token of his intention to buy the property."

Told

all told. Counting every person or everything; considering everything or everyone.

> "There were forty visitors, all told—a rather small number for a day like this."

Tone

tone down. 1. To make less intense in tone or color. 2. To reduce the severity of; to moderate.

> 1. "I think it would be advisable to tone down the reds and the greens."

> 2. "After the elections, the Vice President toned down his attacks on the liberals."

tone up. To strengthen; to increase the tone of muscles.

"A brisk walk in the cool air will tone up your lazy muscles."

tone with. To blend or harmonize with, as colors.

"The new television set does not tone with the furniture in the living room."

tone in with. Same as *tone with,* which see.

Tongue

find one's tongue. To be able to speak again, as after recovering from shock or confusion.

"At last she found her tongue and gave him a piece of her mind."

hold one's tongue. To refrain from saying something, especially to keep onself from scolding or criticizing.

"He knows when to hold his tongue, although he says that with his quick temper it isn't easy."

lose one's tongue. To lose one's power of speech temporarily, as in case of shock or confusion.

"In her embarrassment, she lost her tongue and wasn't able to say a word."

on everyone's tongue. Talked about by everyone; of general concern; of current interest.

"The atrocious crime is on everyone's tongue these days."

on the tip of one's tongue. 1. About to be recalled; almost, but not quite, remembered. 2. Almost spoken or uttered.

1. "His name is on the tip of my tongue, but I can't quite remember it."

2. "The challenge was on the tip of his tongue, but he restrained himself."

slip of the tongue. An instance of saying something in a moment of thoughtlessness; a careless uttering of something.

"When she said 'What do you want?', it was obviously a slip of the tongue, for her greeting was usually much friendlier."

Tooth

armed to the teeth. Fully armed with weapons; armed as much as possible; provided with all kinds of arms or weapons.

"Although it is a small nation, it is a formidable opponent, for it is armed to the teeth."

in the teeth of. Directly in opposition or in the face of; in the worst or most violent part of.

"They wouldn't listen and sailed in the teeth of the storm."

"The cop was in the teeth of the melee when the shot rang out."

"He is determined to maintain his support for the proposal in the teeth of popular condemnation."

long in the tooth. Rather old; far from being young; aged.

"Even in the sixties, she was a bit long in the tooth for a miniskirt."

put teeth in. To make effective; to make it possible to implement a law, order, regulation, etc.

"Unless you put teeth in this law, as by imposing a stiff fine, there is no point in having it."

set one's teeth. To decide or prepare oneself to meet an unpleasant or difficult situation; to become determined to face a challenge.

"In spite of the obvious difficulties, he set his teeth and embarked upon the long course toward his goal."

set one's teeth on edge. To cause one to have an unpleasant sensation; to induce irritation or revulsion.

> "Her shrill voice always sets my teeth on edge."

> "His rude manner is enough to set one's teeth on edge."

put one's teeth on edge. Same as *set one's teeth on edge,* which see.

show one's teeth. To demonstrate anger or hostility; to reveal a concealed animosity.

> "If she feels any resentment at all, this will cause her to show her teeth."

to the teeth. As completely as possible; to the fullest extent; fully.

> "For this particular party she was dressed to the teeth."

throw something in one's teeth. To hurl a reproach, challenge, etc. at someone.

> "As expected, they threw his tardiness in his teeth."

tooth and nail. With all of one's energy or devotion; using all of one's strength.

> "He was determined to win and went at it tooth and nail."

Top

blow one's top. 1. To lose one's temper; to become excessively angry; to become enraged. 2. To become temporarily or permanently insane.

> 1. "He has been so irritable lately that the slightest irritation causes him to blow his top."

> 2. "I can't explain such a statement by him on the basis of logic. He must have blown his top."

on top. At the summit of one's successful career; above others on the ladder of success.

> "Athletes seem to remain on top longer now than they used to, but their careers are still rather short."

on top of. 1. In addition to (something specified). 2. Well informed about a subject or about certain developments.

> 1. "He came late, and on top of that he didn't bring the papers."

> 2. "He is always on top of the latest developments in his field of work."

over the top. Having attained more than the amount aimed at; exceeding a goal.

> "The indicator in front of the local bank showed that the community went over the top a week before the end of the campaign."

top off. To complete something with a final maneuver or touch; to end.

> "He topped off his concert with a song in the native dialect of the villagers."

> "I would not advise you to top off the evening with a drink."

tops. The best (one or something); outstanding in ability, rank, performance, etc.

> "He is always witty, but last night he was really tops."

Torch

carry a torch for. To feel the pangs of unrequited love; to be painfully in love with.

> "Although he is now married again, he still carries a torch for his ex-wife, who also married again."

Toss

toss off. 1. To create quickly or easily; to perform without effort. 2. To consume or drink up.

> 1. "He tossed off a few pages of his next book while waiting at the airport."

> 2. "He tosses off a few drinks before each performance."

Touch

in touch with. In contact or communication with; aware of; informed about.

> "Since they left the neighborhood, we are no longer in touch with them."

> "You may be sure that he is in touch with the latest developments in the case."

out of touch with. Not in communication or contact with; not aware of or informed about.

> "We have been out of touch with them for about two years."

> "It is obvious that he is out of touch with the latest innovations in his field."

put the touch on. To borrow, or attempt to borrow, money from someone, especially without the intention to repay.

> "Let me get out of here before Jim has a chance to put the touch on me for another ten bucks."

touch down. Of an aircraft, to come down and touch the ground; to land, usually at an airfield.

> "A small private plane touched down at the local airfield."

touch off. To begin or initiate some process; to start something, as a conflict, revolution, fight, etc.

> "A flaming cinder from a passing train touched off the brush fire."

> "An innocent remark occasionally touches off a serious argument or quarrel."

touch on *or* **upon.** 1. To discuss or treat a subject briefly. 2. To come close to being (something specified); to verge on.

> 1. "In his lectures, he only touches on the more important topics. You are expected to supplement the lectures with the textbook and additional reading."

> 2. "Such cruel treatment touches on sadism or insanity."

touch up. To improve by minor additions or changes, as a painting, literary work, etc.

> "The drawing is practically finished. All I want to do is touch up the hair."

Tour

on tour. Of a theatrical troupe or company, traveling from town to town in order to give performances.

> "After more than a thousand performances in New York, the company is now on tour."

Tow

in tow. 1. In a condition of being pulled by a rope or chain, as a disabled car. 2. In the role of companion or follower.

> 1. "The car was actually in tow to the shop when it was rammed from the rear."

> 2. "He usually has a couple of underlings in tow, to bolster his ego."

Town

go to town. 1. To do something energetically and efficiently. 2. To overindulge, as in celebrating something; to go out for a good time or on a spree.

> 1. "He really went to town in building that patio."

> 2. "He went to town when the announcement was made about his appointment."

on the town. Enjoying oneself by visiting the theater, bars, night clubs; having a good time visiting various places of entertainment.

> "He is out on the town again tonight, but he said he'll be back early."

Traces

kick over the traces. To rebel against the authority of another; to show lack of subordination; to show independence of spirit or action.

> "She had him under her thumb for many years, but he finally kicked over the traces."

Track

in one's tracks. In the place where one is at a particular or specified time.

> "That telephone call stopped him in his tracks as far as the proposed trip was concerned."

keep track of. To keep oneself informed about something, especially about the doings or whereabouts of another person.

> "He likes to keep track of his former clients and is in touch with many of them."

lose track of. To fail to be informed or aware, especially of the whereabouts of a person.

> "He traveled so much that I finally lost track of him."

off the track. Away from the subject under discussion; straying from the objective.

> "She is a good storyteller, but she has a tendency to get off the track."

on the track. On the subject or goal; not straying from the aim or objective.

> "He may not be a good speaker, but he stays on the track."

on the wrong (*or* right) side of the tracks. In the poorer (or better) part of a town.

> "His parents were opposed to the girl because she was born on the wrong side of the tracks."

track down. 1. To chase or pursue until caught. 2. To search something till it is found.

> 1. "They are still trying to track down the bank robber."

> 2. "He was determined to track down the cause of the food spoilage."

Trade

trade in. To use something, as an old car or television set, as part payment in the purchase of a new item of the same kind.

> "We would not want to trade in the old set because we can use it in the den."

> "He trades in his old car for a new one practically every year."

trade on *or* upon. To use something to one's advantage, especially unfairly; to exploit.

> "Some businessmen trade on the sorrow and gullibility of bereaved relatives."

Tread

tread on someone's toes. To offend someone; to say or do something that hurts another's feelings.

> "Every time he opens his mouth he manages to tread on her toes."

Tree

up a tree. 1. In a difficult situation; in an unpleasant position from which there is no escape. 2. In a quandary; perplexed; unable to explain or understand.

> 1. "Having had so many medical bills to pay, he is now up a tree financially."
>
> 2. "I am up a tree regarding the motive for his action."

Trick

do the trick. Accomplish that which one sets out to do; complete a desired action.

> "One more coat of paint will do the trick."
>
> "We injected some powdered graphite into the lock, and that did the trick."

turn the trick. Same as *do the trick,* which see.

Trigger

quick on the trigger. Reacting quickly, especially with harsh words or angry action.

> "I am not surprised that he acted so harshly. He is known to be quick on the trigger."

Trot

trot out. To display something so that others may admire it; to present; exhibit with fanfare.

"He trotted out his best drawings, knowing that his
visitor is an amateur artist."

the trots. The condition of having frequent bowel evacuations,
usually of liquid consistency; diarrhea.

"The New Year's overindulgence in food and drink
gave him the trots."

True

come true. To become a reality; to occur as expected or predicted.

"His hopes of going in business for himself finally
came true."

Trump

trump up. To prepare a malicious charge or accusation against
someone, for the purpose of discrediting or harming him.

"He was brought to trial on some kind of a trumped
up charge, but he was acquitted."

Try

try on. Of a garment, hat, etc., to put on in order to judge the
size, fit, appearance, etc.

"He often buys shoes without trying them on, and
they fit."

"Before I decide on this coat I would like to try it
on."

try out. 1. To test the quality, suitability, or efficiency of something by actual performance. 2. To demonstrate one's ability in
a particular field, as when applying for a job, membership on a
team, etc.

1. "Try out this new method and let us know how
it works for you."

2. "He plans to try out for the varsity tennis team."

Tuck

tuck away. 1. To put aside as a reserve; to save. 2. To eat hungrily or avidly.

> 1. "He managed to tuck away a few thousand dollars while he worked at the local plant."

> 2. "He can tuck away three or four sandwiches between meals."

Tune

call the tune. To make the important decisions, as in matters of policy; to be in charge; control.

> "Outwardly, he seems to be the boss in the family, but in reality she calls the tune."

change one's tune. To change one's point of view, manner, attitude, etc.

> "She changed her tune when she realized that he can be helpful to her in getting the promotion."

sing a different tune. Same as *change one's tune,* which see.

> "He'll sing a different tune when he finds out that he'll have to work nights."

to the tune of. At a specified price; at the cost of a specified amount.

> "They made the alterations to the tune of some fifty thousand dollars."

tune up. With regard to a motor, especially the motor of an automobile, to adjust certain parts in order to assure smooth operation.

> "He is very sensitive about his new car and likes to have it tuned up several times a year."

Turkey

talk turkey. To speak frankly; to talk about the matters that are of real interest; to talk seriously.

> "All right, now that we have covered the social amenities, let's talk turkey about what really happened."

Turn

at every turn. In every instance or case; all the time; constantly.

> "Although he tried hard to be friendly, he was rebuffed at every turn."

by turns. Alternating one after another; first of one kind, then another.

> "As usual, she was depressed and elated by turns."

in turn. In the expected sequence; in the normal order of succession.

> "Each neighbor in turn keeps an eye on the children walking home from school."

out of turn. Not in the correct order of things; out of the normal sequence; not at the proper time.

> "You'll get your chance. Just wait and don't speak out of turn."

take turns. To follow one another (or each other), as in performing certain duties, speaking, etc.

> "The neighbors take turns in riding the children to school."

turn down. 1. To reduce the degree or intensity of. 2. To refuse to accept; to reject; to refuse to grant.

> 1. "We usually turn down the heat before going to bed."
>
> 2. "He tried to enlist at least twice, but was turned down."

turn in. 1. To submit or deliver, as a statement or declaration of intention. 2. To inform the authorities about someone, especially a person wanted by the police. 3. To go to bed for the night.

> 1. "He was actually fired, since they requested that he turn in his resignation."

> 2. "The fugitive was turned in by his former girl friend."

> 3. "He complained of being tired and turned in early."

turn off. 1. To check the flow of something by closing a valve or faucet. 2. To leave a main road and walk or drive along a side road. 3. To cause antipathy or annoyance; to cause to lose interest.

> 1. "We generally turn off the water when we leave on our vacation, but this time we forgot."

> 2. "In that part of the county, it is not advisable to turn off the main road, as the side roads are narrow and muddy."

> 3. "There is something about her, he said, that turns him off."

turn on. 1. To open a valve or faucet in order to allow something to flow. 2. To cause a light to burn or light up. 3. To cause to become interested.

> 1. "He turned on the hot water by mistake."

> 2. "Let me turn on the porch light before we go out."

> 3. "There is something in her voice that turns him on."

turn out. 1. With regard to a light, to cause it to cease burning or shining. 2. To produce. 3. To end in a certain way.

> 1. "You should turn out the lights before you leave."

> 2. "They turn out more than a thousand cars a month."

3. "Although we did not believe his estimate at the time, he turned out to be right."

turn over. 1. To change the position of the body from one side to the other, as by rolling. 2. To consider; think about. 3. To transfer to the custody of.

1. "He believes that it is advisable to turn over several times during the night."

2. "I turned it over in my mind for several days, but I still don't like the idea."

3. "The private detective turned the man over to the local police."

turn to. To appeal to, as for help or advice; to seek assistance from.

"She always turns to him when she is in real trouble."

turn up. 1. To find or discover. 2. To appear in person. 3. To happen; occur.

1. "There is no telling what the investigating committee may turn up."

2. "He finally turned up, but he was several hours late."

3. "I just wonder what will turn up with regard to the war in the next two years."

turn upon. To change from a friendly attitude to one of hostility with regard to a person; to become angry with someone formerly esteemed or liked.

"We don't know the reason, but she certainly turned upon him recently."

"This breed of dog may suddenly turn upon the owner."

Twiddle

twiddle one's thumbs. To idle; to spend the time doing nothing or trifling.

> "He is busy. He doesn't sit there twiddling his thumbs."

Two

put two and two together. To consider obvious facts and come to a logical conclusion.

> "He didn't tell me that he loves her, but I put two and two together."

U

Unbosom

unbosom oneself. To reveal one's innermost thoughts, feelings, etc., to someone, especially in order to relieve anxiety or a sense of guilt.

> "He found it comforting to unbosom himself, even to a complete stranger."

Under

go under. 1. To lose consciousness; fall asleep. 2. Fail in business. 3. To sink below the surface.

> 1. "He tried to remember his last impressions just before going under the anesthetic."

> 2. "The last of the small grocery stores in this town went under about ten years ago."

> 3. "According to one witness, the man went under as soon as the canoe turned over."

Up

all up with. All hope lost; near a disastrous end; facing defeat or ruin.

"When the bank turned him down, he realized it
was all up with his business."

on the up and up. Frank; honest; dependable; trustworthy; above-board.

"You can take his word for it. He has always been
on the up and up."

up against. Facing something specified; confronted with; forced
to deal with.

"In this case, he is up against his toughest opponent."

up against it. In financial difficulties; in any difficult situation;
perplexed.

"The brokerage firm was up against it for the first
time in its existence."

"He is very resourceful, but this time he was up
against it."

up and about. Sufficiently recovered from an illness to be able
to leave the bed and walk around.

"He was laid up for nearly a month, but he is up
and about now."

up and around. Same as *up and about,* which see.

up for. 1. Facing a court of law; standing trial. 2. Sent to prison;
imprisoned. 3. Considered for a particular office or post; being
considered for nomination or election.

1. "He will be up for the alleged misappropriation,
and the trial is to begin next week."

2. "He is up for two to six years in a federal prison."

3. "He is up for reelection, but I don't think he'll
make it."

up on. Informed about a particular subject; up-to-date in a given
field or science.

"Although he is now retired, he is up on electronics."

up to. 1. Contriving to do something. 2. As far as a specified place, level, time, etc. 3. As much or as many as, but no more than. 4. Having the necessary energy, power, or talent for a given task.

1. "We know they are up to something, but what?"

2. "They intended to climb up to the second plateau."

   "She is up to her neck in medical bills and other debts."

3. "This truck will haul up to four thousand pounds."

4. "He tried, but he just wasn't up to it that day."

ups and downs. Good luck and bad luck; successes and failures; reversals in fortune.

"They are well-to-do now, but along the way they had their ups and downs."

Uppers

on one's uppers. In an impoverished condition; in financial need; dressed shabbily.

"They say that he was a wealthy man at one time, but he is on his uppers now."

Upstairs

kick upstairs. To promote a person to a nominally higher rank or position that is in reality not as important or powerful in making decisions, usually in order to be rid of the person.

"The board of trustees decided to kick the president of the company upstairs."

Upwards

upwards of. More than a specified amount or quantity.

"The repairs cost us upwards of two hundred dollars."

Use

have no use for. 1. To have no need for; to have no opportunity to utilize. 2. To dislike someone or something; to have no fondness for.

1. "We can use this, but we will have no use for the larger sizes."

2. "I have always known that she has no use for pets."

in use. In the act of being employed or utilized; capable of being used.

"The elevator at the end of the hall is now in use."

"The long form is no longer in use, having been superseded by the short form."

make use of. To employ or utilize; to employ for one's own purpose.

"We can make use of the cracked eggs in cooking."

"The organization makes use of old Christmas cards."

of no use. Of no avail or advantage; not likely to yield the desired result.

"It would be of no use to look for it now, in the dark. Let's wait till morning."

put to use. To employ in a useful way; to apply in an advantageous way.

"We have this lumber; let's put it to use and build a storage shed."

V

Variance

at variance. Differing; disagreeing; in a condition of controversy.

"Your account is at variance with the one I received earlier."

"He was fired because he was always at variance with his boss."

Vengeance

with a vengeance. With excessive force; with fury; to an excessive degree.

"On Monday morning he started his job with a vengeance."

"He tore into his dinner with a vengeance."

View

in view. 1. Exposed to one's view or vision. 2. As an aim or goal.

1. "As the sun rose, the shore was clearly in view."

2. "They bought the property with expansion of the business in view."

in view of. In consideration of (something specified); because of.

> "In view of the fact that the accused was a minor, the charges were dropped."

on view. So placed as to be seen; on public display or exhibition.

> "The spring models are already on view in some stores."

with a view to. With the intention or purpose; with the expectation or hope of.

> "They bought the adjacent lot with a view to building a garage."

Voice

with one voice. Speaking at one time or all together; unanimously; without a dissenting voice.

> "The resolution was acclaimed with one voice."

Volumes

speak volumes. To express or mean a great deal; to have obvious importance.

> "Although she said nothing, her very silence spoke volumes."

Vote

vote down. To decide against something by a vote; to defeat, as a bill, by voting.

> "The proposal for a new library was voted down."

vote out. To cause an incumbent to lose his post or office by voting against him.

> "Everyone expected the councilman to be voted out at the next election."

W

Wade

wade in *or* **into.** To begin something with a great deal of energy; to attack verbally or physically.

"He waded into the project with the energy of a novice."

"His mother waded into him for not being attentive."

Wagon

hitch one's wagon to a star. To make one's goal something that is hard to attain; to have lofty aims; have a high ideal.

"In deciding on an operatic career she hitched her wagon to a star."

on the wagon. Not drinking alcoholic beverages; abstaining from alcoholic drinks.

"He is on the wagon again, but he has been there before, many times!"

on the water wagon. Same as *on the wagon,* which see.

Wait

wait on. To attend someone, as in the role of a servant; to offer the services of a salesman to; to serve someone at the table, as a waiter.

> "She loves him and waits on him hand and foot."

> "It seemed to me that the saleswoman was in no hurry to wait on me."

> "We preferred a younger man to wait on us at the table."

Wake

in the wake of. Following immediately behind; coming as a consequence or result.

> "He believes that higher prices come in the wake of higher wages."

> "An investigation is bound to follow in the wake of the rumors."

Walk

walk off. 1. To leave, as a job, without warning or abruptly. 2. To get rid of something by walking.

> 1. "He is liable to walk off the job if sufficiently provoked."

> 2. "I find that I can walk off my anxieties, if I just take the time to do so."

walk off with. 1. To take illegally; to steal. 2. To win, especially without unusual effort.

> 1. "The man walked off with some of the equipment provided by the company."

> 2. "He did even better than we had expected. He walked off with the gold medal."

walk out. 1. To leave a particular place in an expression of protest. 2. To go on strike.

1. "The representatives of the offended country walked out when the opposing speaker took the podium."

2. "The men at the plant walked out when one of their members was fired."

walk out on. To forsake; desert; to depart from unceremoniously.

"She nagged him for years, but one day he just walked out on her."

Wall

drive to the wall. To force into a difficult or desperate situation; to ruin.

"The new supermarket drove the local merchant to the wall."

push to the wall. Same as *drive to the wall,* which see.

Wane

on the wane. Decreasing, as in popularity, severity, intensity, etc.; declining.

"The demand for this item is on the wane."

"His influence as a politician is on the wane."

Want

want in. 1. To have a desire to enter a specified place. 2. To want to participate in a specified activity; to want to belong, as to an organization.

1. "He is a smart dog. He scratches on the door when he wants in."

2. "When I explained the deal to him, he said that he wants in."

want out. 1. To have a desire to leave a specified space or place. 2. To want to leave a particular organization or activity.

> 1. "I could tell by his nervous behavior that he wanted out of here."

> 2. "He knew that the gang does not tolerate anyone who wants out."

Warm

warm the bench. To sit and wait one's turn, as to play; to have an inactive role; to do nothing but sit.

> "You have done nothing last year but warm the bench."

warm up. 1. To prepare oneself for a particular activity, as boxing, dancing, etc., by practicing beforehand. 2. To increase the intensity or fervor of. 3. To develop a liking for something; to become more receptive toward something or someone.

> 1. "Because of bad flying conditions the team arrived late and had no time to warm up before the game."

> 2. "The resentment continued to warm up in spite of all efforts to calm the situation."

> 3. "She didn't like him at first, but eventually she warmed up to him."

Wash

come out in the wash. To become known in the course of time; to be revealed in the course of an investigation.

> "We don't know all the details now, but it will all come out in the wash."

wash down. 1. To cleanse by flushing with water. 2. To swallow some fluid in order to facilitate the passage of food or other liquid previously taken.

1. "The firemen were called and they washed down the spilled oil into the sewer."

2. "He likes to wash down his meal with a glass of ginger ale."

wash one's hands of. See this entry under *hand.*

wash out. 1. To cleanse or rid of something by washing with water or other liquid. 2. To erode by the action of water. 3. To eliminate or be eliminated from, especially a course of study.

1. "The patient's stomach was immediately washed out."

2. "The top soil was washed out by the heavy rainstorm."

3. "He tried college, but he was washed out in the first semester."

wash up. To cleanse by washing, as dishes; to wash oneself, especially one's face and hands, as before a meal.

"She prefers to wash up the dishes before going to bed."

"I'll need about ten minutes to wash up; then I'll be ready for dinner."

washed up. Disqualified; no longer popular; out of the running; out of favor.

"After that outburst of anger, he is all washed up here."

"He ran for office twice and failed both times. I think he is washed up."

Waste

go to waste. To be wasted rather than utilized; to be or remain useless.

"This food will go to waste if we don't take it with us."

lay waste. To destroy utterly; to reduce to rubble; to devastate; to make a wasteland of.

"The marching armies laid waste dozens of villages."

Watch

on the watch. Watching or looking for something; alert, as for the appearance of something or someone.

"I advised him to be on the watch for crossing animals."

watch out. To be careful; to be on one's guard; to look for something in order to avoid it.

"I advised them to watch out for slick spots on the sidewalk."

watch over. To guard and protect; to attend to the needs of someone or something.

"The neighbor promised to watch over her pets while she is away."

Water

above water. Out of a troublesome situation; free from financial worries; not in debt.

"They had a rough time financially for a few years, but they are above water now."

"With prices being what they are, it is difficult for a family to keep above water with one breadwinner in the family."

by water. (Transported or carried) by ship or boat.

"The crude oil is transported partly by pipeline and partly by water."

hold water. To be sound logically; to be able to withstand scrutiny or challenge.

"This explanation seems rather childish. It will not hold water."

in deep water. In a difficult or dangerous situation; out of favor with someone.

> "He spends more than he earns and is always in deep water financially."

> "He is in deep water with his girl friend, since he forgot to buy her a birthday gift."

in hot water. In an uncomfortable or difficult situation; in trouble.

> "His frankness often gets him in real hot water."

like water. As if it were as cheap or abundant as water; freely; in large amounts; lavishly.

> "It was a sumptuous party and vintage wine flowed like water."

> "He never had to work for his money, and he spends it like water."

make one's mouth water. Cause one to desire something; to arouse the appetite.

> "Just the thought of pizza makes his mouth water."

Way

by the way. Incidentally; as a part of one's discourse or remarks; not as a main issue.

> "By the way, have you seen her lately?"

> "He didn't make an issue of this; he merely mentioned it by the way."

by way of. 1. Using a certain route; via; moving or passing through. 2. As a method (for accomplishing a specified goal).

> 1. "We traveled to Los Angeles by way of Chicago."

> 2. "We clipped that hedge shorter by way of marking the boundary between the lots."

come one's way. Happen to one; to occur to one, usually something desirable.

"When she met him, something good came her way."

give way. 1. To yield to something or someone. 2. To collapse or break down.

1. "We finally had to give way to his persuasion."

2. "The roof gave way under the weight of the snow."

give way to. To yield to, as to an impulse; to lose control, as of one's emotions.

"At the sight of her boy, she gave way to uncontrollable sobbing."

go out of one's way. To do something at the cost of inconvenience to oneself; to make an effort.

"On that night she went out of her way to be the perfect hostess."

in a family way. Of a woman, expecting a child; with child; pregnant.

"Although she was still in high school, it was obvious that she was in a family way."

"Some rural folks avoid the word 'pregnant' and use the expression 'in a family way' instead."

in a way. Considered in a certain way; to a certain extent; after a fashion.

"In a way, he may be considered an artist."

in someone's way. Existing as an obstruction or obstacle in someone's way.

"I don't think you can really help him. You'll only be in his way."

in the way. Same as *in someone's way,* which see.

> "I left early, as I felt I was in the way."

lead the way. To be first in a new enterprise or practice; to show the way to others; to take the initiative.

> "This country led the way in the fight against air pollution."

make one's way. 1. To advance, as by walking or riding. 2. To make progress in life without the help of others, i.e. by one's own effort.

> 1. "To get to the other side of the field, he had to make his way through the crowd."
>
> 2. "Although his father was a wealthy man, he preferred to make his way without family assistance."

make way. To clear the way for someone or something; to allow the passage of.

> "He decided to step aside to make way for men with new ideas."
>
> "We had to remove the door to make way for the new desk."

out of the way. 1. So placed as not to hinder or obstruct. 2. Taken care of; disposed of. 3. Not easily reached; not situated along one's usual route.

> 1. "She asked the boy to move the carton out of the way."
>
> 2. "With the overtime work out of the way, I will now be able to spend more time at home."
>
> 3. "It's a very nice store, but it's a little out of the way."

pave the way for. To prepare for something; make something easier to accomplish by doing something in advance; lead to.

"His election to the board of directors paved the way
to the replacement of the old chairman."

see one's way clear. To see something as capable of being accomplished; to regard as a possibility.

"At the present time, we cannot see our way clear
to buying a summer home."

under way. Moving along; in progress; in motion toward a particular place or aim.

"After a long delay, the construction work is once
more under way."

Wear

wear down. 1. To rub away or otherwise reduce in volume or thickness. 2. To cause to become tired; to weary. 3. To overcome opposition by continued effort.

1. "The feet of countless visitors wore down the
threshold of the old building."

2. "Her incessant chatter finally wore me down and
I decided to leave."

3. "He didn't really want to buy the car, but his
wife's persistence wore him down."

wear off. To diminish, as in intensity; to disappear or pass away.

"When the effect of the drug wore off, the pain returned."

wear out. 1. To reduce to a condition of uselessness, as by continued wear or utilization. 2. To cause to become tired or weary.

1. "After many years of service, the lawn mower
wore out."

2. "The long hours at this job will eventually wear
him out."

Weather

keep one's weather eye open. To be alert; to be watchful; to remain on guard.

> "This job is not exactly what I want, and I am keeping my weather eye open for a better opportunity."

under the weather. 1. Somewhat ill; physically indisposed. 2. Slightly drunk; drunk; suffering from a hangover.

> 1. "He phoned and said that he was under the weather and would not come in today."

> 2. "I didn't pay much attention to what he said, since he was obviously under the weather."

weather through. To manage to survive a difficulty, danger, etc.; to live through; to pass safely.

> "Somehow, she weathered through the months of lonely desperation."

> "Do you think we can weather through the winter with our failing furnace?"

Week

week in, week out. Every week; all the time; continuously.

> "We had to drive to the village week in, week out."

Weigh

weigh anchor. To raise the anchor of a ship in preparation for a voyage.

> "He always enjoyed watching ships weigh anchor."

weigh down. 1. To cause to bend or bow, as under pressure or a weight. 2. To depress the spirit; to burden; to weary.

> 1. "The truck was obviously weighed down by the excessive load."

> 2. "The responsibilities of both the business and the home weighed her down."

weigh in. Of an athlete, to have oneself weighed officially, as before a boxing match.

> "The challenger weighed in at 208 pounds, 6 pounds heavier than the champion."

weigh one's words. To choose and use one's words carefully, in speaking or writing.

> "The speaker weighed his words in making the important announcement."

Weight

carry weight. Have influence or effect; to be important or significant.

> "Be good to this man, because his word carries weight around here."

> "He no longer carries weight in the political circles of this state."

pull one's weight. To supply one's share, as of work or effort; to do one's share.

> "Even with his physical disability, he pulls his weight in this business."

throw one's weight around. To assert one's power or influence beyond the limits of decorum or propriety.

> "The new manager used to throw his weight around until he was reprimanded by his superiors."

Welcome

wear out one's welcome. To visit someone so frequently as to make one's presence unwelcome; to make one's visits of such duration that one's presence is no longer accepted with pleasure.

> "We used to like to see him come, but he wore out his welcome long ago."

Well

as well. 1. In addition (to something specified); also. 2. Equally.

1. "We will take this sweater and that one as well."

2. "We like this house as well because of its construction as because of its location on the out-
skirts of the town."

as well as. As much as; equally as.

"In my opinion, he was to blame as well as she was."

leave well enough alone. To abstain from doing anything or making any changes for fear of making things worse.

"Although the colors were not perfectly adjusted by
the television repairman, I advised him to leave well
enough alone."

Wet

all wet. Completely wrong; utterly mistaken; altogther in error.

"You may be right about this, but on the other score
you are all wet."

wet behind the ears. Inexperienced; childish; immature; unso-
phisticated.

"She would never have believed it if she weren't
wet behind the ears."

Whale

a whale of a. An impressively fine or large specimen of something specified.

"This is a whale of a movie. I highly recommend it."

"I have seen beauties before, but she is a whale of
a girl."

What

and what not. And many other things; and other things of all kinds.

> "There was a great variety of food, as roast beef, fried chicken, all sorts of sea food, and what not."

what for. A whipping or beating; punishment of any kind.

> "He'll get his what for when he comes home."

what for? Why? For what reason or purpose?

> "I can't see any point in answering the letter. What for?"

what have you. Other things of a similar kind; many other things, similar or dissimilar.

> "It's an odd kind of store, selling jewelry, novelties, fishing gear, and what have you."

what if. Supposing that; what would be the situation if.

> "What if everyone reasoned as you do and didn't vote!"

what it takes. The talents, the abilities, or the features and characteristics that enable one to be successful or to attain a desired goal.

> "He certainly has what it takes to become the head of this organization."

what's what. The actual facts; the true state of a situation; what is going on.

> "Ask anyone here who has been around for a while. He'll tell you what's what."

Wheel

at the wheel. 1. Handling the steering wheel of a vehicle, ship, etc. 2. In charge or control.

1. "He was not at the wheel when the collision occurred."

2. "The younger man is nominally the president, but
   the old man is still at the wheel."

wheel and deal. To act without restraint or outside the limits of
propriety in order to achieve certain goals; to be influential in
one's sphere of activity.

"He was known to wheel and deal on occasion, but
generally he was a conservative businessman."

wheel of fortune. The unpredictable turns of fate or fortune; the
ups and downs of life.

"The wheel of fortune dealt him another blow when
his business failed."

wheels within wheels. A complex of stimuli, motives, or factors
acting and reacting upon one another.

"Who can understand the enigma of a woman's
mind! It is an example of wheels within wheels."

Whether

whether or no. Under all circumstances; no matter how the
situation may be.

"I told her I am not sure I can get the tickets she
wants, but she wrote that she will come whether or
no."

While

all the while. All the time; all along; during all of a specified period of time.

"He pretended to have a good time, but all the
while he knew that his dismissal notice was in the
mail."

worth one's while. Worth one's effort, time, expense, etc.; advantageous; profitable.

> "You will find it worth your while to read this magazine."

> "We find it worth our while to buy our supplies from them even though it takes them longer to deliver."

Whip

whip off. To compose something quickly and easily; to write, as a letter, hurriedly and without effort.

> "He was able to whip off a short story every two or three weeks."

> "She whipped off a few thank-you notes before going to bed."

whip up. 1. To arouse, as sentiment or feeling; to excite. 2. To prepare something quickly, especially a meal.

> 1. "The speaker knew how to whip up the frenzy of the crowd."

> 2. "She is a good cook and she can whip up a meal in half the time it takes another woman."

Whirlwind

reap the whirlwind. To suffer the consequences of one's own misdeeds or foolishness.

> "He had his fun, now let him reap the whirlwind."

Whistle

blow the whistle on. To cause someone to discontinue a particular activity.

> "The employees used to give away free samples to their favorite customers until the manager blew the whistle on them."

wet one's whistle. To take a drink; to drink an alcoholic beverage, especially for the first time in a given day.

"Many of the workers used to stop in at the local tavern to wet their whistle before checking in."

whistle for. To look for in vain; to seek without success; to use ineffectual methods in trying to get something.

"They refused to satisfy our claim, and we can only whistle for our money."

White

bleed white. To deprive someone of all resources, as by stealing, blackmail, etc.; to become poor, especially as a result of demands for spending.

"A dishonest employee can bleed a business white."

"The repair expenses of his two cars almost bled him white."

Who

who's who. Who is important in a particular region or in a given field; the important people.

"Ask that fellow, he'll tell you who's who in this town."

Whole

as a whole. Regarded as a unit; considered as one thing; everything being included.

"We sustained some losses, but as a whole the move was to our advantage."

on the whole. When all things are considered; in a general way; disregarding a few exceptions and considering the majority of the factors.

"We feel that, on the whole, the changes in management are yielding satisfactory results."

out of whole cloth. Without basis in fact; contrived; fictitious.

"This is a rumor made out of whole cloth, if I ever heard one."

Whoop

not worth a whoop. Worthless; worth nothing; of no value whatever.

"His recommendation is not worth a whoop, at least to me."

whoop it up. 1. To celebrate noisily. 2. To stir up enthusiasm for something or someone.

1. "The townspeople whooped it up following the game in which the local team won."

2. "The author whooped it up for his new book on the television talk shows."

Wild

run wild. 1. To grow exuberantly. 2. To act without restraint; to behave in a wild manner.

1. "We had a lot of rain this summer, and the raspberries are running wild."

2. "She talks a great deal about discipline, but she lets her own kids run wild."

the wilds. A deserted or desolate region; uninhabited land; wasteland.

"She found it both inspiring and awesome to travel by car through the wilds of Australia."

Will

at will. As one desires; when or as much as one wishes; at one's disposal.

"He is allowed to use the premises at will."

do the will of. To do as another person wishes; to obey the instructions or wish of.

"He seems to enjoy doing the will of his wife."

Wind

between wind and water. In a difficult or precarious situation; faced by two unpleasant alternatives.

"In trying to please so many bosses, one is always between wind and water."

break wind. To expel gas or flatus through the anus.

"He was nervous and had to break wind frequently."

get wind of. To get information pertaining to something, especially when the information was meant to be withheld.

"I don't know how they got wind of the proposed merger."

how the wind blows. How things are; what one's intention is; what public opinion is.

"My secretary attended the meeting to find out how the wind blows."

take the wind out of one's sails. To deprive a person of his self-assurance or confidence, as by nullifying his argument, disproving his statement, etc.; to disconcert; deflate.

"The announcement that his contract would not be renewed took the wind out of his sails."

wind up. 1. To cause to be nervous or tense. 2. To bring to an end; settle.

1. "He was wound up, as usual, before the final exams."

2. "We expect to wind up the transaction in another week."

'They wound up the odds and ends in a few days."

Windmills

fight windmills. Same as *tilt at windmills.* See under *tilt.*

"He has some reasonable causes, but most of the time he fights windmills."

Wing

on the wing. Flying; in flight; in motion; moving about; traveling.

"During the Easter recess, the college boys will be on the wing again."

"Spring is here, and the birds are on the wing."

take wing. 1. To begin flying; to move as in flight; to indulge in daydreams. 2. To depart in a hurry.

    1. "This is the time of the year when migrating birds take wing."

    "In the spring, his mind often took wing. He dreamed of travel in foreign lands."

    2. "A soon as I mentioned that he will be here, she took wing."

under one's wing. Under one's care, protection, etc.; under one's patronage.

"You won't be alone there. She'll take you under her wing."

Wink

forty winks. A nap; a short period of sleep.

"He manages to get his forty winks practically every day after dinner."

wink at. To pretend not to see something, as an offensive or illegal act, in order to avoid taking action against it.

"The local authorities winked at certain violations of the zoning laws by some of the merchants."

Wipe

wipe out. 1. To destroy completely; raze. 2. To kill; murder.

> 1. "The entire village was wiped out in retaliation."

> 2. "He was wiped out by the gang who suspected him of being an informer."

Wire

pull wires. To use personal influence or the prestige of one's office to achieve a particular purpose, for oneself or another.

> "His father had to pull wires in order to get the appointment for him."

under the wire. Barely in time; just within the deadline or time limit.

> "By sending the letter special delivery, he was able to get his application in under the wire."

Wisdom Teeth

cut one's wisdom teeth. To become mature; to arrive at the age of wisdom or discretion.

> "What do you expect of him! He is young and hasn't cut his wisdom teeth yet."

Wise

be wise to. To know or be aware of something, especially something that one is believed not to know.

> "She was wise to his duplicity, but she pretended not to know."

get wise to. To become aware of something, especially something that one was not meant to know.

> "She finally got wise to his duplicity, and she told him so."

put someone wise to. To inform or enlighten a person about something, especially something that he ought to know but fails to realize.

> "Somebody should put him wise to what is going on
> in the store after he leaves."

wise up. To become aware of something, especially something unpleasant or detrimental; to inform or caution someone about something he should know.

> "I wonder when he'll wise up and realize that he is
> being taken advantage of."

> "She tried to wise him up about his partner, but he
> wouldn't listen to her."

Wits

at one's wits' end. At the end of one's mental or emotional resources; in a condition of not knowing what to do.

> "She seemed to be at her wits' end, but I was able
> to reassure her and to restore her confidence in her-
> self."

keep one's wits about one. To remain in control of one's emotions; to remain calm, as in face of danger; to remain alert.

> "He is a remarkable man who is able to keep his
> wits about him no matter what the situation may
> be."

live by one's wits. To provide for oneself by cunning; to make a living by wiles or stratagem; to live dangerously or precariously.

> "He had no trade or profession and therefore had
> to live by his wits."

With

with that. Following that; upon it or that; having said or done that.

> "He threw the papers on the table, and with that he
> stalked out."

Wolf

cry wolf. To make a false announcement about being in distress and needing help.

> "It is difficult to tell about him, whether he needs help or not. He may be just crying wolf."

> "She cried wolf so many times before that no one would believe her now if she were in distress."

keep the wolf from the door. To provide just enough means to avert extreme poverty.

> "It isn't much of a job, but it will keep the wolf from the door."

wolf in sheep's clothing. A villain who conceals his evil intentions and hides behind an innocent or benign exterior.

> "She soon realized that he was a wolf in sheep's clothing."

Woods

out of the woods. Extricated from a difficult situation; safe; out of trouble.

> "The bank has given us a loan, but we are not out of the woods yet."

Wool

all wool and a yard wide. Genuine; honest; sincere; devoted; reliable.

> "There aren't too many such people around, all wool and a yard wide."

dyed in the wool. Confirmed; deep-rooted; hardened in a particular opinion or habit.

> "Let me introduce you to a dyed in the wool conservationist."

pull the wool over one's eyes. To deceive; mislead the judgment of someone.

> "He tried to pull the wool over her eyes by saying that he must work overtime."

Word

be as good as one's word. To be reliable or dependable; to be likely to fulfill.

> "If he promised you to do it, he'll do it. He is as good as his word."

break one's word. To refuse to keep one's promise; fail to abide by one's promise.

> "As much as he hated to do it, he had to break his word about joining them on the fishing trip."

eat one's words. To take back what one has said; to recant; make a disavowal.

> "He said that I wouldn't finish the job on time, but I made him eat his words."

give one's word. To promise to do or not do something; to give an assurance.

> "I am sorry, but I'll have to go through with it. I gave him my word."

hang on to one's words. To listen eagerly or attentively to the words of another.

> "She was enthralled by him and hung on to his words with bated breath."

have a word with. To speak with someone briefly; have a short conversation with.

> "I had a chance to have a word with him when we met accidentally at the drugstore."

have no words for. To be unable to summon the words necessary to describe something, as because of amazement, anger, etc.

> "I simply have no words to describe this heinous act."

> "He had no words for the awesomely beautiful sight."

have words with. To exchange words with someone in anger; to argue angrily with.

> "He had words with the supervisor, but it is all straightened out now."

in a word. To summarize; in short; to put it briefly; stated succinctly.

> "In a word, the outline of the story didn't appeal to the editors."

in so many words. In precisely such terms or words; briefly; tersely.

> "He did not say this in so many words, but I feel that he intends to resign."

> "He told them in so many words that he will not put up with such poor accommodations."

man of his word. A man who keeps his promises; a person on whose word or promise one may depend.

> "If he promised you, he won't let you down. He is a man of his word."

of few words. Not talking much; concise in expression; not talkative.

> "You won't get much of an interview with this lady. She is a woman of few words."

put in a good word for. To say something favorable about someone; to commend; to recommend.

> "I happen to know the personnel manager, and I'll put in a good word for you."

take one at one's word. To accept a person's statement to be true without proof.

> "It was impossible for me to check the man's statement. I had to take him at his word."

take the words out of one's mouth. To utter the very words, or say the same thing, that another person was about to speak or say.

> "You took the words out of my mouth when you said that this is not the place for a political discussion."

word for word. Using exactly the same words; quoting or copying every word.

> "He recorded the speech word for word, in longhand."

word of mouth. The spoken, rather than the written, word; transmission by speech.

> "There was nothing in the paper about the incident, but the news got around by word of mouth."

Work

at work. While working; in the process of working; the place where one is working.

> "He sustained the arm injury at work, but he didn't report it at the time."

> "I always wanted to see a cigarette-making machine at work; it's fascinating."

> "In an emergency, I can phone him at work, but I really don't like to do it unless I have to."

get the works. To receive unfair treatment; to become the victim of harsh treatment.

> "On the top of that, he got the works from his boss when he arrived an hour late."

give one the works. 1. To give someone a rough treatment; to be cruel to someone. 2. To kill; murder.

> 1. "The boys at the shop gave the newcomer the works."
>
> 2. "The gang gave him the works because they suspected him of informing on them."

gum up the works. To cause some enterprise to fail, as through ignorance, a silly remark, etc.

> "Be careful now and don't gum up the works by telling anyone about our plans to throw her a party."
>
> "Your smile gave you away and gummed up the works."

make short work of. To dispose of quickly; to accomplish something in very little time.

> "They made short work of his complaint by simply dismissing it."
>
> "He was hungry and made short work of his dinner."

out of work. Not employed; without employment; having no job or work to do.

> "The number of people out of work now is greater than it was last year at this time."

shoot the works. 1. To bet or risk everything one has, as on one play, enterprise, etc. 2. To make the utmost effort.

> 1. "Let's shoot the works and then go home, whether we win or lose."
>
> 2. "He shot the works in trying to land that job, but to no avail."

work in. 1. To make time for, and attend to, between other jobs or chores. 2. To introduce or insert something skillfully or with subtlety.

1. "The doctor might be able to work you in between his other appointments, if you will just wait a while."

2. "This pigment has to be worked in slowly and patiently."

work off. 1. To dispose or get rid of by work or physical effort. 2. To pay a debt by working.

1. "He usually works off his drowziness by taking a brisk walk."

2. "He has no money, but he is willing to work off his check by washing dishes."

work on. 1. To apply oneself to something; to labor; to be engaged in work with relation to something. 2. To exert, or try to exert, influence on someone, as by entreaty, persuasion, etc. 3. To try; attempt.

1. "He is still working on it and expects to have it finished by five o'clock."

2. "He doesn't want to go now, but she'll be working on him, and I'll bet he'll change his mind."

3. "I haven't quite figured it out yet, but I'm working on it."

work out. 1. To materialize; to end successfully. 2. To emerge, as from under the surface of something. 3. To pay off a debt by working. 4. To calculate; solve. 5. To amount to; to total; to add up to.

1. "Our plan worked out very well in spite of a shaky beginning."

2. "The splinter finally worked itself out from under the skin."

3. "He will work out what he owes you by cutting your grass and doing other odd jobs."

4. "I can't give you the answer immediately, but I am sure I can work it out when I get the chance."

5. "All right, but all this works out to no more than five dollars. We have to account for twenty."

work over. 1. To peruse; to read carefully; to examine; to search in. 2. To administer a beating; to punish by repeated blows.

1. "I finally did find the answer, but I had to work over more than a dozen reference books."

2. "I don't think he would have talked if they hadn't worked him over at the station."

work up. 1. To prepare in greater detail; to elaborate. 2. To cause to become excited; to anger; disturb. 3. To better; improve; to increase one's knowledge or skill.

1. "The outline of the story pleased the editor, and the author was asked to work it up."

2. "Your explanation will not satisfy her, I am sure. It will only work up her emotions."

"He got so worked up over this matter that it was impossible to reason with him."

3. "You can surely work up your speed if you practice."

work up to. To advance, as to a higher position; to rise, as in eminence.

"If you have what it takes, you can work up to the presidency of the company."

World

bring into the world. To bear or give birth to; to assist in delivery, as a midwife or obstetrician.

"She brought her children into the world at a time when obstetrics was a primitive art."

"This old lady was once a midwife and brought into
the world most of the children in this community."

come into the world. To be born; to be delivered; come into
existence or being.

"He came into the world in a taxicab, while his
mother was being rushed to the hospital."

for all the world. 1. For any reason; no matter how great the
inducement may be. 2. In every possible way; in all respects;
exactly.

1. "She wouldn't enter a liquor store for all the
world."

2. "This case looks for all the world like the one we
just concluded."

in the world. 1. Ever; at any time; at all. 2. Anywhere on earth;
of all things.

1. "Never in the world would she believe such a
story."

2. "Where in the world did he find this old jalopy!"

on top of the world. Exulted; jubilant; elated, because of achievement, success, etc.

"Since he received a letter from his girl friend he
seems to be on top of the world."

"Having won first prize, he is on top of the world."

out of this world. Exceptionally good, tasty, etc.; so excellent as
to seem not to be found in this world.

"They make deviled crabs that are out of this world."

think the world of. To have great admiration for; to esteem; to
be fond of.

"I think the world of him, but in this case I believe
he is wrong."

Worst

at worst. Even under the worst conditions; even at the greatest possible loss or disadvantage.

> "At worst, the fine will not be greater than fifty dollars."

> "We will not have to complete the work before next Saturday, at worst."

get the worst of something. To lose or be on the losing side; to be defeated or beaten.

> "We always get the worst of the deal when we argue with them."

give one the worst of something. To get the upper hand or the better of; to defeat.

> "He'd better not start anything, or I'll give him the worst of it."

if worst comes to worst. If the worst possible outcome does occur; even if the worst of several possibilities happens.

> "If worst comes to worst and you lose your job, at least I will still be working."

in the worst way. As much or as intensely as possible; in the highest degree.

> "She wanted to give him a piece of her mind in the worst way, but she restrained herself."

make the worst of something. To interpret a statement or a deed in the least favorable way; to regard something in its least desirable aspects; to consider pessimistically.

> "You are making the worst of her remark. I am sure she appreciated our gift very much."

Worth

for all one is worth. To the full extent of one's ability or strength; to the utmost; as fast or as vigorously as one can.

"He swam for all he was worth and got there first."

put in one's two cents worth. To offer one's opinion, as in a discussion, especially when one is regarded as poorly qualified.

"Well, let's give him a chance to put in his two cents worth."

Wrap

wrap up. To finish something one is doing; to put the finishing touches on; to conclude.

"This wraps it up. Now we can go home and get a good night's sleep."

wrapped up in. Engrossed; absorbed in, as in one's work; deeply involved.

"He is so wrapped up in his hobby that he has little time left for reading."

Write

write down. 1. To put a thought, statement, reminder, etc., in writing; record. 2. To write in such a way as to make the writing understandable to readers of a low educational level. 3. To write with the intent to disparage.

1. "I told you a dozen times, write it down and you won't forget it!"

2. "When you write for this magazine, you almost have to write down to its readers."

3. "It does seem that he meant to write down your idea, but I am not sure."

write off. 1. To remove an entry in an account, usually in order to cancel an uncollectable debt. 2. To decide to forget or disregard; to regard as lost or unworthy of consideration. 3. To attribute to.

1. "I'm quite sure that they'll never pay it, so let's write off the amount and forget it."

2. "They decided to write off the demonstration and go home."

3. "He suggested that we write it off to bad luck."

write out. 1. To write in detail or in full. 2. To put in writing; record. 3. To exhaust a topic or oneself by excessive writing.

1. "In this office we usually write out the word 'doctor'."

2. "I would suggest that you write out your complaint in duplicate."

3. "The press has written itself out on the subject of pollution."

write up. 1. To report in writing, in full detail. 2. To describe in writing, as in a newspaper.

1. "One of the witnesses was asked to write up the incident as he saw it."

   "I still have to write up the history before I can leave."

2. "The editor chose one of his best reporters to interview and write up the distinguished visitor."

Wrong

get in wrong. Fall into disfavor; become implicated in some difficult situation.

"He got in wrong with some of his friends because of his outspoken opposition to the war."

get someone in wrong. To cause someone to fall into disfavor; to cause someone to become involved in a difficult situation.

> "You'll get him in wrong with his boss if you keep calling him at the office."

get someone wrong. To misinterpret the intention of another's statement or deed; to misunderstand someone's motive.

> "Don't get her wrong, she still loves him, but she is understandably cautious."

go wrong. 1. To fail; to turn out badly or unfavorably. 2. To turn from a moral way of life to an immoral; to become criminal or depraved.

> 1. "Something went wrong and he didn't get our message in time."
>
> 2. "Being away from home increases the chances that a youngster will go wrong."

in the wrong. Not right or just; in violation, as of a law; in a situation that is sinful or wicked.

> "He is a careful driver, but this time he was in the wrong."

> "He isn't often in the wrong, but he is this time."

Y

Year

year by year. As each year passes or passed; each year; as one year succeeded another.

> "One could see the neighborhood deteriorate year by year."

year in and year out. All the time; continuously; continuing through the years.

> "Year in and year out they went hunting together."

Young

with young. Pregnant; with the abdomen distended by a gravid uterus.

> "Being with young, she received a preferential treatment."

Z

Zero

zero in. 1. To bring an aircraft into a desired position, as for bombing. 2. To come upon someone or something suddenly or pointedly; to aim at the substance of a thing.

1. "After circling the ship several times, the plane zeroed in."

2. "We did not expect her. She just zeroed in on us."

   "The man in the audience waited for the right time to zero in on the speaker with the embarrassing question."